T0301526

The Economics of the Mind

to Giovanni

The Economics of the Mind

by Salvatore Rizzello

Department of Economics, University of Torino, Italy

Edward Elgar

Cheltenham, UK • Northampton, MA, USA

First published in Italian as *L'Economia Della Mente*
by Gius. Laterza & Figli Spa, Roma-Bari
© Gius. Laterza & Figli Spa, Roma-Bari 1997

English language edition arranged through mediation of the
Literary Agency Eulama
This edition © Salvatore Rizzello 1999

Translated from the Italian edition by Elena Pasquini

Published by
Edward Elgar Publishing Limited
Glensanda House
Montpellier Parade
Cheltenham
Glos GL50 1UA
UK

Edward Elgar Publishing, Inc.
136 West Street
Suite 202
Northampton
Massachusetts 01060
USA

A catalogue record for this book
is available from the British Library

Library of Congress Cataloguing in Publication Data
Rizzello, Salvatore, 1963–
        The economics of the mind / by Salvatore Rizzello.
            p.   cm.
        1. Austrian school of economists.   2. Neoclassical school of
    economics.   3. Institutional economics.   I. Title.
    HB98.R59   1999
    330.15'7—dc21   99–34496
                                                                  CIP

MIX
Paper from
responsible sources
FSC   FSC® C013604
www.fsc.org

ISBN 978 1 84064 163 9

Printed and bound by CPI Group (UK) Ltd, Croydon, CR0 4YY

Contents

Contents

Foreword

by Massimo Egidi

The Economics of the Mind is addressed to both the educated reader and specialists in the disciplines that study the mind and human action: economics, psychology, the cognitive sciences.

The book is able to communicate with such a diversified audience because it is structured to show the close conceptual connection between the human sciences and the sciences of the artificial. The history of this connection, and of how it has been broken and then restored in the course of this century, is set out in the book. But this is not its specific purpose, since it is a history that emerges spontaneously whenever investigation is made of the key problem that concerns the author: the role of knowledge in the explanation of human action inside social institutions.

This problem is emerging today with renewed strength, after a long walk with many vicissitudes, in economic analysis: the role of knowledge has been considered crucial since the debate on planning between academic socialists and the Austrian School in the 1930s. The exponents of the Austrian School - mainly Menger and Hayek - denied that it was possible to construct a planned economy that was as efficient as a market-based economy, arguing on the basis of an original analysis of the role of knowledge.

According to Hayek, in order to understand whether an artificial order - the planned society - is able to replace the market, it is first of all necessary to investigate how an economic structure like the market can "spontaneously" arise, where "spontaneously" means non-deliberately and unconsciously. Understanding the nature of the market and the other economic institutions therefore requires inquiry into how a social order that has not been deliberately designed by an architect can emerge and establish itself.

Explicitly taking the partly unconscious nature of human decisions and the limited extent of human knowledge as their analytical premises, the Austrian School suggested that the social institutions perform the role of a collective mind whose knowledge is dispersed and therefore partly unconscious. The problem is understanding how this collective mind works. That is, how it is possible for the institutions to function in the absence of a planner or a dictator when the knowledge that they require to do so is scattered and fragmented in the social structure.

An important component in this position - which Rizzello's book rightly stresses - is the suggestion that the economic institutions function successfully because they enable a radical simplification of individual tasks. This comes about through the division of knowledge and work, so that the bulk of people's everyday tasks are performed semi-automatically and without complex individual calculation. The complexity is "distributed" within the institution through the division of tasks and knowledge.

On this view, what we understand about the nature of the human mind is fundamental for comprehending the nature of the social institutions, and vice versa. This profound philosophical assumption, which traverses much of European economic thought, is the *leitmotif* that runs through *The Economics of the Mind*.

The book surveys a "vision" of the role of the social sciences, and economics in particular, which is the antithesis to the paradigm that predominated until the 1980s, namely the neoclassical-traditional approach. It directs attention to the fact that there is a link between economics, psychology and the artificial sciences. The matter is by no means obvious, because one of the most important principles on which neoclassical economics was based was the idea that the two disciplines of economics and psychology should be treated as entirely distinct.

According to the Neoclassical School, in fact, the theory of rational choice provides economic subjects with the model of optimal action, and it therefore proposes a set of norms which it is in everyone's interest to obey. Thus economic actors were prescribed the best way to achieve their goals, and it is assumed (Milton Friedman) that those who failed to conform would be gradually excluded by a process of selection which permitted only "rational" operators to survive. It is therefore pointless to investigate the psychological aspects involved in decision-making, because at most they could only aid explanation as to why certain individuals are unable to behave in an entirely rational manner.

The theory of rational action is well known, and here I shall merely make some remarks before resuming my argument. The theory was limpidly expounded in Lionel Robbins' *Essay on the Nature and Significance of Economics* (1932), in which he defined economics as the *science of choice*.

This is a highly general and abstract definition. It can be applied in all the settings of human action and precisely because of its generality still today finds numerous proponents. Robbins' essay was the belated systematization of a long process of analytical inquiry into the purposes and nature of the human science that pervaded late nineteenth-century European culture and whose frame of reference was provided by such outstanding thinkers as Weber, Menger and Pareto. In that period, the notions of economic action and rational action underwent profound scrutiny: it was above all Weber, the Linnaeus of the social sciences, who provided the first exhaustive classification of the types of social and economic action in *Economy and Society*.

Thereafter, an immense amount of analysis was undertaken to translate the notion of rational choice into well-defined and operational mathematical models. During the process, the paradigm of rationality progressively spread: the meaning of *rational action* was gradually restricted to that of *optimal choice*, while its range of action was extended to all the domains of the social sciences.

Yet this paradigm - now paramount after half a century of exceptional analysis and conceptual extension - was increasingly undermined by the systematic inaccuracy of its predictions and by its lack of explanatory capacity. Precisely at the moment when the paradigm received its most thorough formulation (principally in the theory of rational expectations), it came up against its limits, to predict human economic actions. Why was this?

The standard model of rational action had already been called into question in the 1950s by experimental results. Allais's experiments and paradox ("Le comportement de l' homme rationel devant le risque: Critique des postulats et axiomes de l'Ecole Américaine", *Econometrica*, 1953, 21, pp. 503-46) were published in 1952, and thereafter a broad array of results in psychology and experimental economics demonstrated the extreme fallibility of human behaviour, compared with the behavioural norm envisaged by the theory of rationality. Even if discussion is restricted to the branch known as the theory of expected utility - the theory, that is, which predicts rational behaviour in conditions of uncertainty - the work of cognitive psychologists, most notably Kahnemann and Tversky, showed that the theory's main predictions were invalidated by the majority of the experimental subjects studied.

Curiously, however, although these facts are generally accepted, and even included in the economics textbooks, there are few attempts and great difficulties to draw all their consequences. It is very difficult to go beyond the passive reception of these results, if one remains within the conceptual frame of the rationality model and the epistemology on which it rests. A risky but potentially promising solution is to change the conceptual frame of reference. The orthodox theory takes it for granted that the rationality model prescribes the best line of action, and that experimentally observed deviations from it provide a measure of human error. But how could one be certain that the discrepancies between observed attitudes or behaviours and the predictions of the rationality model reflect an inadequacy or incapacity of actors?

The question could be answered in two ways. One option is to develop new models of rationality which correct the standard model by making slight adjustments to the axioms of choice. This option has been widely taken up, but still today the success hoped for has not been achieved.

Although the variants proposed - Prospect Theory, Regret Theory, and so on - correctly predicted certain forms of behaviour that the traditional theory had failed to capture, their range of validity was still restricted.

A more radical option is to assume that the abilities deployed by economic actors reflect an intellectual capacity of greater complexity and richness than envisaged by the standard theory of rationality.

A massive amount of experimental work was undertaken to clarify this point and to identify the mental abilities employed in economic and social action - and much work still remains to be done. It was shown that human rationality - defined as the capacity to perform a mental calculation in order to achieve pre-established ends - had marked limitations, which depended essentially on the human mind's restricted capacity for representation and memorization. Thus it was that the notion of *bounded rationality* was transformed from a mere hypothesis formulated by Herbert Simon in the 1960s into a branch of experimental psychology which studied the nature and difficulties of the human mind in problem-solving. But at precisely the moment when the limits to the human capacity for mental calculation were realized, it became clear that this ability was an aspect - an important but not crucial one - of the mind's more general capacity to manipulate symbols and to create mental models of reality.

Research thus rapidly shifted to a different version of the problem: the various mental abilities that are essential for explanation of human action - memorization, categorization, judgement, problem-solving, induction, deduction - were subjected to increasingly intense experimental scrutiny. In parallel to the experimental work, we have had the rise of formal models of intelligence which generated a new discipline, namely artificial intelligence and, more generally, the cognitive sciences.

Besides restoring the connection between economics, psychology and the cognitive sciences, this line of research suggested that the actions of decision-makers in the real economic world should be studied, not in terms of rationality, but in the light of the capacity of the human mind to create mental models (in Johnson Laird's formulation).

This observation offers a possible answer to the question of why systematic discrepancies arise between the predictions of the theory of omniscient rationality and human behaviour: they occur because the human mind is at once more limited and more powerful than envisaged by the rational action model. It is limited in its ability to perform the procedural operations of symbolic manipulation, but more powerful in generating new symbolic representations of the problem addressed. To coin a phrase, the road opened by Herbert Simon's path-breaking work suggested that the old idea of the *rational* agent should be replaced by that of the *intelligent* actor. And it is discussion of this crucial point that forms the core of Rizzello's book.

In proposing a re-reading of one of the central problems of the social sciences - the role of knowledge in the evolution of the social institutions - *The Economics of the Mind* (which could be retitled *Mind and Institutions*), rightly goes back to the crucial issues that engendered the theory of omniscient rationality, and then traces the features of an alternative account spread by the debate of the 1930s and which laid the basis for the growth of the cognitive sciences.

While doing so, it once again encounters an important contribution from Hayekian thought. In 1952, Hayek published a book, *The Sensory Order* (conceived in the 1930s but then set aside), which covers numerous themes of cognitive psychology. The work appeared almost simultaneously with D. O. Hebb's *Organization of Behaviour* (1949), which laid the basis of modern neurophysiology and experimental psychology. The two works had so many features in common that Hayek was tempted not to publish his book.

These same years saw the explosion of computer theory founded by Alan Turing, Alonzo Church, John von Neumann, Warren McCulloch and Walter Pitts. It is unfortunately not possible here to discuss that extraordinary chapter in the history of science, but it should be pointed out that the attempt to analyse human intelligence, and formulate a representation of it, involved the joint efforts of mathematicians, neurologists and psychologists. Here, therefore, at the origins of the cognitive sciences one finds the close linkage mentioned at the outset between the human and artificial sciences.

Thus, rational choice is no longer the central component of the decision-making process. Rationality is studied as a process of procedural rationality, or in Simon's terms, the ability to develop and manipulate mental symbols in order to solve problems.

Much work has been done in this area in the last thirty years, especially within the cognitive sciences, as I have sought to show. With the onset of the idea of procedural rationality, and with the empirical study (protocol analysis) of how individuals behave in complex strategic situations, it has become evident that, due to the limits on the transmission of information and knowledge, and on their classification, strategic behaviour involves a constant process of learning and problem-solving. The focus of analysis has therefore shifted to learning and its distinctive characteristics, among which path-dependency is essential. Rizzello uses this feature to propose an explanation of the cognitive asymmetries and uncertainty that systematically characterize human decisions. It an interesting proposal because it suggests the causes of information asymmetries rather than taking them as given, as usually happens in economic analysis. In the book, of course, Rizzello merely proposes a hypothesis for further research, without seeking to construct an outright model. But in so doing, he notes the impasse in which the neoclassical micro-foundations have left us, and proposes a line of inquiry to resolve it. With a wealth of detail he describes the challenge to which the cognitive and social sciences have reacted by reasserting their status, seeking out new avenues of inquiry, and discovering their shared foundations. Consequently, even the reader who does not agree with some of the author's arguments will read the book with curiosity and interest.

To conclude, I believe that we should recognize that we do *not* know enough about the mental processes that give rise to social action, and consequently that we cannot claim to predict, on the basis of a soundly-established model, how humans will behave in every important circumstance. The model of rational decision-making is still too weak and too restricted to be applied - as some have improperly sought to do - to the whole of economic and social action.

The models with which we interpret economic reality are a highly partial and incomplete representation of that reality, and consequently the actions that they prescribe are unable to achieve the goals set. It is therefore ingenuous to assume, in a world about which we have systematically incomplete knowledge and information, that there is a privileged observer in possession of the only model that can prescribe the correct course of action.

The path marked out by the artificial sciences, following the pioneering work of Cyert, March and Simon, takes direct account of the cognitive limits that I have discussed. Precisely because it prompts us to conduct analysis of human behaviour and the evolution of the institutions in a more penetrating manner, less laden with theoretical prejudice, than the traditional approach, it obliges us to investigate the workings of human intelligence and the origins of knowledge to gain understanding of the institutions. And it thus forces us to shake off the fetters of well-established but fallacious and hidebound knowledge.

Introduction

There never was nor will be a person who has certain knowledge about the gods and about all the things I speak of. Even if he should chance to say the complete truth, yet he himself knows not that it is so. But all may have their fancy.

(Xenophanes, *fragment* 34)

The economics of the mind is the economics of creativity, uncertainty and complexity: the economics of the mind is the economics of man. Not the abstract man, the social actor or the economic agent. The economics of the mind deals with real men and women. It tells us how they assess things, how they decide and act. The main thesis of this book is summed up in the title. Economics implies choices. A choice is the result of psycho-neurobiological acts. The assumptions that are at the basis of economic theory must be consistent with the mechanisms that guide the workings of the human mind.

Yet, is it true that the main role of economic theory is describing the mechanisms of choice? Though I do not want to run the risk of starting a dispute on the definition of economic science and on its object (it might be the subject of a whole book), I deem it necessary to specify this concept.

In one of her last works, J. Robinson wrote that one of the conditions of human life is that "life as we experience it would not be possible if the future was known for certain" (1980a, p. 86). The hypotheses contradicting this simple principle have certainly been, in the past, detrimental to economic politics.

Since the end of the nineteenth century, economic theory has tried to explain producers' and consumers' behaviour within the theory of exchange, which can be synthesized in the theory of prices. The essential characteristic of this science can be found in Hayek's definition "pure logics of the choice". Thus - as Coase wrote (1988b, Chapter 1) - instead of people who choose, we have orders of preferences, and instead of manufacturing firms, we have curves of costs and demand, and the logic of price fixing and of optimum input combination. "Exchange takes place without any specification of its institutional setting. We have consumers without humanity, firms without organization, and even exchange without markets" (Coase 1988b, p. 3).

In the traditional approach, therefore, choice is the main object of economic theory. I consider this assumption as fully valid, but I also think that the analysis should not be restricted to consumption and production.

When we make choices, we do not act in an isolated context. We often act within a hierarchical structure and we are conditioned by its rules. We are in an institutionalized context, and we contribute to its evolution with our behaviour. Moreover, we live in a dimension of historical - rather than logical - time, and, unlike the latter, historical time is irreversible. All these elements characterize human nature, inducing us to behave according to mechanisms that are much more complex than the ones assumed by orthodox economics; this makes the outcome of our actions quite uncertain. Such unpredictability of future scenarios is due to human creativity. Only where uncertainty and complexity coexist can human creativity be exerted; creativity is, in turn, the source of social and individual development, at an organizational and institutional level.

As we live in a world that is characterized by scarce resources, we cannot help making choices. This is why I agree with the idea that economic theory should deal, first of all, with the issues of problem-solving and the theory of decisions. In doing so, it should go beyond the excessive simplifying, typical of the traditional theory, and take up the challenges of complexity and uncertainty. I will illustrate that part of the theory - known as heterodox - which is aimed at explaining how people act, in a situation of complexity and uncertainty and within the limits and potentialities peculiar to human nature. In order to spot such limits and potentialities, we cannot leave the psycho-neurobiological dimension out of consideration. In fact, the research should start from that dimension and develop consistently with these principles. Therefore, mind and its workings will be our constant reference point, while trying to develop an economic theory that can be applied to our world, which is made up of rules, hierarchies and unpredictable individual actions.

Every day we experience how complex reality is. Along with situations which repeat themselves, thus becoming routines, we encounter other situations, which draw our attention. They are unexpected and problematic situations, urging us to look for solutions. We carry out routine actions unconsciously. Facing an unexpected event, on the contrary, we immediately retrieve our mental faculties and use them in a mainly conscious way, in order to overcome that impasse. In a few chapters of this book, such processes are explained in detail. What I want to underline now is that we operate in a complex and uncertain context.

Complexity is connected to unpredictability; and the latter arises from the former. The world is far more complex than the human mind can imagine and predict. This is why it is often impossible to predict future events with absolute certainty, since they arise from the choice of one of the possible options.

A few renowned authors have considered the theory of probability valid: an individual, who is facing a series of alternatives, chooses the one which is more likely to make him succeed, on the basis of the information he/she owns. I see at least two faults in this approach. The first one arises from the absolute lack of interest in how the individual "builds" the alternatives among which he/she chooses. Since we cannot be sure that he/she has more than one alternative, he/she might choose the only possible option. In this case it becomes important to understand whether this is due to the impossibility of finding other alternatives, or to a voluntary decision not to look for them. Here the most relevant difference with the preceding approach consists, in my opinion, in the fact that the alternatives are not given to the individual, but he/she builds them up, and the analysis should focus on this aspect. Another fault of the probabilistic approach lies in the fact that - as psychologists and neurobiologists teach us - apparently our mind works on the basis of mechanisms that are incompatible with that theory. In the following pages I shall try to explain such mechanisms and to assess their economic importance.

I believe that a high number of the answers we are looking for are to be found in the limits and potentialities of the human mind, and in the way they allow us to act.

To start with, this book offers the reader critical remarks on the microfoundations of economic theory, through a quite original path, i.e. a systematic picture of the heterodox approach. This will shed light on how ineffective the explanations of the traditional theory are, because of its unrealistic hypotheses.

If our goal were to mention - in a rather extensive perspective - all the scholars who questioned the prevailing theory, we should draw up quite a long list. We should include celebrated authors, such as Menger, Schumpeter, Keynes, etc., to mention only the few names of the most renowned and closest in time to Walras. But, when I refer to the heterodox approach, I mean only those authors who rejected the validity of the microfoundations of the Pareto-Walrasian model, and who contributed, with their studies in the space of almost fifty years, to the development of an alternative paradigm, i.e. the neoinstitutionalist paradigm.

Today economic research certainly follows many different lines, and I do not expect to review them all. I have assumed a guideline, a kind of "file rouge" of my analysis, and I have tried to follow it. It is my firm belief that the most effective criticism can be traced back to two separate lines; they both deal with the unreality of the foundations of the neoclassical paradigm, emphasizing the discrepancy between ideal analysis and real data.

In 1937, *Economica* published two articles that are the cornerstones of these two lines of research: "Economics and Knowledge" by F. Hayek, and "The Nature of the Firm" by R. Coase. For our analysis, it is important to underline that the value of these articles was acknowledged only several years after they were published. This was probably due to their being innovatory, or even revolutionary, as compared to the prevailing theory.

One of these lines of research was started in Austria, its foundations are Menger's works, and F. von Hayek is its major representative. The origin of the other line is more composite and its foundations are to be found in the institutionalist tradition of the studies of organizations (J. Commons and C.

Barnard), and in the analysis of the processes of social coordination between market and extra-market institutions (R. Coase). H. Simon is the forerunner of this second line, in which the attention is focused on the comparison between psychological theory and economic theory.

The criticisms of the neoclassical paradigm centre on two main issues. The first issue concerns the mechanism of acquisition and use of knowledge on the part of economic agents. As mentioned above, in the traditional theory the process of choice is carried out by perfectly informed individuals and results in a maximizing mechanism. This hypothesis is rejected by Hayek, in that it is based on unrealistic assumptions. In fact, he thinks that one of the most interesting problems economic theory deals with is explaining the process of acquisition and handling of information: information, in fact, - far from being given - is scattered, idiosyncratic and implies a cost. All this has relevant consequences. First of all, Walras' view on competition and market is to be reconsidered. Besides, the possibility of achieving general economic equilibrium is thus disputed.

The second criticism is linked to the first one and concerns the intrinsic limits of human rationality. In the neoclassical hypothesis, agents are assumed to be endowed with substantive rationality and to be perfectly informed. Thus, a choice becomes a mere maximizing act, which takes into account neither individual computational capabilities, nor individual information handling capabilities. Yet, also this assumption is quite unrealistic. A comparison with the results obtained by psychology shows that individuals have cognitive and computational limits. In short, the hypothesis of substantive rationality is confuted by the empirical data on the cognitive and computational limits of human rationality. This subject was studied by Simon, who developed an alternative method of rationality, which he defined as "procedural", after a well-founded criticism of the neoclassical theory. This model emphasizes the *process* through which alternatives are generated, and the individual and collective learning mechanisms, with relevant consequences on the comprehension of the role of organizations.

According to the traditional theory, exchanges are carried out at no cost, the institutional context is unimportant, firms are "black boxes" in which input is turned into output and for which change is an external factor, and the institutional context of transactions is of no importance for the analysis. In my opinion, on the contrary, by studying the peculiar features of the workings of the human mind, we understand why transactions can occur only within an institutional context, and why firms spring up and develop near the market. One of the reasons is that organizations and institutions are established in order to offset the limits of human capabilities in handling information. In other words, institutions simplify the context within which rationality is exerted, and convey the knowledge necessary to communicate; organizations cut transactions costs, which are due first of all to the scattering of information.

These issues are essential in the neoinstitutionalist paradigm, towards which - according to the thesis I have introduced - these two lines of research converge and reach a satisfactory synthesis. If this can be said with reference to Simon, I think that it is also coherent and consistent with the outcome of Hayek's thought (or even that it is its natural outcome). I will therefore try to shed light on how the methodological and economic aspects of this new approach have their roots in Hayek's theory of knowledge and in Simon's theory of bounded rationality.

There are certainly relevant differences between these two authors, but the points of convergences seem to prevail over the point of divergences.

I hope that the following pages duly explain what I have just stated. Nevertheless, I will now underline a few relevant common elements of these two authors, for the readers, who might find my bringing them together too hasty, since they are usually perceived as quite far from each other.

Both Hayek and Simon, in their criticism of the neoclassical paradigm, try to find the object of economic science and they both find it, first of all, in the dynamic process of individual behaviour, which is the opposite of the prevailing static approach. They both consider the psychological dimension important, in order to discover the foundations on which the models of economic theory are to be based. If this is evident enough as regards Simon (who is also known for his applying psychological theory to economics), I will demonstrate that it is as evident with reference to Hayek. One of the purposes of this work is to make Hayek's psychological and neurobiological methodological assumptions explicit, as they are especially relevant for a full and all-encompassing comprehension of the work of the Austrian Nobel prize-winner. Such assumptions stayed in the background in the literature, except for isolated cases.

As these issues are very important, we will briefly enter the field of the history of psychology, so as to understand what kind of studies these authors could draw on. Therefore the part of this book called "Interlude" should not surprise the reader: it illustrates, also from an historical point of view, the psychological aspects we are dealing with and, more generally, the relation between economics and psychology.

Moreover, acknowledging the subjective cognitive limits and looking for a more realistic explanation of the mechanisms of action and choice, the two authors are urged to focus their attention on the workings of the mind, in order to explain human behaviour. This is what Hayek and Simon do; and this is why I will systematically illustrate their models of mind.

As regards Hayek, this is especially important, since in the literature I found no systematic description of his model. It is also important because it will help us better understand - and maybe with a new perspective - the methodological foundations that are at the basis both of the mechanism of information acquisition and use, and of the "spontaneous" origin of institutions.

In the light of these considerations, I will try to define the final purpose I aim at. My purpose is that the last part of this book may confirm the validity of the hypothesis I am working on. This will be accomplished only if we manage to stay within the paths branching off the microfoundations of the process of human mind, while developing a realistic theory of choice. The methodological approach that is more consistent with economic theory is based on a synthesis of two convincing views: on the one hand the psychological analysis, developed especially by Simon, which dealt with the handling of complex information; on the other hand, the neurobiological or subjectivistic approach of the Austrian School, developed by Hayek, which has highlighted the creative aspect of decisions.

In this way, by finding a link between non-homogeneous learning, imperfect knowledge and technological diversity, we might be able to understand what is the origin of the endogenous change in organizations (Dosi-Kaniovski 1994). I am referring to the kind of change that is being studied by those scholars of the economics of innovation who belong to the school of evolutionary economics, founded by Nelson and Winter.

In brief, the implications of this approach might demonstrate the following:

i)   the nature of organizations and institutions can be fully understood only by referring to the specific features of human mind and to the way individuals behave in a situation of complexity and uncertainty;
ii)   every transaction implies costs;
iii) agents always act on the basis of imperfect information;
iv)   hierarchical organizations play an alternative and complementary role to market in cutting costs and reducing the risks arising from the uneven distribution of information;
v)   any exchange can occur only and necessarily within an institutional framework defining the context within which individual and organizational rationality is exerted;
vi)   the change in individual behaviour, organizations' structure, and institutional context is linked with human nature and arises from the individual ability to process information in an original way, thus generating knowledge;
vii) these processes have both an exogenous and an endogenous nature;
viii) in order to understand such processes, it is necessary to analyse individual and organizational learning processes in detail.

My initial hypothesis is that the neoinstitutionalist approach, in a broad sense, is finding solutions for these open issues. These solutions can be found, first, in the new theory of the firm and in particular in innovation economics, and above all in the studies of the emergence of rules in individuals and in economic organizations. Moreover, all these issues are linked to the studies of transaction costs, market failures, asymmetrical information, bounded and procedural rationality, of the various processes of coordination of information within a firm and on the market, of the processes of organizational learning, of the development of path-dependent models of technological and institutional change and, more generally, of the spreading of evolutionary models offering a unitary explanation of dynamic processes, both at a macro and at a micro level.

Acknowledgements

This book is the result of five years of research, and also of manifold discussions with friends and colleagues. I am extremely grateful to Vincenzino Caramelli, Massimo Egidi, and Cosimo Perrotta, who in these years have supported and critically spurred me in my research and writing. I am also grateful to Cristiano Antonelli, with whom I have long discussed the topics concerning industrial economics, and whose advice has proved helpful. The preliminary draft of this work has been read and commented upon by G. Clerico, R. Cubeddu, G. Fornengo, R. Marchionatti, P. Terna, V. Valli, and - as to specific parts - by J. Birner, A. Brero, M. Catalani, U. Colombino, B. Contini, F. Cugno, P. G. Motta, W. Santagata, and R. Viale. I wish to thank all of them for their pieces of advice and criticism, which I have profited by. Special thanks to my "travelling companions" Stefano Fiori and Alessandro Innocenti, with whom, several years ago, I took the decision to sail the arduous sea of scientific research.

This book deals with several interdisciplinary issues. I have often profited by discussing them with experts of various disciplines. In particular I wish to express sincere thanks to Paolo Legrenzi and Maria Teresa Marcone for their repeated enlightening pieces of advice concerning the psychological aspects. Special thanks to Magda Fontana, who has discussed law issues critically.

I did research in several libraries, whose staff I wish to thank. I have especially appreciated the kindness and professional competence of the staff of Fondazione "L. Einaudi" of Turin.

Particular thanks to the II Faculty of Law of the University of Turin, which funded part of this research.

Finally, I dedicate this book to my son Giovanni, with the explicit hope that it might be for him a viaticum in a future where heart and mind coexist more and more harmoniously.

(S.R.)

PART ONE

HAYEK'S CRITICISM OF THE NEOCLASSICAL PARADIGM

I will start my exposition by illustrating Hayek's thought. His chief merit was to point out the role of the process of acquisition of knowledge in economic analysis. His analysis starts from the real characteristics of agents, their intrinsic cognitive and computational limits and the heterogeneous distribution of information. These aspects are at the basis of Hayek studies on the role of market and competition. Market is regarded as a cybernetic tool that has developed historically, allowing agents to use more information than they actually own. The study of competition starts from a real situation, in which individuals are unequally informed. The main role of competition is creating knowledge (these aspects will be dealt with in the second chapter).

For a long time now, scholars have focused their attention on the use of information in the economic process (see Luini 1994). Few of them paid special attention to knowledge, distinguishing it from information. The difference is remarkable: knowledge is the result of an active creation by individuals, who interpret, process, check and re-process external stimuli; information means external data; knowledge is the subjective interpretation of those data.

This idea is at the basis of "constructivism", a word coined by epistemologists and then borrowed by cognitive logic (Watzlawick 1981). The peculiar elements of this approach can be summed up in the idea that individuals actively process external data to "construct" their models of the world and, with the help of feedback,[1] they continuously adjust these models of interpretation to external discrepancies. The basic idea is that knowledge is not the image of the surrounding environment, it is rather the image of our experience of such environment (Maturana - Varela 1984).

This idea is important, because at the core of economic theory lies the problem of understanding how markets and organizations contribute to create

---

[1] The concept of feedback is borrowed from cybernetics. See also Section 8.2.1.

a situation of equilibrium or simply of social order in spite of heterogeneous agents and firms.

Hayek can be considered one of the main exponents of this approach. A major part of his works are part of the "Austrian tradition", which is different from the Walrasian tradition. Therefore I will start from the criticism of the neoclassical standard paradigm on the part of the Vienna School and in particular from Hayek's thought.

An element present in Hayek's thought as well as in that of his maestro Menger, and distinguishing them from the orthodox approach, is the constant attention paid by the Austrian School to institutions and to their importance for understanding economic processes. Besides, Hayek sheds light on the important link between potentialities and limits of the mind and the origin of rules of behaviour. I will deal with this in depth at the end of the third chapter, since I reckon it especially important for the thesis I propose in this book. I will introduce Hayek as the founder of a neurobiological approach, whose implications for economic theory will be dealt with in the first three chapters of the third part.

In my opinion, the breakthrough in Hayek's thought is that he sheds light on the link between the micro-dimension (the mental process of acquisition of knowledge) and the macro-dimension that guarantees homogeneity and continuity (the development of a spontaneous order). I also wish to point out that the two dimensions are both characterized by the activity of problem-solving: at an individual level as regards learning processes; at a social level as regards the role of institutions, which on the one hand guarantee identification among individuals and on the other simplify the environment by making it standard.

1. Neoclassical Paradigm and the Anomaly of the Austrian School

1.1 Introduction

The fundamental works of Jevons, Menger and Walras, published around 1870, represented a turning point in economic theory that is considered revolutionary by many.[1] The fundamental analysis of the Classical School concerns the process of wealth production and accumulation. The background is the relation man/nature within a macroeconomic context. In fact, the economists' interest is always focused on aggregated wealth and every macroeconomic concept is subordinate to the idea of the creation of "national wealth" or the idea of "system". For neoclassical authors the centre of analysis shifts from production process to consumption. The main agent is the individual-consumer and the concept of scarcity becomes the heart of their analysis. The background changes, as well. Instead of the relation man/nature, the background is the relation between individuals and between individuals and social institutions (Vannucci 1990).

The Classical economists do not deal with individuals but with the aggregation of individuals in classes. The individuals' interests are the capitalists', the workers' and the landowners' interests and they act according to the laws of production.

The neoclassical authors, instead, put at the heart of economic science the behaviour of the single agent, with his specific choices, determined by the pursuit of his personal interests within a social background where every agent pursues his own interests. This different perspective brings new results in economic analysis. Yet, not all the results are homogeneous.

Carl Menger's view, in particular, includes peculiar elements which will lead to a sharper differentiation of the "winning" outcome of the Marginalist School. The Austrian School[2] that he founded was a faithful interpreter of

---

[1] Nevertheless, it is important to underline that historians are not unanimous as to the "revolutionary" character of the emergence of marginalistic doctrines (as Vannucci wrote, 1990, p.141, note 1).

[2] For a brief definition of "Austrian School of Economics", a thorough list of its components and of the various generations, see Donzelli, 1988, note 1, pp. 11-12. For a more detailed picture, see: Hayek 1958; Mises 1969; Zamagni 1982; Negishi 1989, ch. 8; De Vecchi 1986b; Cubeddu 1993; Boettke 1994. As regards in particular the founder of this school, see the interesting essay by Hayek (1934), and the one by

methodological individualism - understood as subjectivism. The outcome of
Walras' analysis contradicted it (Negishi 1989, p. 279).[3]

1.2 The rationality of agents in the neoclassical theory

Let us now focus our attention on the main differences between Walras'
approach and Menger's.

The economic agent has a complete set of preferences and can gather
perfect and free information. He makes choices, according to his preferences,
so as to optimize his utility. His behaviour is considered rational as long as he
arranges the necessary means to reach a given goal; the origin of the
preferences is not examined. In short we have:

  a) maximizing rational behaviour of the agents, who optimize according to
     their (given) preferences;
  b) absence of chronic problems regarding information, radical uncertainty,
     diffused ignorance of structures and parameters in a complex world;
  c) movement towards a static[4] equilibrium rather than a continuous process
     of transformation in real time (Hodgson 1988, p. xviii).

If we also consider the relation with the environment and focus our
attention on choice, we find that the agent makes the best possible choice in a
rigorously and sharply determined environment:

  i) all the alternatives are "given" to the economic agent, but we do not
      know how he obtained them;

Alter (1990). I wish to underline that the authors I will refer to are C. Menger and
Hayek.
[3] According to the representatives of methodological individualism, all social
macrolaws can be traced back to the theory of individual behaviour, whose
explanations are teleological-motivational (see Donzelli 1986, ch. 2, to whom I refer
the reader for a systematic and critical illustration of this concept). With reference to
the word "methodological", Donzelli (1986, p. 35) specifies that methodological
individualism deals with the procedures, rules, investigation techniques (in short, with
methods) which scientific research must follow in the context of social phenomena.
Donzelli mentions the neo-Austrians and Hayek in particular among the main
supporters of methodological individualism.
Actually, with the Vienna School, we shift to the field of subjectivism (see section
3.3). The modern representatives of subjectivism – including the Austrians - extend
subjectivism to every field of research. It is present in every analysis of time,
uncertainty, entrepreneurial activity, rules (O'Driscoll-Rizzo 1986, pp. 252-67;
O'Driscoll-Rizzo 1985, pp. 22-27; Kirzner 1986). Unlike Menger's thought,
individualism – which is a feature of the marginalistic economic theory – is here
confined to the consumer theory.
[4] As to the difference between static and stationary equilibrium and the concept of
equilibrium in general, see Donzelli 1986.

ii) he knows the consequences of each alternative: he is in a situation of complete absence of uncertainty but in the presence of risks, as defined by Knight (see section 7.5);

iii) the economic agent has a function of utility or preferential disposition with a minimum and a maximum level of preference;

iv) the agent chooses the alternative which he knows will lead to the preferred consequences (March-Simon 1958).

Therefore the theory of human action in economic activity can be considered aprioristic; the economists created models of analysis in which agents behave "as if" they had the same constraints and the same view on the world. Thus rationality means paradigm rather than theory (Hogarth-Reder 1986a). The agent decides rationally whether his action is consistent with the paradigm of *rational choices*. Therefore rationality and reality do not coincide. Because of its being aprioristic and arbitrary, the theory of rational choices lacks the ontological aspect, the constitutive dimension of human action. Thus, "rational" is what is consistent with a given kind or pattern of behaviour (and of relation), and its meaning is correlative to that pattern (Calabrò 1980). In economics "rational" is a quality of the action in a choosing process rather than a quality of the process. "An action is rational to the extent that it is 'correctly' designed to maximize goal achievement, given the goal in question and the real world as it exists" (Dahl-Lindblom 1953, p. 38).

As regards market, in Walras' model it has an "ideal" form, reaching its highest point in Pareto's optimum. Nevertheless - as we shall see in depth later - it does not really explain reality (Simon 1969).

1.3 The general economic equilibrium

One of the main goals of the Walrasian School was the attempt to "purify" economics. To reach this goal it was necessary to borrow the methods of physics, in order to create indisputable and axiomatic laws, interrelated by the principle of necessity. The result was an "atomistic" model, based on the behaviour of the single agent, aimed at finding the necessary criteria to maximize pleasure and minimize efforts. The conflicting actions of the individuals are brought into harmony by the mechanism of perfect competition. Such mechanism, governed by the rules of demand and supply, guarantees the best allocation of scarce resources (Gee 1991).

Walras demonstrated that: if in the economic system there are three categories of agents - landowners, workers and capitalists *stricto sensu*; if they own a capital in the form of, respectively, lands, personal capital and capital *stricto sensu*; if a fourth category exists, the entrepreneurs, who buy the factors of production and combine them; if all these individuals are well informed, self-interested and rational (substantively)[5] then a situation of general economic equilibrium can be reached.

The agents adjust their behaviour to the price changes. The equilibrium will be reached if, in every market, prices can make demand and supply equal and if in the markets there is completeness of goods, information included. To estimate the price vector guaranteeing equilibrium, it is sufficient to know the initial supplies of resources, the preferences of consumers and the production methods (Screpanti-Zamagni 1989; Napoleoni-Ranchetti 1990). This implies that, thanks to the market, rational agents pursue their goals making use of the necessary means.

The agents are highly interdependent because everyone's actions are influenced by the others'. The result is a complex framework of interaction, which is simplified by the atomistic market of perfect competition.

1.4 The Austrian School's different view on equilibrium

If, for Walras, general economic equilibrium is a logical and consistent outcome, we cannot maintain the same as regards Menger. In the analysis of the Austrian School's founder there is no room for a perspective of general economic equilibrium.[6] One of the main differences concerns one of the foundations of the theory: the concept of scarcity. For both Jevons and Walras this concept is objective, while for Menger it becomes subjective. According to the Viennese economist, scarcity arises from the relation between individuals and goods, i.e. from the way the individual sees the object, according to his own interests. An increase in quantity of the good does not necessarily change the "subjective" condition of scarcity. This is because needs are boundless and cannot be confined to a merely quantitative relation (Vannucci 1990).

In more general terms, while for Jevons and Walras methodological individualism is confined to the consumer's behaviour, Menger extends it to the whole sphere of analysis. As a result, some simplifications of the models developed by the school of Lausanne become unacceptable. One aspect above

---

[5] Simon (1976, pp. 129-45) makes a distinction between substantive and procedural rationality. Procedural rationality deals with the methods through which the decision-making process is carried out; substantive rationality aims at finding the most adequate behaviour in conditions of environmental determinism. Behaviour is substantively rational when it is adequate for the achievement of given goals, within the limits due to given conditions and constraints. It is procedurally rational, instead, when it is the outcome of an adequate decision. In the first case, rationality depends on the goals: once the goals are given, rational behaviour is determined by environmental constraints. In the second case, rationality depends on the process generating it (Simon 1976, pp. 130-31). These aspects are dealt with in detail in Part II of this book.
[6] Vannucci 1990, p. 166; according to Negishi (1985a and, above all, 1985b), Menger is the first great non-Walrasian economist.

all becomes the common denominator of the Austrian School: they agree that the criterion of choice in conditions of perfect knowledge is unacceptable. The cornerstone of the Viennese economists' theories is the problem of *how* information is gathered and *how* the single agents' decisions are made in conditions of *uncertainty*. This is a crucial point. Walras' "agent" is simply "economic", i.e. his behaviour aims at maximization. Menger's agent is "acting" (Garofalo 1990): he gathers information to decide upon his behaviour. Since individual action is the heart of the marginalistic theory, a difference in this concept implies different and autonomous developments.

The new idea is relevant. For the Austrian School, knowledge is not available to everyone and individuals acquire it in different ways. Knowledge is spread among all the agents and each of them owns only fragments. Knowledge is conveyed by economic institutions among the agents. They, in turn, sort out, retain and convey again *only* the part that is necessary for pursuing their personal interests.[7] Therefore the analysis is focused on relations between individuals and between individuals and institutions.

1.5 The rationality of agents in the Austrian School's models

In the perspective of general economic equilibrium, the agent is characterized by a model of "Olympian rationality"[8] (Simon 1983). The only limit of his choice is also the limit of the whole system: the environmental constraint due to scarce resources. The model is so structured because it has to be "scientific". This is the reason why axiomatization and the principle of causality become its core. There is an evident connection with classical mechanics. The main limit of this approach is just as evident. The general economic equilibrium system is impersonal. The agents's role becomes being "re-agents", i.e. reacting to changing data with the only possible choice: maximization. Every choice becomes an introjection of the only possible choice, according to a mostly deterministic view. Hayek criticized it as "pure logics of choices" that has little to do with human behaviour (Garofalo 1990).

Paradoxically, therefore, in Walras' approach there is a contradiction with the assumption of methodological individualism. The extreme objectivization of conditions cancels the central role of the agent-individual - of his individual behaviour, that is conflicting with other agents' interests - from which the reasoning had started. Here is another difference between the Walrasian School and the Austrian School. The model of rationality in Menger's approach is consistent with the model of methodological individualism and is quite close to what Simon defined as *"procedural rationality"*. The agents are studied according to their *real behaviour*, in a context characterized by *scarcity of information and uncertainty* (Simon

---

[7] De Vecchi 1986b, pp. 319 and 324; De Vecchi 1986a; Loasby 1989, pp. 155-167.
[8] It is thus defined by Simon, because it is a kind of rationality typical of gods, rather than of people.

1983).[9] The individual acquires, acts, modifies, interacts with others and with institutions in a context of goals/means. His choice, far from being optimizing, is only satisficing (*Satisficing* approach is dealt with in Chapter 4).

It is evident that the perspectives are quite different. In this approach there is no room for general economic equilibrium and the principle of causality. The time in which the economic process takes place becomes the heart of a dynamic perspective, while for general economic equilibrium the perspective is necessarily static. Time is *real*, it is no longer the time of neoclassical mechanics. To sum up, there is no room for a concept of equilibrium, which Hayek abandons completely in favour of a concept of spontaneous order.[10]

1.6 The object of economic analysis

There is another relevant difference between Menger's approach and Walras'. In a perspective of general economic equilibrium, the subject of economic analysis is limited to the optimun allocation of "objectively" scarce resources. In Menger, instead, it has other characteristics and "economic" behaviour first of all regards the adjustment to changing situations. In general, the agent gathers information through the market or through financial and economic institutions, plans his choices and, by implementing them, he influences other agents' choices. In a "static" situation, characteristic of the neoclassical theory, if no unexpected external shock takes place, the agent behaves repetitively, but when he receives a new piece of information, such as, for example, a drop in the price of a good he is interested in, he immediately develops new economic plans for his choices.

This is certainly true also for Walras' approach. But the Austrian economists' merit consists in shifting the attention from the estimate of a vector of prices able to guarantee equilibrium in given conditions, to the dynamic process of acquisition of the means necessary for planning economic action. The mechanism of individual action planning, necessary to adjust and

---

[9] According to Loasby (1991, p. 53), the assumption of limited and incomplete knowledge in the Austrian School is quite similar to Simon's concept of bounded rationality.

[10] Hayek follows an intellectual path, leading him to abandon the concept of equilibrium, in favour of a concept of order. This path has been synthetically described by Garofalo (1990, pp. 47-50) and, in more detail, by Donzelli (1988, pp. 16-43). According to the latter, Hayek is urged to look for an alternative solution by his awareness of the empirical limits and the logical difficulties in the stationary equilibrium theory (p. 31): an alternative solution, which might overcome the problems of the model of equilibrium (it proves incapable of incorporating the processes through which knowledge is spread, and of coordinating the individual levels). Such alternative solution is the concept of order (p. 37).

With reference to this point, see also the final part of the next chapter. As concerns the concept of order in Hayek, see also Hayek 1976, Chapter 4.

to control a changing system, becomes the most relevant and interesting economic problem and market becomes the institution that can guarantee the best distribution of information spread among the agents.[11]

1.7 The role of institutions

While in the neoclassical theory there is no reference to the role of institutions, in the analysis of the Austrian School their role is considered quite relevant. According to Menger, institutions are not the result of social contracts of any kind. In fact, he does not exclude this event, but restricts it only to a few institutions. Other institutions, instead, arose spontaneously from the actions of individuals, pursuing their own interests. This is the origin of language, money, market and States. These institutions are able to carry out their functions best as long as individuals are free to act and pursue their own interests. Here is another characteristic element of the Austrian School: liberalism (Vannucci 1990; De Vecchi 1986b). Any obstacles or hindrances to agents' free actions or to the mechanism of information transmission is detrimental to the correct functioning of the system.[12]

According to Menger, therefore, institutions arise and develop spontaneously (Menger 1883; De Vecchi 1986b; Vannucci 1990; Cubeddu 1986; see also DeVecchi 1986a). Once institutions have developed, they play a crucial role that need to be acknowledged and protected, since institutions guarantee social evolution. In this approach, market in particular is seen in the historical perspective of its development. The mechanism of competition is not aprioristic; its specificity is to be found in the interrelations among individuals pursuing their own interests.

---

[11] With reference to the concept of "market order" in Hayek, see Hayek 1976, Chapter 4. This aspect is also dealt with in the next chapter.

[12] Moreover, the Viennese economists are the forerunners of economic liberalism and of the market system and the most convinced opponents of centralized economic planning. Opposition against Socialism is a constant element in the Austrian School. Among the authors who chiefly dealt with the matter, see Mises (1981, first German edition 1922) and Hayek (the three essays on the subject in Hayek 1949).

If, in the objective perspective of general economic equilibrium, centralized planning may be considered as a necessary consequence (Napoleoni-Ranchetti 1990, pp. 10-11), nevertheless the neo-Austrian criticism shows its limitations. The subject is still the same: the process through which information is divided and conveyed. Such process works "remarkably" only as long as the market is allowed to work freely, with the contribution of every single agent, who influences the prices with his own choices; thus prices become the most immediate pieces of information for the economic planning of the single individual levels.

In a centralized perspective, this mechanism would not work as effectively. It would clash with the quantitative, qualitative, and timely impossibility of concentrating all the necessary information in a single decision-making mind.

Still another consequence has to be highlighted: if this is the origin of institutions, the general system does not necessarily guarantee the general welfare spontaneously. Nevertheless, institutions must be protected just as they are. Any attempt at "improving" them artificially would hinder the "prodigiousness" of these mechanisms. Their prodigiousness is due to their spontaneous nature (this aspect becomes especially relevant in Hayek's thought, as we shall see in the third chapter).

1.8 Concluding remarks

The Austrian School focused its attention on some debatable aspects of Walras' paradigm. They analysed the role of rationality and knowledge, as well as the role and nature of institutions. Generally speaking, we can maintain that their criticism regards the foundations of general economic equilibrium. For this reason, I share the view of scholars like De Vecchi and Zamagni, who - in spite of the differences among the authors belonging to this school - think that a common element can be found in the reference to a particular research model, aimed at interpreting the methods of generation of those decisions that are at the basis of the system and of society's evolution, and at stirring consistent social behaviour (De Vecchi 1986b; see also Zamagni 1982).

This aspect, though, is in turn characterized by another preliminary assumption: considering economic processes as cognitive processes means applying methodological individualism consistently to every aspect of economic reality. As mentioned above, in other approaches methodological individualism was confined to a single aspect of that reality. This is the reason why the results were so different.

In conclusion, there are two critical points, which are complementary and interrelated: the dynamic process of acquisition of knowledge and the bounds of rationality. The first point was stressed by Hayek and the second one by Simon. Both topics regard the process of learning as the key to explaining microbehaviour and the problem of coordination. I will now deal with these aspects in depth, starting from the most important representative of the Austrian School of our century.

2. Hayek on Competition and Knowledge

2.1 Introduction

F. A. Hayek is one of the main representatives of the Austrian School, who interpreted Menger's theory of the spontaneous origin of institutions with a coherent application of methodological subjectivism. His research developed along two main lines. The first one regards the analysis of the mechanism of generation of knowledge, through the study of the mental representations of the world. The second line regards the explanation of the origin of social order in a context characterized by exogenous circumstances, such as the unpredictable consequences of individual actions. These lines are not separated, they often cut across and influence each other.[1] In order to fully understand Hayek's thought, it is necessary to examine his ideas at a micro-level. We shall first examine the mechanism of acquisition of information and then the theory of the spontaneous order (catallaxis).

Hayek criticizes interlinked aspects in the neoclassical paradigm: knowledge and competition.

2.2 The theory of knowledge

The theory of knowledge is probably Hayek's most important contribution to economic theory. In order to study the microfoundations of his analysis, it is necessary to take into account the strict link between theory of knowledge and subjectivism. With his article of 1937, *"Economics and Knowledge"*, Hayek raises a new methodological problem. He maintains that the economic process must be conceived in different terms from the neoclassical tradition. The theory of equilibrium makes economics mere logic of choice, based on a deductive process of self-evident propositions. Between representation and reality of the economic process there is an unbridgeable gap, since no empirical element guarantees a link between theory and system. Hayek finds this empirical element in the process of acquisition and transmission of information. What was considered given to all agents at no cost in the neoclassical theory is, in fact, the result of a dynamic process of acquisition of information and of adjustment of every agent's actions to the others' behaviour. Information, far from being complete and given, is incomplete and

---

[1] Ferry (1990) thinks that Hayek's whole theory can be summed up in his considering the process of acquisition of information as a tool for interpreting social events.

spread, and every agent uses only what he considers relevant. Thanks to the market and to the use of only the pieces of information that are considered relevant - which are conveyed by means of the information indexes - every agent uses, without knowing it, much more knowledge than he actually owns (Hayek, 1937).[2]

Therefore the problem of social sciences becomes understanding how the spontaneous interaction between individuals, who have different information, might result in a situation of order which does not arise from a centralized and planned process.

Hayek thinks that, in order to give an answer to this question, it is necessary to study the real behaviour of real individuals in an economic context, and to understand their limits and their capabilities. Studying Hayek's thought, we face at least two problems. The first one is a microbehavioural problem and consists in understanding how individuals acquire and use knowledge. The key to this research is neurobiological, since it concerns the problem of how individuals perceive stimuli and react. Behaviour is different in every individual and finds its deepest roots in this context. Free markets work because individuals own different information. Their actions (i.e. the use of the information they own) along with other elements, including good luck, lead to failures or to corroborations of their individual plans.

Yet, if we carry out a logical survey, we discover that not only do individuals own different information, but they also give different interpretations to identical stimuli. The resulting actions are necessarily different.

Here comes the second problem. How can social order arise spontaneously from the actions of many individuals, each with his own unique rationality as to both reactions to stimuli (actions) and acquisition of knowledge (interpretative classification of stimuli)? It is necessary, therefore, to explain the passage from the microbehavioural to the holistic level. Observing that individual behaviour is regular is not sufficient to conclude that social order arises automatically. Thermodynamics, in fact, teaches that a set of regular individual behaviours produces a situation of perfect disorder (Hayek 1967a). It is rather necessary to understand what elements lead to spontaneous

---

[2] According to Tamborini (1991), the theory of knowledge is now a central aspect in economic theory. In particular, he underlines the fact that he does not consider valid an objective view on knowledge on an inductive basis, while he is in favour of a form of knowledge seen as an individual creation.

Another Austrian author, O. Morgenstern - who shares Hayek's view on several subjects - has often criticized the Walrasian School, thinking that, when developing models, it is necessary to take into account agents' computational limits and actual ability in handling information (Morgenstern 1935). For details on Morgenstern's criticism of Walras' theory, see Innocenti 1995.

formation of institutions like language, money, market, States, etc., i.e. institutions that enable social organizations to be as effective as possible.[3]

Hayek's answer is antithetical to the contractualistic or rationalistic or constructivistic tradition,[4] according to which individuals deliberately set social rules that everyone must abide by, in order to guarantee the protection of the group. According to the tradition of spontaneous order, followed by Hayek, institutions are the result of thousands of individuals' actions (actions rather than plans) by means of a long process of adjusting and sifting, rather than the result of rational decisions.

The point I want to shed light on, is that - in order to fully understanding economic phenomena - it is necessary to understand how decision-making and human action work, i.e. how mind works. This is the starting point in order to understand social interaction.

As we shall see in depth further on when illustrating his model of mind, Hayek's subjectivism starts from the physiology of the mind. Human behaviour is the result of neurobiological reactions and interpretations with a prevalent meta-conscious nature. These concepts are expressed in Hayek's "logical" works and in *The Sensory Order* in particular. In my opinion this work is an integral part of his production and represents the key to understand his unitary methodological view.

Hutchison's view is different. He maintains (1981, Chapter VII) that Hayek, after 1937, makes a U turn abandoning Mises' apriorism to reach Popper's falsificationism. Hutchison even sees two almost incompatible Hayeks (in this respect, see also Dufourt-Garrouste 1993). The first Hayek - up to 1937 - uses and accepts general economic equilibrium as a reference point for all of his economic theory. Later, Hayek abandons this analytical perspective as a result of Popper's influence. According to Hutchison, Hayek I, following English Classical economists, believes in the existence of social laws; Hayek II, instead, rejects the existence of laws in social sciences and in economics and the idea that these sciences might make predictions. Caldwell criticizes (1988) Hutchison's view, finding methodological continuity in the Austrian economist's works. Caldwell thinks that it is the theory of equilibrium that leads Hayek to new methodological developments: Hayek, as a technical economist, accepts the theory of economic equilibrium and continues to consider it valid as a preliminary analysis for explaining the real world in 1941, when *The Pure Theory of the Capital* is published. The change takes place with the passage from the individual aspect (compatible with the theory of equilibrium) to the social aspect (overall equilibrium). In

---

[3] According to Cubeddu (1996, Chapter 6), the idea that individual actions are at the basis of the organic origin and development of unintentional social institutions is one of the major contributions to social sciences made by the Austrian School, in particular by Menger, Mises, and Hayek.

[4] Hayek considers the contractualistic, rationalistic and constructivistic traditions as synonyms .

"Economics and Knowledge" he does not abandon the idea that every legitimate economic theory should contain concepts of equilibrium. The difference consists in the stress on subjectivism and the mechanism of knowledge acquisition. Hayek never abandons the idea that there is a certain tendency to equilibrium in the reality, yet he cannot explain how the agents' different actions and interests can lead to a situation of equilibrium. This is the reason why Hayek turns his attention to studying the origin of institutions and spontaneous orders (Caldwell 1988). Here another limit has been highlighted. J. Gray and Diamond do not agree with the idea of Hayek as a falsificationist, yet they maintain that in his reasoning there is no evidence that he believes that a spontaneous order of society (cosmos) must necessarily contain moral and political principles of Classical liberalism. In his thought, opposite and incompatible elements can be found (conservatism and libertarianism; traditionalism and individualism; scepticism and rationalism). His works of political philosophy contain unsolved and incompatible problems. Besides, he cannot explain how spontaneous order is created outside the sphere of the market (Gray 1980, in Wood-Woods 1991, III; Diamond 1980, ibid). As shown in this paragraph, there is a lively debate on the methodological aspects of Hayek's thought, and critics are not unanimous. This will be the subject of the next section and especially of the next chapter, where I will deal with the origin of rules of behaviour and of the phenomenon of cultural selection.

2.3 Subjectivism and the criticism of constructivistic rationalism

Hayek's individualism follows the eighteenth century Anglo-Scottish tradition of "spontaneous" order (Hayek 1949).[5] But Hayek also follows the tradition of critical rationalism and he claims to be a follower of Kant, and, much more so, of Hume. His view on the cognitive process is therefore linked to criticism and scepticism. He rejects the idea of the persistence of inborn categories and accepts the idea of the world as the result of the creative action of mind. The mind is, in turn, the result of a peculiar evolution process that will be dealt with in depth. Sensory perceptions come from physical reality and are *interpreted* by the mind; at the same time the mind itself changes and

---

[5] According to Shearmur (1986, p.210), this tradition – including Mandeville, Hume and parts of J. S. Mill - was somehow "created" by Hayek, who grouped these authors, ascribed common ideas to them and later developed these ideas. In his theory of spontaneous order, Hayek often mentions the thought of authors belonging to the Scottish Enlightenment (Macfie 1955, Dow 1987), in order to prove that his own ideas are nothing but a corroboration of what Mandeville, Hume, Hutcheson, J.S.Mill, and above all A. Smith had maintained (Hayek 1967a and 1978). As to the differences between Hayek's thought and the assumed Scottish tradition, see also Gray (1983 and 1988).

develops. The following action ensues from the interpreting activity and the "view on physical reality" developed by the mind.

Certainly this phenomenon is more complex, as we shall see. What I wish to underline now is that a kind of dualism is to be found here between physical reality and mental interpretation and that the latter cannot be explained thoroughly, because it cannot be reduced to a physical dimension. Mind is an instrument used for interpreting reality; mind changes reality and changes itself as a consequence of its own actions.

The knowledge of the outside world is, therefore, a strictly subjective phenomenon, because the "interpretation" of sensory perceptions is subjective. The act of perceiving and learning is limited by every individual's capability to interpret reality, which implies a need for rules and decisions. If these rules are "rational", this is not due to their being the result of a theoretical process of induction and deduction, but the result of a long adjusting process to the surrounding environment.[6]

Along with theoretical (scientific) knowledge, empirical knowledge exists, and it is just as important. This knowledge is gathered unawares every day and it is the most effective knowledge in order to pursue one's goals. Usually people are unaware of this knowledge, since it is acquired spontaneously. It arises from a process of contamination, from individuals imitating other individuals' actions. Individuals find it impossible to describe such process (Hayek 1963). This practical knowledge arises from a long process of cultural selection of the species (Schotter 1981) and from individuals' histories. It is also the key to interpreting sensory reality, a key individuals are unaware of. It is therefore subjective. Here is a new explanation of human actions. They arise from a simultaneous use of two different kinds of knowledge: theoretical and practical knowledge. And no matter what the context is in which the individual acts, decisions are made on the basis of incomplete knowledge, that is considered, nevertheless, complete and indisputable when actions are carried out (Hayek 1967b).[7] What allows individuals to decide and act is a "know how" arising from unconscious practices and customs and only secondarily from theoretical knowledge (Polanyi 1967).[8] This practical knowledge - on which social, economic and political life is founded - changes

---

[6] Please note that there are links between this (Hayek's) concept and Simon's inductive learning, which I will illustrate further on.

[7] Hayek draws on Ryle's distinction between "knowing that" and "knowing how" (Ryle 1949, p. 28). Lachmann (1990, p.31) underlines the importance, in Hayek's thought, of "being able to, without knowing how". Also Oakeshott (1962) mentions Ryle's distinction and maintains that (p. 11) rationalism goes as far as to deny the existence of practical knowledge. For a synthesis of this subject, see Lavoie 1985, pp. 103-4.

[8] With reference to tacit knowledge, which cannot be codified and conveyed to others as pieces of information, see also Hodgson (1988, p. 6): he thinks that these aspects – which are familiar to psychologists, philosophers and social scientists - are not taken into consideration by economists.

along with society and seldom can this change be expressed explicitly. It is, in fact, the result of a selection process and of "genetic heredity", passed on from parents to offspring. For this reason the mechanism of information acquisition and processing is such important an abstract component of decision-making.

This allows us to reject any rationalistic or "constructivistic"[9] (as Hayek used to call it) hypothesis, according to which man creates institutions deliberately and he can control and modify them by means of his mind and of a project. Hayek associates these ideas - from Descartes to Rousseau, from Socialist to Positivistic tradition - since they share the view that only what can be explained rationally can also be accepted as a basic principle for social laws; the problem of knowledge is taken into account only at an intellectual and objective level. Hayek, instead, thinks that mind is not pre-existing. It develops along with society. Institutions have not been created. They are the result of a spontaneous evolution: "they are the result of human actions but not of human design".[10]

Therefore there is no room in Hayek's ideas for a scientist view on social sciences: the individual's behaviour cannot be understood objectively, according to precise mathematical rules, because of the structural limits of our mind. For the same reason a central mind - that is capable of developing effective rules of social behaviour - cannot exist. Such rules are the result of a long evolution of society, during which the experience of a lot of attempts and mistakes has been selected and stored (Hayek 1967b).

The structural limits of mind are at the basis of Hayek's methodological subjectivism, as well of his understanding of the social dimension. According to Hayek, there are simple phenomena, such as the phenomena of the physical world, that can be reduced to formulae, and other phenomena, regarding the mind and the social dimension, that are more complex (*The Theory of Complex Phenomena*, in Hayek 1967a). Therefore we cannot look upon economics by the same standard as physics, since the human mind is not able to "bear" all the necessary information for a correct prediction, some aspects being unknowable. In economics, for example, we cannot leave the interactive process between mind structure and surrounding environment out of consideration (Hayek 1967a).

---

[9] The use of the word "constructivism" might cause misunderstanding. Above, I have referred to Hayek as one of the major representatives of constructivism, while in these pages he is considered as an implacable critic of this approach. The possible misunderstanding can be overcome by keeping in mind the difference between the social and the individual level. Hayek supports the subjectivistic thesis which considers the individual as a "builder" of knowledge, but he categorically rejects the idea that institutions are the result of a process of social engineering. It is therefore possible to maintain that Hayek is a follower of constructivism at a micro level, while the same cannot be said at a macro level.

[10] See "The Results of Human Actions but not of Human Design", in Hayek 1967a; and "The Errors of Constructivism", in Hayek 1978.

In social sciences, scientific knowledge is hardly sufficient to assess future results of present actions. For a correct prediction, the knowledge of unknowable and incommunicable dimensions would be necessary. Individuals, therefore, cannot but act in conditions of uncertainty. For the followers of situational determinism, instead, human behaviour is rational when it pursues its goals within the limit of given conditions and circumstances (Simon 1967). Mind is considered a passive sieve, through which the data concerning decisions are perceived. This is the static subjectivism model (O'Driscoll-Rizzo 1985). Such is the neoclassical approach to human behaviour in microeconomics. On the contrary, Hayek thinks that it is necessary to study the individual decision-making process, rather than its results. The model underlying this approach is dynamic subjectivism, in which mind is conceived as a creating entity (O'Driscoll-Rizzo 1985; Witt 1992; Vanberg 1994).

Hayek maintains that constructivistic rationalism conceives conscious mind as the determinant of every specific action. Evolutionary or critical rationalism, on the contrary, in Karl Popper's terms, "recognizes abstractions as the indispensable means of the mind which enable it to deal with a reality it cannot fully comprehend" (Hayek 1973, pp. 29-30; see also Hayek 1967a).

2.4 The meaning of competition according to Hayek

The different meaning and role of competition at the origin of the neoclassical and the Austrian Schools has already been underlined. Now we shall focus our attention on Hayek's contribution. He often deals with this problem and writes two articles on the subject (Hayek 1946 and 1968). I will now illustrate their contents (a good résumé of Hayek's thought on competition can be found in Ferry 1990).

Hayek starts from the contradiction between the concept of perfect competition in economic theory and what in reality is experienced by, for example, the businessmen. According to the neoclassical theory, perfect knowledge is considered the right model to assess competition in the real world. If reality is different from the model, it is necessary to intervene to adjust it (Hayek 1946).

As stated above, in the static model of competitive equilibrium,[11] conclusions are implicit in the initial hypotheses. Economic action depends

---

[11] As stated by Donzelli, the concept of equilibrium Hayek applies to his analysis of the cycle is the stationary concept. Stationary economic equilibrium refers to an equilibrium indicating the trend, the "theoretical rule", which prevails in a system characterized by an invariant configuration of data, and in which any adjustment is carried out in real time. It differs from static or instantaneous equilibrium (*à la* Walras-Pareto) in that here adjustments are fast and are carried out in logical time (Donzelli 1998, pp. 24-26). See also Donzelli 1986, Chapter 4, and Garofalo 1990, Chapter 1.

on a great number of individuals, who try to develop their individual plans of action by adjusting the data they have at their disposal to objective facts of their own environment. The followers of Walras presume that data are already adjusted, while Hayek thinks that the main problem is understanding how such adjustment takes place. The neoclassical model is static, whereas competition is a dynamic process by its very nature. In standard economic theory, the fundamental characteristics of dynamism are eliminated by hypothesis.

The presuppositions of perfect competition are:

  i) that a homogeneous good is dealt with by a sufficient number of sellers and purchasers and that they are small enough, so that none of them can significantly influence the price independently of the others;
  ii) full freedom of entrance into the market, without constraints to price and resource movements;
  iii) complete knowledge of all relevant factors on the part of market operators (Hayek 1946).

Hayek's first criticism to this approach concerns the paradox that, if everybody knows everything, actions are subject to paralysis. None of the expedients that are used in everyday life would be possible. Perfect competition implies the absence of all the activities characterizing competition. Real data show that the goods sold by two producers are never really the same, at least because the goods are located in two different places. These differences are at the origin of competition and economic issues.

Thanks to competition, goods are produced by those who can do it in the best possible way. The real problem of political economics is not finding out whether it is possible to obtain given goods and services at given marginal costs; it is finding out which goods and services can meet people's needs in a less expensive way (Hayek 1946). In well-organized markets of standardized goods, such as wheat, there is no need for competition. There is no need for a great number of actions, either, since the situation is such that the conditions at which competition aims are fulfilled from the very beginning. Innovations spread quickly and economic analysis usually considers these transitional periods irrelevant. Yet, only in these intervals can the mechanism of competition work (Hayek 1946). The more complex and imperfect the objective conditions in which competition works, the more relevant its power.

Hayek's idea is that, should the circumstances known as perfect competition exist in reality, all the activities connected with competition would become useless. In reality, this motive power of economic life has hardly been studied at all. The real problem is understanding how the knowledge owned by economic agents can be used in the best possible way. For example, the knowledge of the lowest price at which a good can be produced, can be acquired only by means of the competition mechanisms. It cannot be reasonably maintained that, in a situation of free competition, consumers have the necessary knowledge at their disposal before the competition process starts. In fact, the information upon which agents base their actions is spread by means of the market.[12]

Therefore competition is essentially a process of opinion formation. "It creates the views people have about what is best and cheapest." Competition "is thus a process which involves a continuous change in the data and whose significance must therefore be completely missed by any theory which treats these data as constant" (Hayek 1946, p. 106).

Competition brings about a kind of impersonal constraint, compelling individuals to modify their actions. Neither an explicit command, nor any deliberate order could possibly reach the same goal. According to the concept of equilibrium, though, all the facts to be discovered have already been discovered and competition is no longer working (Hayek 1968).

Hayek's development of the theory of spontaneous order - following Menger's tradition - is strictly connected with the meaning of competition. Before examining this aspect, it is necessary to study the subjectivistic roots of social process, concerning the mechanism of communication, imitation and selection of rules of behaviour.

2.5 Communication

Communication is the fundamental act of social interaction. Hayek believes that communication works through affinity. There are common patterns that have developed through a process of imitation. According to such patterns, everybody can interpret other people's thought and language, put himself in their place and look at the world through their categories of interpretation (Hayek 1952a). Without these patterns, neither affinity nor communication is possible. This is the case for deviant individuals. We cannot understand their behaviour because we have no common patterns and we cannot put ourselves in their place. Their behaviour does not match with our world and our past experience, therefore it is perceived as a situation of danger (Hayek 1952a).

The common patterns of behaviour, which Hayek defines "rules of correct behaviour", simplify the complexity of the world (they lower its level of entropy) and allow us to act with a certain level of predictability. Yet, they do not allow us to predict the specific action of every individual. It will always be unpredictable or only partially predictable, since the patterns, in spite of their being similar and common, are organized subjectively.

The crucial aspect allowing different individuals' instruments of knowledge to be similar, is their common origin, since these instruments arise from a process of imitation of other individuals' most effective actions. This

---

[12] According to this approach, the role of competition is even more important in those countries, which have not yet discovered unknown opportunities. Generally a high growth rate means that, in the past, several potentialities were neglected (Hayek 1968).

process takes place at a meta-conscious level because individuals learn how without knowing why. A child - says Hayek - learns how to speak correctly without any knowledge of grammar rules (Hayek 1963).

In any unknown circumstances, individuals learn by imitating other individuals.[13] This ability to understand the rules of other individuals' actions is the "physiognomic perception", which is the result of a process of imitation as well as of identification. Individual behaviour is perceived as belonging to the same species of behaviour as the other components of the group.

This is a crucial point of our reasoning. We found out that Hayek's main contribution to economic theory is the process of acquisition of knowledge. It is now necessary to study the link between such process and the origin and role of institutions. Yet, some aspects have to be examined first. They concern the role of learning and of *problem-solving*. I will dedicate a whole chapter to these aspects, that I consider fundamental in the framework of this research: I will illustrate Hayek's model of mind along with the link between mind and institutions.

---

[13] Like Hayek (1952a, p. 224), also Knight (1947) refers to an unconscious individual mechanism by which customs and traditions are acquired, through imitation.

3. Mind and Institutions

> The structure of men's mind, the common principle on which they classify external events, provide us with the knowledge of the recurrent elements of which different social structures are built up and in terms of which we can alone describe and explain them.
>
> (Hayek 1942, pp. 283-4)

3.1 Introduction

Hayek and Simon criticize the neoclassical paradigm, taking, as a source, the results of neurobiology and logic and giving, in turn, important contributions to these sciences. They both find useful elements for the comprehension of economic phenomena in the same theories: gestaltism[1] and cognitivism.[2] In other words, the two scholars study how the mind works in order to explain human behaviour, which is the basis of economic activities.

Both in Hayek's and in Simon's models, man is not conceived according to the classical abstract concept of *homo oeconomicus*,[3] rational and

---

[1] Unlike behaviourism, Gestalt psychology deals with whole systems and the dynamic correlation between their components. The main idea is that the whole is greater than the sum of its components and has an autonomous meaning with respect to its components. A typical example is a melody, which can be recognized even when its tonalities are changed (the single notes are changed, but the distance between sounds is kept): this is a symptom of the autonomous meaning of the whole. With reference to the origin of Gestalt theory, especially as regards its development as an opposite theory to behaviourism, see Kohler (1947).

[2] Since the 1950s, cognitivists have maintained that each individual is endowed with cognitive functions, allowing him/her to interact with the environment. Not only does the organism adjust to the environment, it also changes it according to its own needs. The attention is focused on the processes of acquisition of information through perception, processing and interpretation of the surrounding world. In this approach a central role is played by the process of feedback between perception and "adjustment" of the subjective patterns, which in turn change on the basis of external stimuli (Gardner 1985). For further details, see Chapter 8 of this book.

[3] It is well known that J. S. Mill, in his essay *On the Definition of Political Economy; and on the Method of Investigation proper to it* of 1836 introduced the concept of *homo economicus*. According to Mill – unlike, for example, Marshall - economists should not deal with the "real" man but with a fictitious man, who maximizes his own wealth.

maximizing. He is rather considered as an individual, endowed with a limited instrument, i.e. his mind, which is the subject of their analysis. This assumption brings economics to a new field of investigation, also from a methodological point of view. It can no longer be considered in the scientist terms of "physics of society", but in terms of continuous exchange with other sciences such as philosophy (Hayek refers to Kant and Popper[4] and Simon refers to Dewey), logic, cybernetics and systems theory.

In this chapter, I will try to shed light on the relation between mind and institutions in Hayek. Afterwards I will deal with the role of mind in Simon's theories. Before illustrating these authors' thought on the subject, I will go back to the nineteenth century, to some pages by Alfred Marshall, that are of great significance in this context and whose importance has not been duly underlined yet.

3.2 The model of mind according to Marshall

Around the 1860s, i.e. long before developing his main contributions to economic theory, Marshall studie philosophical and neurological issues (Raffaelli 1994).

These aspects of Marshall's thought, that have not been duly studied, show that Walras' thought represents an involution with respect to the theoretic wealth of Marshall's works. One important aspect, that did not leave a trace in Walras' works, is the concept of organization as the fourth factor of production, along with the three traditional ones.

Marshall has his own idea of organization, strictly connected with the way the mind works. References to the relation between mind and organizations can be found in *Principles of Economics* (Marshall 1961). Moreover, he wrote a specific work on the subject: *Ye Machine*, of 1867-68. The book deals directly with the relation between mind processes and organizational structures, referring to his contemporary neurological theories. Marshall is convinced that the firm is a result of the organization of production processes, which either develop mental mechanisms, or are the results of such mechanisms.

Marshall thinks that the mind is a multi-level structure, basically made of cerebrum and cerebellum. They constitute two different but interlinked levels, carrying out two distinct functions: a creative function and an executive-adjusting function. When an individual faces a new problem, he uses his mind to solve it. Once the problem has been solved, it is codified into a routine. Now the individual can handle the same problem, every time he faces it, mechanically and without paying much attention. Marshall thinks that, at this

---

[4] I will go back to the relationship between Hayek and Popper, further on. As regards the relationship between Kant and Hayek, the matter is more controversial. According to Cubbeddu (1996, II, Chapter 7), for example, we can talk of a Menger-Aristotelian influence rather than a Kantian influence on Hayek.

point, these procedures are physically conveyed from the cerebrum, that is conscious, to the cerebellum, that is a kind of container of meta-conscious activities. In the cerebellum all the activities are stored which have been experienced and codified by the cerebrum, and they are retrieved and adjusted every time a similar problem arises (Marshall 1867-68).[5]

The following neurobiological research (Gregory 1987) showed that cerebellum is the co-ordinating centre of man's physical equilibrium; it is not what it was thought to be in Marshall's times, i.e. the container of already developed procedures. Yet, what I am interested in is not the validity of neurobiological theories in Marshall's time; it is rather the analogy he brings to view between the work of the mind and the structure of organizations.[6] From this point of view, his theory is still valid.

Marshall thinks that a firm has several levels, just like mind. The higher levels make the new decisions, codify and transmit them to the lower levels. Lower levels do not merely execute (Marshall 1961). When carrying out the codified routines, the cerebellum does not work mechanically. It adjusts the routines - with little effort and unconsciously - to very similar real situations, by means of a *feedback* process. According to Marshall, the "lower" levels of organizations act in a similar way, by adjusting, with a certain degree of freedom, already codified routines. This process, carrying matters to extremes, is quite interesting, since it helps to explain two aspects. At a micro-level, the mind is described as a formidable instrument that is able to carry out several functions. According to this model, the mind keeps releasing new energy towards the higher levels. It develops and codifies a series of procedures, which become significant knowledge for the individual who uses them. Once the procedures have been stored, the energy used to codify them is released. This energy can be used to solve other - probably more complex - problems at a higher level (Marshall 1867-68 and 1961). This approach implies an idea of mental progress and development that can be applied to the development of mankind, also in generational and organizational terms.

And now the second aspect. Organizations often face new and more and more complex problems, just like the mind. Through their hierarchical multi-level structure, organizations solve, codify and release energy, that can be used for solving more complex problems (Marshall 1961). This analogy

---

[5] Of course, Marshall's concept of mind is far more complex and richer than this simplified description. For details, see Raffaelli 1994.

[6] For a more exhaustive definition of the role and nature of organizations and institutions I refer the reader to Chapters 11 and 13. Nevertheless, I deem it necessary to point out now that I follow D. North's definition (1990): institutions are the rules that give a structure to human interaction, while organizations are the "players", who follow those rules. While organizations are tools which are created to reach given aims, institutions have no aims of their own, but they have a spontaneous and organic origin.

between mind and organization can explain the internal evolution of the organization itself and the process of technological development.

We can now point out a few common elements between Marshall and Menger. Marshall's organization has the same organic nature as Menger's institutions. Organizations and institutions are the result of the same limits and potentialities of mind and human behaviour. In the context of a general approach to the problem, Hayek represents a valuable combination of these two theories. Though he does not devote much attention to the concept of organization, he assimilates Marsall's idea of the central role played by the mind in the comprehension of social phenomena. Moreover, he underlines the connection between mind and institutions, which in Menger's theory was in the background. This is how Hayek combines Marshall's ideas with the ideas of the founder of the Austrian School. The Viennese Nobel Prize Winner is less interested than Menger (and this is Hayek's main contribution) in the "genetic" aspect of the formation of social order; he is convinced that natural laws and environment are the result of a process of interpretation by the human mind. The real problem, then, is understanding whether it is possible (and how) to proceed from individual representations to social order (Cubeddu 1996).

3.3 The model of mind according to Hayek

Explaining how mental processes work is fundamental for understanding Hayek's thought. We might even say that it is the unifying element of the explanation of the micro-aspects as well as the macro-aspects. I will try to demonstrate that in the Viennese economist's works there is a strict link between explanation of the mental processes of knowledge acquisition and the origin of institutions. In 1952, he published a book that is of great importance from this point of view: *The Sensory Order.*[7] In this book, Hayek expresses the idea that human mind is structured into general categories with a genetic and sometimes inborn nature. Through these patterns, individuals interpret the sensory data they perceive from outside. These patterns change

---

[7] This text has been little considered by most scholars. A few authors even consider it as separate and different from the rest of Hayek's works (among them Machlup 1974, Runde 1988, Tomlison 1990). Others, instead, think that this text contains the most coherent, complete and systematic description of all the methodological aspects used by Hayek (Gray 1983; see also Miller 1979, Nadeau 1987, De Vries 1993; Vanberg 1994; Witt 1989, and, in Italy, Rizzello 1993 and Cubeddu 1996). As Hayek himself acknowledged (1988b), several psychological considerations contained in *The Sensory Order* are at the basis of his social and economic theory. This acknowledgement alone would be enough to underline its importance. Although it was published in 1952, its origin dates back to thirty years before (Hayek 1952a, Preface). This work was conceived and written in German in the 1920s, when, after studying law, he hesitated over whether to study economics or psychology (Hayek 1983, p. 9 and 1994).

along with our changing perceptions of external data.[8] This process is influenced by genes as well as by the experience of the individuals and of his species. Hayek is referring to Kant's model of mind. Each individual has his own *framework*, where all the patterns necessary to organize the worldview are contained.[9] Such *framework* is the representation of the world the organism has lived in, up to that moment. It contains the classifications and the interpretations given to past stimuli. These patterns are semipermanent. Being the result of past experiences, on the one hand they are steady as to new experiences, on the other they are also influenced by the same new experiences and change slowly, adjusting to individual actions and responding to new external stimuli. Hayek's patterns are not rigid and a priori like Kant's categories. They are rather the result of dispositions, that are probably inborn and certainly reshaped and adjusted by experience.[10]

Thanks to the interactive relation between individual and environment, the mind structure is not rigid and aprioristic. It develops incessantly, according to mechanisms that are spontaneous and unknowable, since they belong to a sphere defined by Hayek as "supraconscious", out of reach for our thought. This is the seat of that implicit and unconscious knowledge that is located at a higher level than traditional, deliberate and intelligible knowledge (as to this concept, Hayek is influenced by M. Polanyi 1967). Individual action is, therefore, the resultant of two forms of knowledge: conscious and unconscious.

Hayek refers to many of Kant's themes, especially the "rationalistic criticism", which he presents in an interpretation that is similar to Popper's. Hayek underlines the importance of studying the structural limits of mind, while abandoning every scientistic claim for a mind endowed with potentialities beyond these limits. In the following pages, you will find some epistemological foundations of Hayek's criticism of constructivistic rationalism and of his agreement with the Anglo-Scottish tradition of spontaneous order.

According to Hayek, mind is a *framework* arranging the perceptions from the outside world by means of neurological phenomena of classification and association of classes of stimuli to classes of responses. Mind does not perceive sensations passively, but through an act of *interpretation*. Each perception and each action (presented in a binding link) are unavoidably

---

[8] Popper (1965) confirms what he has already written: when one observes, a selection is always carried out. A fleeing animal finds new ways out. A hungry animal divides the world into two parts: things that are fit to be eaten and things that are not.

[9] In the years of his education, Hayek was influenced by Ernst Mach (Hayek 1952a, Preface; Hayek 1994).

[10] Miller (1979) underlines that Hayek, in *The Sensory Order*, assumes that the mind is a framework of categories, evolving through the experience of the single individual and of the group, while in his works of the 1940s (Hayek 1952b) he accepts Kant's model of mind, where categories are fixed and unchangeable.

modified by the genetic structure of every individual and by the preceding classifications and associations (acquired experience, varying from individual to individual). Individual behaviour is unpredictable, because it is a creative act with its roots in a perceptive phenomenon. Sensation, as well, is *essentially dependent* on experience (Hayek 1952a) and every individual stores different experiences and creates links between different stimuli. Therefore the same phenomenon cannot be perceived in the same way by different individuals, since each of them associates that specific stimulus to a unique class (as to the role of interpretation in Hayek, see Burczak 1994 and Gray 1994). Thus Hayek gives us a key to the reason why individual cytoarchitecture (the arrangement of cells of various kinds in a tissue and specifically in the cerebellar cortex) is different in every individual: because individuals are genetically different, and above all because everyone lives particular and unique experiences, leading to a different neural structure.

These intuitions have been later confirmed. Neurobiology (Patterson-Nawa 1993; Calissano 1992; Damasio 1995) is demonstrating empirically what Hayed had already understood in the 1920s and then published in 1952. In this work, Hayek explains the microfoundations of the differences in individual behaviour.[11] Moreover, he underlines the physiological bases of methodological subjectivism, according to which the agent is the creator and user of knowledge, the master of economic processes and, above all, the engine of change. If the problem at the heart of economic process is how an individual acquires (learns) and uses (acts) the relevant knowledge, the preliminary study of the mental processes of learning has its *raison d'être*.

Here is the first methodological directive: the foundations of economic theory need to be corroborated by the new developments in logic and neurobiology.

3.3.1 Knowledge and institutions

The most interesting implications of this work are to be found probably in the application of the theory of knowledge to economic process. Market works not only because individuals own different relevant information, but also because they *interpret* the same data in a different way; classifications and *feedback* are, in fact, entirely subjective processes, based on the *genetic tradition* and acquired *experience* of every individual. Difference and freedom become, carrying subjectivism to extremes, the two *necessary* elements for a correct working of market mechanism and for the emerging of spontaneous institutions.

---

[11] F. Knight (1921) had anticipated Hayek as to this aspect: we are not capable of perceiving the present as it is, in its wholeness, as we are endowed with bounded intelligence. Therefore, we cannot predict the future with high degrees of reliability, not knowing all the variables of the present (p. 201).

Describing how the mind works and what its physiological limits are, helps us demonstrate that the economic process has a catallactic nature.[12] Individuals act pursuing their interests and obtain results that cannot be predicted. The necessary elements to reach a "spontaneous order" - based on free and deliberate individual actions - are the following: learning, which occurs at a certain level by means of a process of meta-conscious imitation of other individuals' actions (know what without knowing how); communication between individuals through affinity; constant adjusting to the environment, i.e. adjusting to rules and to their developments. Therefore social order is the unwitting result of the actions of individuals who act pursuing subjective goals.

A few remarks are now necessary. The first one is understanding why Hayek publishes *The Sensory Order* as late as 1952 and not before that. He writes in the preface that he decided to publish the book then, because his theories, developed 30 years before, were still up-to-date, especially as regards the idea that sensory order is at the basis of logic and neurobiology. Probably, a meeting in London at the end of the 1940s with M. Polanyi had an influence on this decision: Polanyi was then developing his theory of monocentric order and polycentric order (Polanyi 1951), which corroborates Hayek's opinion on the microfoundations of spontaneous order.

Along with these influences, there is a link between Hayek's theory of the evolution of social rules and the selection process. This is a mechanism of *cultural selection* based on man's ability to learn through imitation.

Many of the aspects dealt with, directly concern another problem that was extensively studied by the Austrian School: the problem of the origin of institutions. Yet, there are other quite relevant and up-to-date themes that I have not explicitly dealt with yet. I will try to do it now. I will begin by explaining all the implications of Hayek's model of mind.

The cognitivist approach to the problem of choice stands out among the characteristic aspects of a large part of today's economic theory. This approach, along with the subjects of knowledge and bounded rationality, urge scholars to find new microfoundations for economic analysis. Thanks to the growing application in economics of the discoveries in the field of logic, neurobiology, cybernetics, and artificial intelligence, the approach started by H. Simon in the 1950s has had a fast development in the last decade.

Hayek's analysis of the physiological limits of the work of mind is close to the results of modern cognitivist psychology and also, implicitly, to other aspects that in the future will prove relevant for both bounded and procedural rationality.

Moreover, in the specific fields of neurobiology and psychology, the extremely detailed descriptions of cognitive process in *The Sensory Order* anticipate the empirical results reached by Soviet neurobiology as well by the followers of Piaget on cognitivism in the last decades. These results underline

---

[12] As regards catallaxis, see next Section 3.4.

the importance of the social dimension in building individual intelligence (this topic is exhaustively dealt with in Chapter 8).

Therefore Hayek's approach has to be taken into account within the broader context of the contributions to the development of cognitive science. Hayek's approach is quite important for economists, especially those who decide to take up the gauntlet and try to find alternatives to neoclassical microfoundations for economic theory.

I will now more closely examine the perception, action, adjusting and knowledge mechanisms along with the role of the meta-conscious dimension in Hayek's model of mind.

3.3.2 Perception

Human behaviour is unpredictable and the reasons for that are to be found in the phenomenon of perception. This is a part of a continuous process, through which the microcosmos of the brain obtains a reproduction of the external macrocosmos by means of successive approximations (Hayek 1952a). Thus knowledge is representation and the actions carried out by the mind are acts of classification and re-classification of perceived stimuli. Past *experience* plays a key role: it creates a system of links which records the situations when - in the history of the organism - the different groups of stimuli have worked together (Hayek 1952a). Everything we perceive is immediately compared to other classes of recorded events. Every perception of a new stimulus or class of stimuli is influenced by the already existing classifications. A new phenomenon is always perceived in association with other events it shares something with. A single event that cannot be compared to a recorded and classified something, will not be perceived (Hayek 1952a).

Every individual stores different experiences and creates a different system of links among stimuli. It is evident that Hayek's methodological subjectivism is deeply rooted. This approach is antithetical to Russel's approach, who maintains that the essence of a sensation is its being independent of past experience. For Hayek, on the contrary, a sensation is *essentially dependent* on experience. This topic is worth being investigated thoroughly. A simplistic interpretation might lead the reader to think that past experience modifies or adds something new to a sensation that is originally pure. This is not true. The "integrity" of sensory qualities itself is an "interpretation" based on the experience of the individual or of his race (Hayek 1952a).

As mentioned above, Hayek thinks that the mind has semi-permanent patterns, since they are modified by experience: not only by individual experience, but also by what we unwittingly receive from the group and the environment we belong to. Routine individual action corroborates the customs of the group; innovatory individual action contributes to the development of the group *framework*.

3.3.3 Perception-action

Perception is strictly linked to action through an adjusting process. The perceptive patterns adjust to (are influenced by) behavioural patterns and vice versa. Between perception and action there is a continuous *feedback* process and the resulting sensory order is simultaneously input and output of the activities of the higher nervous centres (Hayek 1952a). The meaning of our perceptions and images springs from the rules of the already experienced actions they are associated with. If in the past, when facing a problem, we experienced effective patterns of action, we are ready to use them again if we associate these selected patterns to new perceived phenomena.

This is due to the circumstance that our nervous organs always perceive not a single stimulus but a class of stimuli, which these organs associate to a class of responses, and classes of classes of stimuli, which they associate to classes of classes of responses (Hayek 1952a).

In brief, association is the main phenomenon of knowledge and it is present both in perception and in action. Classification by means of individual association of stimuli leads to quite different individual interpretations (and, as a consequence, actions). This happens because the combination of stimuli and actions is linked to every individual's *history* and *specific experiences*.

3.3.4 Adaptation-knowledge

Knowledge means adjusting situations that do not correspond to what has already been acquired. In other words, knowledge is a continuous adjusting process of perceived data that do not match preceding experiences.

As mentioned above, the same situation is never perceived identically by different individuals. Adjusting actions, consequently, can never be exactly predicted by an external observer (theses concepts and behaviourism are poles apart).[13] Hayek describes a specific "physical" interaction between internal and external stimuli bearing out his theory. Internal stimuli are the "spontaneous reactions" of an organism to external stimuli and are further differentiated from individual to individual (Hayek 1952a). When mind faces a problem, it focuses its attention only on the aspects that do not correspond to already acquired knowledge. Our mind - Hayek says - is like the captain of a ship, who cannot contemporarily be engaged in all the sailing activities: he focuses his attention on the situations that the sailors report as unusual. With his decisions, he tries to adjust what is incongruous (Hayek 1952a), by means of a process of association with past experiences.

Our higher centres focus their attention only on what is incongruous. *Déjà vu* is considered acquired knowledge. What is new, is to be adjusted.

In the process of knowledge acquisition of new phenomena, therefore, two mechanisms work contemporarily: the synchronous multiple classification of

---

[13] For details, see Chapter 8.

perception and action and the time dimension linked to *feedback*. The resulting knowledge/adjustment is neither logic nor conscious. That is to say, it is not scientific knowledge of any kind. It is rather a kind of *ésprit de finesse*, an actually natural knowledge. It arises· from everyday practical actions, from experimented and selected past experiences: it is our spontaneous and immediate actions, that are based on behavioural mechanisms of our fellow-creatures.

This kind of knowledge has two interesting aspects. On the one hand, it is a selection process on the part of the species, learned by every individual through unconscious imitation; on the other hand, it is also, and above all, based on the individual association of perceptions, which makes knowledge personal and differentiated.

3.3.5 Meta-conscious

Individuals act by using two kinds of knowledge. One of them is concrete and well defined, deliberate, logically determined. The second one is unconscious, spontaneous, and - in Hayek's words - abstract. Hayek focuses his attention on this second kind of knowledge, this non-conscious reality which he defines as meta-conscious.[14] This dimension represents subjective intuition, know-how and ability. Meta-conscious knowledge is also made up of our own rules of behaviour, which we cannot explain in well-defined scientific terms, since one brain can never fully know another brain, being knowledge dependent on brain mechanisms. In this case, subject and object coincide and the implicit dimension incorporates the explicit one (Hayek 1952a). This aspect can be better understood, after further outlining Hayek's model of mind.

Mind is a system of abstract rules arranging our perceptions of the world, like a "sieve". Every sensation, perception and image is produced by overlapping several "classifications" of events, perceived according to differentiated meanings. Abstractions are dispositions making the organism inclined to respond to certain stimuli; inclinations to action arise, in turn, from the overlapping of a lot of such dispositions. The general models of actions work like moulds in which external perceptions are shaped. It is important to underline that the models of actions are not created by the mind a priori, but arise from a selection process: they correspond to specific structures of the nervous system (neural interactions), selected according to their effectiveness and consequently abandoned or stored. Abstractions are neither "deliberate" nor "built", since the selection process is "spontaneous". There is a continuous feedback between mind structures and external factors and the emergence of a new abstract rule means changing the mind system by means of an "adjusting-adapting" process based on external impulses.[15]

---

[14] Hayek 1952a, pp. 111 and 138.
[15] Hayek 1978.

The creation of a new abstraction, therefore, is *never* the result of a conscious process, something the mind might accomplish deliberately. At the most, the mind can *a posteriori* discover something that is already regulating its actions.

Certainly a process of transfer of learned rules exists and is based on the association model. Recognizing a correspondence between patterns built on different sensory elements, presupposes a mechanism of multi-pattern sensory transfer. It is a transfer of the ability to distinguish an abstract order or disposition, from one field to another (Hayek 1963). A neural process is responsible for this transfer: it consists in correlations between different neurons (impulses between neurons excited by sensations) creating a hierarchical order of classification. When we recognize that in a given order we find the same features leading us to our concept of large, high, intense, etc., then we transfer an already known pattern onto another. Once again this is a subjective process. The subjective and differentiated structure of relationship among these abstract characteristics leads to considering the patterns similar or different (Hayek 1963).

These rules of intelligibility may not be explicitly known or communicated (Polanyi 1951). They belong to the supra-conscious, that may not be known, because it is too high a level for the limits of the cognitive ability of human mind. When watching other individuals, we do not perceive single movements, but intentions, moods and attitudes, i.e. we perceive only abstract combinations. We do not perceive single clues, but clues arranged in an abstract meaning. The great number of subjective combinations of rules (abstract propensity) make new and differentiated actions possible. Every action of a mind-regulated organism is something new.

3.3.6 Analogies between Hayek's and Popper's models

Hayek's and Popper's models show numerous similarities. These two scholars were friends and they met frequently, sharing similar views and influencing each other. An exhaustive exposition of Popper's concept of mind can be found in the first of the three volumes *The Self and Its Brain* (Popper-Eccles 1977). Popper's Self, as well as Hayek's, is an active concept. The brain is owned by the Self and not vice versa (Popper-Eccles 1977). Popper uses Plato's metaphor of the mind as a pilot, who observes, assesses, decides and acts. This concept is, for him, in complete contrast with Hume's concept of the mind as the total amount, beam or stream of his experiences. The first concept has an active dimension, while the second one is quite passive (Popper-Eccles 1977). Our mind draws from two equally important sources of knowledge, one of them is inherited, the other one is acquired. Popper underlines the importance of acquired experience, in contrast with empiricist tradition. "Without the background of inherited knowledge, which is almost all unconscious, and which is incorporated in our genes, we would not, of course, be able to acquire any new knowledge" (Popper-Eccles 1977, p. 121).

The empiricist tradition of the mind as a *tabula rasa* before sensory perception starts, is therefore, for Popper, absurd, grotesque and unacceptable.

Moreover,.Popper, like Hayek, thinks that the mind has a conscious and an unconscious dimension. Information implies a modification of the already acquired knowledge. Most of the acquired knowledge that is perceived through senses is also unconscious. Conscious knowledge is the knowledge of world 3, where worlds 2 and 1 interact.[16]

Our willing behaviour is mostly produced without any intervention of consciousness. It intervenes, instead, when we face new problems. Consciousness is necessary to select new expectations and theories critically (Popper-Eccles 1977).

3.4 Spontaneous order

One of the main problems Hayek deals with is understanding how social order can be created if not deliberately. The hypothesis is that social order is spontaneous and arises from individual free acting.

By communicating, individuals can establish a series of social relations through "sympathy". Yet, communication alone does not account for the emergence of order. The elements acquired so far, confirm that individuals act using the knowledge arising from their personal interpretation of external stimuli. Social order hinges on individual rules of correct human interaction, which all the individuals share. These rules are not the result of the will to set up an ordinate coexistence, but a result of individuals' actions. These rules themselves are meta-conscious patterns in continuous development. They are not in-born, they are the result of a selection process.

3.4.1 The origin of rules of behaviour and their selection

The mechanism is quite simple. The actions that are useful for the group development persist and are replaced as soon as more useful ones are experienced. All the actions that are harmful for the group development are eliminated (Hayek 1973; Hayek 1952a).[17] The freedom of individual action is thus limited by the condition that it must not clash with the group interests.

---

[16] Popper-Eccles (1977). It is well known that Popper thinks that three different worlds exist. World 1 is the world of physical objects and it is different from world 2, i. e. the subjective or psychological one. They both differ from world 3, created by man. This is the objective world of the products of human mind: myths, tales, scientific theories, and works of art.

[17] For a better comprehension of what follows, it is useful to draw readers' attention to the fact that the evolutionary and selective view on institutions is one of the major aspects of the institutionalist approach (compare Veblen 1899). As to the importance of these aspects in Hayek, see the last chapter of this book.

Vice versa, opposite mechanisms might exist: there are action of the group that are unfavourable for some individuals. These mechanisms persist and are handed down from generation to generation. New rules of behaviour arise through an interactive process of adjusting existing rules that are subject to selection (Hayek 1960).

Order arises from two aspects. One is individuals' free actions, by means of subjective interpretation of the external world; the second one, laws and moral rules that individuals use spontaneously, since they received them almost at a "genetic level". Naturally individual action may upset the group equilibrium and a pre-active knowledge should be assumed in order to contribute to preserve order. Understanding how rules of behaviour are selected, can help us answer this question. The selection mechanism - as I shall explain in detail in Chapter 13 - is different from the natural or genetic one. Unlike the latter - which is slower - the former develops thanks to the individual's ability to learn though imitation, which allows him to behave in a certain way without knowing "why" and yet behave in the right way, since he follows rules that have consolidated over a long time. Usage, custom and convention, i.e. the "culture" of a nation or of a social group, is the memory of actions that have proved useful for the group itself and are capable of preserving order (Hayek 1967b).[18]

3.4.2 Monocentric order and polycentric order

To define spontaneous order, Hayek borrows the word "cosmos" from Greek language, as opposed to deliberate and artificially created order, defined "taxis" (Hayek 1973). On this point Hayek is influenced by Polanyi:[19] his differentiation between polycentric and monocentric order becomes an integral part of Hayek's theory.

According to Polanyi, order is established by individuals' spontaneous interaction, each individual being a centre of free decision. In monocentric order, instead, every individual action is subject to a central authority (Polanyi 1951). Polycentric order is a better system than monocentric order, since in the context of polycentric order large and complex modern societies are organized more effectively. In monocentric order, to better manage social organization, it is necessary to concentrate all the knowledge at one point before making decisions. This requirement implies the slowing down of the decision-making process and it is inconsistent with the limited capacity of the human mind: the mind is able to handle only a certain number of pieces of information and to control directly only a certain number of people (Polanyi estimates no more than five).

---

[18] With reference to social institutions that have been established by means of recurring practices, see also Giddens 1982.

[19] For details on this interesting author, see the brief biographical essay by Allen (1990).

In polycentric order, instead, every agent continuously and spontaneously adjusts his actions according to the other agents' actions: he can act immediately, there is no need to wait for instructions. He does so by using only the few indexes of knowledge he considers relevant, and he transmits, in turn, more information other interacting individuals will adjust their action to wich.

In the case of few individuals, planning is certainly possible and is, in fact, the best possible organization. But in a large system or society, planning becomes impossible and order can be reached only through continuous adjusting of individual actions to other individuals' behaviour. In this way an absolute optimum is not obtained, yet a situation of efficiency is established, which no other form of cooperation might yield (Polanyi 1951).

A formidable mechanism for establishing order is the market, characterized by polycentrism: if somewhere a variation takes place, adjustment will take place in the rest of the market and so on. Polycentrism is believed to be also a characteristic of human beings, who can continuously interact and adjust to their surrounding environment.

3.4.3 Catallaxis

The analogy between Hayek's and Polanyi's theories should not pass unnoticed. Hayek's spontaneous order is established through evolution.[20] Artificially created order (taxis) is similar to monocentric order and is characteristic of small-size organizations, which have well-determined and specific goals and whose organizational complexity does not overcome the limits of its founders. In spontaneous order there are no specific goals, it allows individuals to pursue their own interests.

Within organizations, every agent has his strategic, specific, determined and hierarchical position. The relations are regulated by the decisions of the central authority ruling the organization. In spontaneous order, there are no rigid positions. Roles are interchangeable and actions are free. Spontaneous order, though, is less precise and more difficult to control than organizations.

Every agent plans his own economic actions, when he develops his plan of behaviour. Catallaxis, instead, is the resultant of free individual actions and

---

[20] This is not a Darwinian selection. The selection Hayek refers to is of a "cultural" kind and it is closer to a Lamarckian selection. In fact, Hayek considers the selection of institutions more interesting than individual selection. Moreover, unlike what is generally held, he thinks that the concept of evolution belongs to social sciences, rather than to biology. According to Hayek, the idea of evolution was developed long before Darwin, who used this idea neglecting the most relevant aspect, concerning the evolution of institutions (Hayek 1973; Hayek 1988a, pp. 23-24).
In the recent literature, Hayek has been accused of ambiguity, with reference to his concept of evolution. I will deal with this in the last section of this chapter and in Chapter 13. A valuable illustration of Hayek's theory of spontaneous order can be found in Gissurarson 1987, Chapter 2.

can neither be planned nor controlled. Certainly, catallaxis does not guarantee the best possible social organization. Yet, for large societies or open societies, where in every moment a great quantity of pieces of information are exchanged, there is no better way for individuals to interact. Through this mechanism, individuals who do not know each other get in touch and unwittingly contribute to everybody's interest.[21]

Agents do not look for scientific and all-encompassing information, they look for specific information, concerning where and when. This skin-deep information implies a series of circumstances the agents do not and will not know anything about. Market, as a spontaneously developed mechanism of social coordination, is considered a cybernetic tool, ruling the agents and allowing a certain degree of coincidence of predictions. Variables act like signals, indexes, incorporating and pointing out the factors of endogenous evolution (Ferry 1990). Market arises spontaneously, it is due to a casual discovery; it was not created by man deliberately, because it is beyond man's capacity. The more complex a society becomes and the more generalized its exchange circuitries, the more unaware of its functioning can be its components.

Let us now go back to the premises of our reasoning. Theory of knowledge and subjectivism are the foundations of Hayek's criticism of social constructivism, scientism and theory of planning. The study of mind and its limits in relation to agents' actual behaviour stirred up a new debate in economics. Some contributions to this debate that have been developed by other authors (H. Simon, first of all) are worth examining thoroughly. Before that it is necessary to illustrate some criticisms of this subject that have been put forward in the last few years.

3.5 Criticisms of the Hayekian idea of spontaneous order

Hayek's theory of cultural evolution of group rules has been criticized by Vanberg, who underlined that the group selection process is inconsistent with methodological individualism (Vanberg 1986 and 1994).

As mentioned above, Hayek thinks that there is no spontaneous market order as such, which might be considered efficient and useful, apart from the rules and institutions regulating participants' behaviour. His aim is not understanding what the best criteria are for such rules to follow. He insists, instead, on the origin and the process of development of cultural rules. Vanberg makes the following remarks. The emergence of rules in an evolution process is determined by the interaction of two processes: change (continuous transmission of new variations) and selection. We cannot take it for granted that, from a process based on individual innovation and on selection (based on imitation), there emerge rules useful for the group.

---

[21] As to this point, besides the already mentioned Hayek (1973), see also Donzelli 1988, pp. 45-47.

Vanberg thinks that Hayek has neither developed systematically, nor pursued consistently an evolutionary-individualistic analysis of the following problem: why and how rules that improve the group efficiency and help to solve social problems can be considered spontaneous. On the contrary, in Hayek's theory there is a blurred boundary between two quite different ideas: on the one hand, the idea that the rules of behaviour emerge and prevail because they are useful for the individual observing them; on the other hand, the idea that rules are observed because they are useful for the group (Vanberg 1986).

Vanberg maintains that, once a rule has been established in a group, it cannot be taken for granted that it will develop into the most efficient rule for the group, by means of a spontaneous process. Some consolidated rules need a deliberate and organized action to be changed. In other words, if the market is not independent of the rules observed by the participants, it is necessary to understand what mechanism can select the rules leading to the emergence of order. Hayek excludes the possibility of a mechanism "establishing" rules because the agents' behaviours change along with the change of social reality. Yet, Vanberg maintains, the concept of cultural group selection is theoretically vague, inconsistent with Hayek's individualistic approach and incomplete. This concept of cultural evolution has a restricted range of applicability, since a great number of basic rules of market order are implemented and limited by organized systems; and also because certain rules may not arise from a spontaneous process, if not under limiting conditions. The idea that spontaneous forces, if let "alone", can give rise to useful rules is not convincing.

Criticisms concern also Hayek's idea of egoistic *self interest* as the criterion regulating spontaneous interaction. Axelrod underlines that the mechanism of reciprocity is the main source of cooperation between individuals with conflicting interests (Axelrod 1984 and Axelrod-Hamilton 1981); this topic - he adds - is part of the Scottish economists' social theory which Hayek refers to (Hayek 1984).

Following Vanberg, Hodgson also criticizes Hayek's concept of selection on the grounds that selection always operates in a structured context, i.e. the market (Hodgson 1991). He suggests that the analysis should be shifted to selection at structure and substructure level, which leads not only to different groups and agencies, but also to different economic systems or subsystems. His ideas draw on modern theoretical works in the field of biology, which study, along with group selection, different levels of selection (Hodgson 1991).

In a socio-economic context, the selecting criterion ought to include also a number of models of economic structures, not only a number of groups and individuals in a free market system. This system is in contrast with both the absolute trust in the market and centralized planning. Therefore criticisms of Hayek's theory should concern the absence of additional selecting processes beyond the group level - including different types of institutions, among which market and non-market - rather than the fact that, by embracing group selection, he abandons consistent individualism.

Moreover, Hodgson considers Hayek's mechanism of rule selection ambiguous, since he does not indicate whether it occurs phylogenetically or ontogenetically. The distinction is especially relevant - he continues - since, with selection of the first kind, there would be a contrast between Hayek's individualism and the idea of selection (Hodgson 1993).[22]

Jossa (1993) criticized Hayek with reference to a different aspect: the possibility of planned activities in a market economy, which Hayek excludes. He thinks that Hayek does not explain with convincing arguments why a spontaneously created order should not be modified rationally. Jossa supports Popper's opinion, who accepts the idea of market economy as a spontaneous order, but thinks that such order may be modified step by step, according to rational and specific plans. But, though market order emerges spontaneously, man can intervene and does intervene to improve it (Jossa 1993).

Jossa refers to an idea generally shared by scholars, that state intervention aimed at reducing social imbalance is always possible and advisable, as long as it does not slow down production. The problem is, therefore, finding the best *trade-off*, rather than refraining from state intervention.

Shackle (1972) writes that Hayek, by insisting on the limits of human knowledge and on the subjective character of human expectations, introduces an unbalancing factor, which is not duly accounted for in the explanation of market processes. His theory, for example, does not explain market failures, which play a crucial role in contemporary economic theory.[23]

---

[22] Tomlinson (1990) and Barry (1979), too, think that the concept of selection in Hayek is ambiguous.

[23] These are situations in which the market is not able to bring about an optimum allocation of resources of the system, because of the peculiar nature of specific goods, such as information or inventions, or as a result of the presence of externalities. This word was introduced in the 1950s as a substitute for (but with the same meaning as) the word used by Pigou in 1920, i.e. external economies and diseconomies (Coase 1988b, p. 23). The presence of such diseconomies in the economic system is seen as the cause of unbalances hindering the correct allocation of resources. This justifies Government's intervention. In the literature, a classical example is the one proposed by Pigou in 1920, which concerns the damage caused by fires in the fields and woods around railway lines, due to sparks coming from locomotives: since the railways, and specifically the train service, cause external diseconomies for the landowners, the Government's intervention aimed at eliminating such diseconomies is considered justifiable (Pigou 1952, p. 134). This is one of the fundamental principles used to justify the regulating role of Government in the economic system. Coase (1960, Section 8) criticized Pigou and put forward the idea that the mere existence of externalities does not imply a necessary intervention by the Government. At the most, Coase maintains, we should talk of generalized externalities, since several effects of economic transactions are not "synthesized" by the market. According to this author, in order to understand such phenomena, attention should be focused on the presence of transaction costs (see Chapter 12 of this book). Moreover, since also Government's intervention implies costs, a Government, in the presence of externalities, should

Finally, Hayek's theory shares the limits of the Austrian School, i.e. it does not account for organizations (Loasby 1991a).

As to the alleged ambiguity of Hayek's idea of evolution, we refer the reader to the last chapter of this book, where the problem is dealt with thoroughly. I wish to anticipate here that I do not see any ambiguity, but an original equilibrium between ontogenesis and phylogenesis, a unitary principle of selection, which is applicable to both individuals and institutions.

As regards Jossa, I would like to point out that, according to his criticism, Hayek's theory seems to exclude State intervention *tout court*. It is therefore worth underlining that, for Hayek, market cannot work without a State, intervening in extra-market economic activities, guaranteeing social security and preventing the risks due to the presence of monopolies. Rather than considering him against any kind of State intervention, it is more correct to say that Heyek is against contamination between public and private law and that he believes in a nomocratic society (governed according to the law) rather than in a telocratic society (governed pursuing specific goals).

Finally, I share Shackle's and Loasby's critical views. The aspects underlined especially by Loasby, represent Hayek's main limit, that is probably the limit of the whole Austrian tradition. These problems - that will be dealt with later - are nowadays finding solutions within neoinstitutionalism, a line of research Hayek contributed to creating.

---

decide whether its intervention is advisable or not, on the basis of the cost-effectiveness (and social convenience) of that specific intervention. But, such an extensive presence of externalities makes it advisable for the Government not to intervene, rather than making such intervention necessary (Coase 1988b, p. 26). Stiglitz (1989), in turn, criticized Coase, in that from his consideration the idea arises that groups of individuals are able to agree on how to solve this kind of inefficiencies, without any State intervention. According to Stiglitz, Coase underestimated the problems arising from free-riding, opportunism, and inefficient individual assessment of the cost which might derive to the group (Stiglitz 1989). More generally, Greenwald and Stiglitz (1986) demonstrated that it is not true that the State can never operate better than the market.

PART TWO

SIMON'S CRITICISM: FROM SUBSTANTIVE RATIONALITY TO PROCEDURAL RATIONALITY

In Part One, I dealt with the issue of the role of knowledge in economic process. The refutation of the standard theory, in which agents are characterized by perfect information, seems to me the main goal achieved. The analysis I carried out has highlighted a strict link between mental processes and the role of institutions, which is at the origin of knowledge. We may now use these results as a basis for a new way of studying economic events. Another general aspect that I have mentioned in the introduction is worth considering.

Neoclassical theory conceived its models also on the basis of an assumption, strictly connected to the idea of perfect information: economic agents' substantive rationality. Being perfectly informed, individuals will certainly act so as to maximize the outcome of their actions. If we were able to imagine all the possible scenarios ensuing from our actions, it is easy to predict that we would choose the optimizing alternative.

In order to explain how a choice is made, it is necessary to define in advance the rational criteria individuals follow in their acting. If, as assumed in the standard economy, individuals are perfectly informed from the very beginning, they behave rationally only if they choose the option implying the best possible result (optimization).

The rationality of this kind has been defined absolute or substantive by many authors. According to the conclusions of Part One, though, the hypothesis of perfect knowledge is undoubtedly unrealistic. As a consequence, also the assumption of rational behaviour is to be rejected. Hayek thinks that individuals acquire knowledge on the basis of partial and idiosyncratic information. This means that they seldom follow the criteria of absolute rationality, and only in very simple and uninteresting situations. In the light of these remarks and in contrast with the orthodox tradition, Herbert Simon coined a third word to define rationality, as conceived in neoclassical models. He defined it, a little ironically, "olympian", since it is peculiar to gods, who live on Olympus and are omniscient, but it is not peculiar to man, who has to bear costs in order to obtain the necessary information.

Several issues arise from the conclusions of the first three chapters. It is necessary to define alternative criteria of rational behaviour, to explain how the agents make their choices and what the results are. In fact, if the hypothesis of perfect knowledge is refuted, the same will happen with the hypothesis of optimizing result.

In this Part Two, I will try to give an answer to these problems, that had already arisen while illustrating Hayek's thought. I have repeatedly referred to the cognitive and computational limits of human mind. Studying such limits was one of Simon's main interests. He used the word *bounded*, to define the kind of rationality that is actually peculiar to people. Chapter 4 deals with the characteristics of bounded rationality and its main implications for economic theory.

Simon has also carried out studies in the psychological field. Refuting the idea of perfect knowledge made it necessary to define economic agents' new criteria of behaviour. The problem to be solved was explaining how individuals - who are intentionally rational, but who are in reality endowed with bounded rationality - may be able to make effective choices. Being interested in studying behaviour in conditions of uncertainty and bounded rationality, Simon had to deal with the problem-solving process directly (see Chapter 6), and he developed a new criterion: procedural rationality. Unlike bounded rationality - that may be considered a criticism of neoclassical models - the introduction of "procedurally rational" criteria of action is the *"construens"* part of his research. Chapter 7 deals with the characteristics of procedural rationality and its implications for economic theory.

One more aspect needs defining: the outcome of choosing processes. Once optimization has been excluded, it is necessary to find an alternative criterion. Simon develops the *satisficing* criterion. These aspects are dealt with in Chapter 5.

Simon's thought seems complementary to Hayek's, as much as the criticism of perfect knowledge is complementary to the criticism of substantive rationality. Certainly, there are several differences between the two authors. One difference is that Hayek highlighted, above all, the link between mind and institutions, while Simon highlighted the link between mind and organizations. Simon thinks that organizations are an effective answer, given individual limits, to the issue of work organization. The division of competencies, resulting from the division of knowledge, helps to solve organizations' problems: routines are developed as a result of individual and collective learning processes. Once again, the understanding of learning processes proves to be the most relevant aspect of this work and another complementary element between Hayek's and Simon's studies.

4. Bounded Rationality

> Bounded rationality is natural rationality; it is the assumption of infinite capacity to handle infinite quantities of data which is artificial.
>
> (Loasby 1976, p.3)

4.1 Definitions

For the last few years, the theory of bounded rationality has been drawing several scholars' attention; H. Simon had the merit of introducing this concept into economic theory. His theory lays a stress on the discrepancy between perfect human rationality, as conceived by neoclassical theory, and real human behaviour in economic reality, which is visible to everybody. Such discrepancy does not mean that people are irrational; it means that neither computing ability, nor acquired knowledge enable individuals to reach optimum, as conceived in the neoclassical theory (Simon 1992).

Simon examines the difference between unrealistic assumptions and empirical facts, in the light of the results achieved by cognitive psychology, which explains that human beings think in conditions of limited knowledge and computing ability (Simon 1992). He focuses his analysis on human thought and on the real choosing processes, concerning cognitive and procedural mechanisms. His model explains the processes through which alternatives are formulated, compared and assessed, in conditions of uncertainty (Simon 1987a), i.e. consistently with cognitive psychology.[1]

According to the principle of bounded rationality, in his original form, computing and cognitive abilities are limited.[2] As a result, economic agents are not capable of making the best possible choices, when (in most cases) they are very complex.

These ideas have spread with difficulties. This is due in part to the fact that, in the 1950s, optimization techniques had reached levels of high formal precision, and proved to be effective, though very complex. But the theorizers

---

[1] With reference to the ineffectiveness of equilibrium theory, B. Loasby (1976, p.22) wrote: "the apparatus of equilibrium theory serves to conceal our ignorance, and thereby accentuates our ignorance". See also Loasby 1989, Chapter 9, illustrating bounded rationality.

[2] Already, several years before, F. Knight (1921) had maintained that we are endowed with bounded rationality, though it can develop with the world.

of optimization did not take into due account the problems arising from the time needed and the computing ability required to achieve results. Moreover, those economists who have repeatedly drawn on these models, have neglected the evident fact that the hypothesis of unlimited computing ability - invalidated in a lot of relevant real examples - is analytically inconsistent with the traditional economic theory. In this context, in fact, gathering information and computing are considered activities at no cost (not even time-consuming), thus implicitly crediting individuals with the ability of gathering and processing information. This is an evident violation of the principle of scarce resources (Egidi 1992a).

I will now examine the genesis and development of the theory of bounded rationality. Later, I will illustrate its main applications and consequences for economic theory, which will be dealt with in depth in the following chapters.

4.2 Genesis and development: from Commons and Barnard to Simon

Simon's education and cultural development was deeply influenced by J. Commons and C. Barnard (Simon 1979a; Simon 1991).[3] This is especially evident as regards the theory of organization and the theory of bounded rationality.

The core of these two authors' interests is human action. More specifically, Barnard thinks that people aim at changing the surrounding environment. This implies constantly experiencing the existence of physical, biological, mental, cognitive and social limits (Barnard 1938). He starts from this consideration in order to define his theory of cooperation. What I am interested in here, is underlining the influence of this approach on Simon's theory of bounded rationality. In this regard, it is important to illustrate the concepts of "bounding factor" and "strategic factor", which Barnard, in turn, has learned from Commons.

In *Institutional Economics*, Commons introduces the concept of bounding factor, applying it to the managerial operations of transactions (Commons 1934). In the case of routine transactions, the agent does not need to pay special attention, because he is performing an "automatic" action, based on experimented and corroborated mechanisms. When a problematic situation occurs, the transaction is no longer routine, it becomes strategic. The manager, in this case, ought to focus his attention on the element/s (bounding

---

[3] J. Commons and T. Veblen are among the major representatives of American institutionalism. Commons' name is still linked to *Institutional Economics* of 1934, in which the role of institutions is considered fundamental in order to understand economic and social processes. He thinks, in particular, that institutions simplify the collective action which brings about economic development, almost like a vital strength, similar to technology (Foster 1991, p. 210). C. Barnard's name, instead, is linked to the development of administration science. His most famous book *is The Function of the Executive* of 1938, which, as we shall see, deeply influenced Simon.

elements) he has to cope with, in order to overcome the impasse. As regards the concept of strategic factor, Barnard explains its meaning in detail.[4]

A system is made up of elements. Strategic factors are those elements which, if they are changed or absent, make it impossible to reach a goal. All the other factors are complementary. If the factor is a physical element, then the definition "limiting factor" should be preferred. If it consists in an action carried out by a person or an organization (as in the case of efforts aimed at specific objectives) then the best definition is "strategic factor". A strategic factor may, of course, derive from a limiting factor: the presence or absence of a physical factor, which hinders the functioning of the system, urges the manager to undertake a series of (strategical) actions, in order to solve the problem and find a routine solution. In every decision-making process the decision-maker has to focus his attention only on the strategical factors. Besides, the existing biological, mental and cognitive limits allow him to face only one problem at a time in a sequence.

In their approaches, Commons and Barnard underline the fact that human action is voluntary and central. They also focus their attention on the real mechanisms of action; they start from limits and potentialities of intelligence, intelligence being the only instrument capable of spotting limiting factors (Commons 1934).

Simon formulated the theory of bounded rationality on these bases.[5] In a broad sense, rationality implies behaving so as to reach specific goals, within the limits due to given conditions and constraints. Constraints may be: objective characteristics of the surrounding environment; perceived characteristics; characteristics of the organism itself, which considers them fixed and out of its control. In the first case, rationality is defined as objective, in the others, as subjective or bounded (Simon 1964b).[6] In the case

---

[4] Barnard 1938. Also Commons mentions a strategic factor, but he does not distinguish between it and the limiting factor.

[5] He mentions bounded rationality for the first time in the first part of Chapter 5 of *Administrative Behaviour* (Simon 1947) and he gives further explanations of this concept in several later works. Among the most important works (besides the ones I have already mentioned), see Simon 1955; Simon 1957, Chapter 4; March-Simon 1958; Simon 1969, Simon 1976 and 1983. In Simon 1971, the author refers in particular to computational and time limits of the internal environment, i.e. human mind, conceived as a scarce resource in a world full of information. In Simon 1972, he refers to the implications, in economics, of the acknowledgement of the intrinsic limits of rationality (risk theory, uncertainty, etc.). Finally, in Simon 1979b, also the uncertainty concerning exogenous elements is taken into account among the limiting elements.

[6] Marris (1992) criticizes the use of the word "bounded", which seems to imply that a form of "unbounded rationality" exists (p. 198). This kind of rationality should be referred to as "intelligent", rather than bounded. Intelligent rationality is a concept which can be taken into consideration. On the contrary, the assumption of an

of objective rationality, the decision-maker is asked to formulate all the possible alternatives of actions and their consequences. For a single individual, though, it is impossible to reach a sufficient level of objective rationality, because his ability to formulate alternatives is limited and he cannot predict all the possible scenarios deriving from each choice. Far from being precisely formulated, future consequences can only be imagined and assessed approximately. As concerns predicting all the possible alternatives of actions, in reality only a few of them can be formulated and compared by the individual (Simon 1947). Human mind is incapable of taking into account all the relevant aspects of value, knowledge and behaviour for every single decision (Simon 1947). It - as cognitive psychology teaches us - can generate only a limited number of alternatives and can assess only few of the resulting scenarios.

Modern cognitive psychology has analysed not only the processes through which individuals formulate alternatives, but also the processes aimed at finding possible solutions for problems (problem solving). By observing how a decision is made, it becomes clear that the individual uses most of his time for formulating alternatives and assessing their consequences. Little time is used for the final action (the choice), once the alternatives have been formulated and selected. For this reason, it is necessary to focus our attention above all on the process leading to the choice.

4.3 Implications

The first relevant aspect is that not all the agents can gather the same kind of information, while standard models assume that information is equally spread. Yet, if bounded rationality is at the basis of human behaviour, as a consequence asymmetrical information is the most widespread reality. Each individual, very often, owns different pieces of information as to their quality and quantity. The implications for the theory of exchange are relevant, as pointed out by Akerlof (1970). Moreover, if information is asymmetrically spread among agents, transactions may often take place with the possibility of opportunist behaviour on one side or on both sides (Williamson 1986).[7]

Another important implication of the approach of bounded rationality is that markets are incomplete. In standard models, the assumption of Pareto's optimum implies that markets are complete with all goods. This means that the market, free from external interferences, is capable of allocating all the resources perfectly. Nevertheless, some anomalies might emerge, due to the peculiar nature of some goods. One of these goods - as Arrow pointed out as

---

"unintelligent" rationality is an unacceptable concept. Neoclassical rationality is an example (ibid., p. 199).

[7] This aspect is dealt with in detail in Chapter 10 of this book.

early as 1962 - is information.[8] Information is quite a peculiar good, since it can be only imperfectly gathered, it cannot be perfectly divided and it can be only imperfectly assessed, as a consequence of the limited human ability to acquire and use it. Another problem, connected to this aspect, is the allocation of this kind of resource. Often it is not convenient to invest in new information, since - being easily doubled - it is difficult to allocate at production cost; sometimes it is not convenient to transfer it, being profitable to own it exclusively (Egidi 1991). Because of the peculiarity of this good, there is a need for institutions (such as laws protecting inventions by means of patents) that make its production and allocation possible, by acknowledging monopolies. This might lead to market failures. It is evident, though, that the causes of market failures are to be found also in human limited cognitive and computing abilities (Williamson 1975). The concomitance of uncertainty, opportunism arising from unequal distribution of information and bounded rationality brings about a blackout of information, occurring when relevant information concerning a given transaction is known only by one contracting party, while the other one can find out about it only by bearing a cost.

Among the implications of agents' bounded rationality, there is the necessary role of institutions when transactions are carried out. As mentioned above with reference to Hayek, the main role of institutions is to simplify the context in which individuals make use of their cognitive abilities in order to make a choice. Moreover, in an exchange process, the risk of an opportunist use of the different information owned by one of the parties, accounts for the role of institutions: guaranteeing that transactions are carried out correctly (Williamson 1986; Egidi 1992b).

Acknowledging the existence of human actions due to bounded rationality is at the basis of another major aspect of recent neoinstitutionalist works: the transaction costs.[9] The subject will be dealt with below.

It is impossible to list all the implications of this approach: I will deal with them in the following pages and chapters. Yet, it is now important to point out the influence of this theory on industrial economics. Also in this regard, Simon gave the first contributions. He considered firms as hierarchically structured organizations, in order to overcome the limits due to individual rationality. Organizations use successful routines and procedures, arising from tested and codified knowledge. Their origin and use have been dealt with in works on organizations. The evolutionary theory of firms, that has developed from Nelson and Winter's work (1982), has brought the most relevant contributions. Moreover, if we take in due account the link between dynamics of routines and technological change, the implications of the theory

---

[8] Arrow 1962. See also Egidi 1991 and 1992a, p. 8. As regards the importance of institutions guaranteeing that transactions may actually be carried out, see Coase 1960 and 1988b; Williamson 1986; North 1990.

[9] They are those costs (like information gathering, contract drafting, etc.), which must be paid in order to carry out an exchange.

of bounded rationality for the economics of innovation become more and more evident.

4.4 Main applications

4.4.1 Markets as imperfect institutions

In the neoclassical model of the market, information is implicitly considered a scarce resource: the market is assigned the role of carrying out those complex computing operations that individuals are not able to carry out themselves. Without an alternative social mechanism for coordinating individual decisions, rationality - as an estimate of the necessary means to accomplish specific aims - would work in a context of strict interdependence of decisions. It is a situation of strategic choice, where individuals are required to perform complex rational computing activities. The problem is if (and how) this complexity may be reduced systematically and completely (Egidi 1992a).

One of the main drawbacks in this mechanism is that the indexes of information (prices) do not contain all the relevant information. Most of the information concerning the goods' quality, dislocation and technological characteristics is given. This assumption, though, is unrealistic, since it does not take into consideration that the process of information gathering implies costs.

A tentative solution might be considering these information-goods as endogenous, within production processes. Still, another already mentioned drawback would show up: markets are incomplete and information is a peculiar good. In the major example of innovations, information is usually copied at a very low cost, rather than bought. This is an early-stage market failure, affecting one of the most relevant aspects of the economic process: the development of innovations.

4.4.2 Markets and hierarchies

If the market is subject to failures and it is not a reliable instrument for the coordination of information, it is necessary to find other mechanisms allowing this process to take place among individuals. It is important to understand how knowledge is gained and relevant information is selected and, above all, how information complexity is simplified, in such a way that a single individual may handle it.

The role of institutions ought to be studied within this framework.[10] Institutions handle information more effectively than a single individual,

---

[10] Arrow (1974, pp. 33 and 37) links the reasons for the existence of the firm to the existence of uncertainty and market failures. Organizations are the means by which the favourable effects of collective actions are obtained whenever the price system fails. An organization with a more limited range of action is to be preferred to the

every time information handling goes beyond individual capacity. The coordination of information - handling is carried out hierarchically in several circumstances, since this proves to be a more efficient instrument than the market. Thanks to this kind of structure, complex problems can be solved, by decomposing them into sub-problems that are coped with by functional subsystems.

This approach is the starting point of Coase's pioneer article in 1937, in which the Nobel prize-winner to-be faces the problem of why the firm exists and what its actual role is. He reaches the conclusion that its *raison d'être* and role are the profitable costs of transactions and that this can guarantee social coordination[11] along with the market. Williamson has further developed this subject: he thinks that the entrepreneurial activity consists in the ability to plan new forms of division of labour. The role of the firm differs from that of the market in that the firm exists in order to reach specific aims, which can be, at the most, partially intentional, while the market is an unintentional institution (according to the meaning of the word in Hayek). As an unintentional institution, the firm embodies the ability to plan ways of cooperating, in order to reach its aims.

4.4.3 The new role of the firm

Coase's idea that both firm and market - in different ways - coordinate individuals' activities, has been further developed by Williamson.[12] The models of behaviour characterized by bounded rationality - one of the major aspects of Williamson's approach - imply that the agent can control neither all the consequences of his decisions nor the influence of other agents' decisions on his own. Asymmetrical information may favour phenomena of

---

market as a whole, also because of the features of the information networks created by firms.

[11] "Although production could be carried out in a completely decentralized way by means of contracts between individuals, the fact that it costs something to enter into these transactions means that firms will emerge to organize what would otherwise be market transactions whenever their costs are less than the costs of carrying out the transactions through the market. The limit to the size of the firm is set where its costs of organizing a transaction become equal to the cost of carrying it out through the market. This determines what the firm buys, produces, and sells. As the concept of transaction cost it is not usually used by economists, it is not surprising that an approach which incorporates it will find some difficulty in getting itself accepted. We can best understand this attitude if we consider not the firm but the market (Coase 1988b, p. 7).

[12] It is also necessary to mention Nelson's work of 1981, in which the problem of the relationship between market and organizations is directly dealt with. It is Nelson's firm belief that neither market nor planning as such are the best possible forms of economic organization. Planning and market are to be organized in mixed systems, in order to respond to different situations most effectively.

opportunism, that is, a selfish use of a preliminary advantage in transactions. The role of a hierarchically structured firm consists also in cutting down the risk of opportunist behaviour. Moreover, the firm is no longer defined according to mere technological characteristics, as in the neoclassical approach. The entrepreneur fixes the boundaries of the firm by comparing two organizational methods: he can either produce by integrating the phases of production outlined in the plan of production or he can decentralize intermediate production on the market (Egidi 1992a).

These are the bases from which the evolutionary theory of the firm has developed. Especially thanks to Nelson and Winter's work, it laid a stress on the process of development of competencies, on the acquisition and shaping of decision-making procedures, which characterize the work of the firm-organization. It must be able to learn and adjust to continuous environmental change and to modify its production goals continuously.[13]

4.4.4 Procedural rationality

In conclusion, there is another implicit aspect in the approach of bounded rationality that is worth underlining. Cooperation among individuals takes place according to assigned tasks and within a well-determined structure of division of labour. Division of labour is the result of a human innovating activity, consisting in intelligent research rather than in rational choice. This topic is connected with the development of Simon's studies on problem-solving.

Human cognitive abilities consist in the symbolic representation of reality. This is obtained by processing and manipulating the symbols through which individuals represent their reality, create their beliefs, develop and assess their alternatives. Therefore, economic decision is not a mere choice among alternatives, but the result of a process of symbolic representation. This process consists in gathering and assessing the information and knowledge necessary for individuals to interpret the relevant data referring to a problem. Since rationality is bounded, symbol manipulation is a process subject to time, cost and energy limits. It is a slow and demanding process and only a few alternatives are actually examined.

Thanks to the developments in the field of artificial intelligence, Simon and his fellow-researchers can put the problem-solving activity in the centre of the decision-making process (which I will briefly mention). The main stages are the acquisition of information and the genesis of alternatives. This is accomplished by decomposing problems into sub-problems, by means of a process of mental division of labour, concerning individuals as well as

---

[13] The pioneering article on this approach to the evolutionary theory of the firm is Alchian 1950. A literature on the subject has developed, especially now in the last few years (this subject will be dealt with again further on, in particular in Chapters 12 and 13).

organizations. The solutions are procedures, i.e. sequences of steps to be taken in order to reach the desired goals. Within organizations, these solutions consist of organized administrative procedures, which become routines. Every new problematic situation stirs the development of new routines, according to new problem-solving processes.

Simon coins the word "procedural rationality", after empirically observing how problems arise and how solutions are developed within economic organizations. In order to fully understand the meaning of procedural rationality and how it differs from bounded rationality, it is necessary to refer to the contributions Simon has given as a psychologist. For this reason, I refer the reader who wishes to read on these aspects in detail, to Chapter 7, where Simon's model of mind is illustrated.

4.5 Concluding remarks

The assumption of the criterion of bounded rationality is the cornerstone of contemporary economic analysis, that is alternative to neoclassical analysis. Contemporary analysis focuses its attention on what was considered marginal in the neoclassical approach.

Bounded rationality was the starting point of the theories of asymmetrical information, of various theories of the firm and has helped the theory of transaction costs to develop. All these elements are at the basis of neoinstitutionalist economics, of the evolutionary theory of the firm and, generally speaking, of the research on the emergence of rules within economic organizations.

I will deal with all these aspects in the following pages. Now, it is necessary to examine in detail H. Simon's thought, so as to understand his contributions systematically.

5. Optimizing and "Satisficing"

> Most human decision-making, whether individual or organizational, is concerned with the discovery and selection of satisfying alternatives; only in exceptional cases it is concerned which the discovery and selection of optimal alternatives.

> (March-Simon 1958)

5.1 Definitions

A decision-maker who chooses the best valid alternative, is optimizing; a decision-maker who chooses an alternative equalling or exceeding specific criteria, though with no guarantee that it is the only one or the best one, is satisficing his own wishes (Simon 1987b). The word *satisfice*, of Scottish origin, is used by Simon as a synonym of *satisfy*, "to denote problem solving and decision making that sets an aspiration level, searches until an alternative is found that is satisfactory by the aspiration level criterion, and selects that alternative" (Simon 1972, p. 168).[1] H Simon, after his criticism of the neoclassical paradigm, and consistently with the assumption of the criterion of bounded rationality, proposes - as an alternative to *optimizing* approach - a *satisficing* approach.

5.2 Optimizing and the satisficing "alternative"

In the works on the economic and statistical theory of decision, rationality has usually been defined in such a way as to imply some forms of optimization, such as the maximization of subjective utility under constraints. But - as proved by Simon's and his fellow-researchers' empirical studies - in many, if not all, situations of the real world, the real optima - whether they are a minimum or a maximum - are very difficult to estimate. This is especially true with reference to decisions to be made without using powerful computing instruments, such as a computer.[2]

---

[1] See also Simon 1957, part IV, pp. 196-279; and Simon 1987b and 1969.

[2] Simon maintains that if one tries to multiply 1776 by 1492 without using paper and pen, while taking a shower, one immediately realizes that our computing capacities are limited. In Slote 1989 you can find a good illustration of the difference between optimizing and satisficing, and of A. Sen's ideas against optimizing.

Because of these difficulties and impossibilities, in the choosing process the decision-maker is content with a satisfying option, though it is not optimizing. Simon gives the example of the needle in a haystack. Two research processes are possible. In the first one, an individual looks for the sharpest needle (maximizing process). In the second one, an individual looks for a needle that is sharp enough to sew. This is the process that Simon defines as satisfying (March-Simon 1958).[3] The two crucial moments of a choice, in conditions of uncertainty and imperfect knowledge, are research and satisfaction. The decision-maker, who does not know all the alternatives of choice, explores the field of the possible actions and acts in a way he considers satisfying with respect to his wishes.

Simon's first important work on the subject is his article of 1956,[4] where he describes how an organism can meet its needs in a satisfying way and survive, though it is endowed with neither superhuman powers nor a computational intelligence. The orthodox paradigm failed to explain the decision-making process because it overestimated human rationality and described behaviour in mechanicist terms. Simon, instead, suggests an alternative approach to the description of rational behaviour, which is more strictly related to the psychological theories of perception and cognition.[5] The central point in his approach is that the interactive relation between individual needs and environmental influence produces levels of aspiration (Simon 1969).[6] At a formal level, a satisfying process of research may certainly be converted into an optimizing process, up to the point when the expected profit arising from one more minute of research exactly equals the opportunity cost of that minute. A new burden, though, is put on the agent from such conversion: he is supposed to be able to estimate the marginal opportunity cost and expected profit (Stigler 1961). Simon thinks that estimating these figures might be as difficult as solving the original problem of the choice to be made.[7]

---

[3] For a debate and a development of this example, see Marris 1964.

[4] In one of his preceding articles (Simon 1955), he had made a first attempt at formalizing the psychological theory of bounded rationality. The concept of satisficing is already present there, though it is not yet conceived as "good enough action" as opposite of optimum.

[5] "By giving up optimization, a richer set of properties of the real world can be retained in the models. Stated otherwise, decision - makers can satisfice either by finding optimum solutions for a simplified world, or by finding satisfactory solutions for a more realistic world" (Simon 1979a, p. 498).

[6] Simon's studies mainly deal with the psychology of cognitive processes, paying special attention to chess and to strategy and information processing procedures implemented by a good chess-player. Compare Newell-Shaw-Simon 1958b; Newell-Simon 1965; Newell-Simon 1972; Simon 1972.

[7] "Stigler poured the search theory back into the old bottle of classical utility maximization" (Simon 1979a, p. 503). Marschak and Radner (1972) tried to answer to Simon from a neoclassical point of view, by developing the "theory of teams". In

According to the neoclassical view on rational behaviour, two complementary aspects can be distinguished: internal consistency and *self-interest*. As regards the first aspect, "rational" is synonymous with "consistent": behaviour is consistent when it fulfils given requirements of consistency. Yet, this theory is a tautology: behaviour is explained in terms of preferences and preferences are, in turn, defined by behaviour.

The second aspect concerns *self-interest* or instrumental rationality: every agent is driven only by self-interest. The core of this approach is that economic agents - whether they are consumers or firms - maximize. According to the theory of subjective expected utility a choice can be made: between given alternatives with the possibility of subjectively picturing to oneself each configuration corresponding to an alternative, so as to maximize the expected value of one's function of utility. If, instead, we acknowledge the limits of human rationality, a new psychological analysis of behaviour becomes necessary. Every action is aimed at reaching tacit or explicit goals. There are routine actions, which we are often not aware of, and deliberate actions, which we control and manage consciously.

In order to explain these concepts more effectively, Simon (1972) gives us an example referring to chess. The complete tree of all the possible moves for a player, in an average game of chess, equals 10 raised to the 120th power. It is too high a number to examine them all, as even an amateur player knows. Besides, the different options are not given; it is necessary to formulate them. Therefore, a player, because of time and computational limits, has to make a choice after taking only very few moves into consideration. Since it is impossible to compare all the possible options, an alternative criterion of choice is necessary. *Satisficing* criterion is a possible alternative (Simon 1972). Besides, the level of satisfaction is determined by the level of initial aspiration. An individual keeps working until he finds a satisfying solution (March-Simon 1958). But how are these levels of aspiration generated?

5.3 The levels of aspiration

Simon thinks that the most relevant limits of neoclassical theory concern the deductive process, which does not require empirical data. It is enough to assume a basic element of psychological theory, to develop a completely renewed perspective. In psychology, actions arise from needs and they come to an end when such needs are met (Simon 1959). To find out whether an event is satisfying, it is necessary to compare the real acquired data with the level of aspiration. If data exceed the initial level of aspiration, satisfaction level has been reached; if, on the contrary, the level of aspiration is not

---

this case, decisions are made by groups of individuals, in a context in which also the organizational structure is taken into consideration. Yet, according to Simon, this approach implies enormous mathematical difficulties, it does not go beyond a mere illustration of the situation, and it can be applied only to simple cases (Simon 1979a).

reached, the individual is dissatisfied: the individual can either lower his level of aspiration or continue trying.[8]

The levels of aspiration arise from the interactive relation between an agent and his environment, on the basis of the needs the individual thinks he can meet in that context (Simon 1956; Simon 1969). In this connection, dynamic mechanisms exist, which continuously adjust the levels of aspiration to reality, on the grounds of information on the environment (Simon 1972). The process can be described as follows. The action continues until the previously-set levels of aspiration are reached. If, after a number of moves, the goal has not been reached, a lowering process of the levels of aspiration begins. The action continues, until a satisfactory alternative is found. Positive satisfaction is recorded if experience exceeds the level of aspiration, otherwise dissatisfaction is recorded (Simon 1969).

Of course the opposite process may occur, as well. If the settled levels of aspiration are too easily reached, the individual is likely to raise them, in the following action. The levels of aspiration are frequently lowered or raised, according to different experiences. If the environment is perceived as favourable and it offers several positive alternatives, the levels of aspiration are raised; in an unfriendly environment such levels are lowered (Simon 1979a).

5.4 *Satisficing* **within organizations**

The *satisficing* approach has also remarkably influenced the theory of the firm.[9] "The basic features of organization structure and function derive from the characteristics of human problem-solving processes and rational human choice. Because of the limits of human intellective capacities in comparison with the complexities of the problems that individuals and organizations face, rational behavior calls for simplified models that capture the main features of a problem without capturing all its complexities" (March-Simon 1958, p. 169).

According to the studies carried out by Simon, March, Cyert and Trow and published in the 1950s (Cyert-Simon-Trow 1956; March-Simon 1958) the *decision-maker* does not assess the alternatives only by following the criterion of profit, and - rather than the "best" alternative - he looks for a "satisfying" alternative (Cyert - Simon - Trow 1956; Simon 1979b). According to these authors, numerous empirical data confirm that also firms stop looking for new alternatives as soon as a satisfying solution is found.[10]

---

[8] Simon 1969 and 1972. See also Giva 1985.

[9] Simon 1969 and 1979a. With reference to the introduction of the satisficing approach into the theory of the firm, see also Loasby 1967.

[10] Empirical corroborations of a satisficing approach on the part of firms: Hayes 1950; Cyert and March 1963; Katona 1951, Chapter 11. On the contrary, Machlup 1946 and Mason 1952 criticize Simon. According to these authors, his review of the theory of

In traditional models, the entrepreneur has to make a decision only as to the quantity of goods he wants to produce. The environment consists in the curves of costs and proceeds and the only goal is maximizing profits. In such circumstances, rational behaviour means estimating the quantity which maximizes the difference between proceeds and costs. In reality, the entrepreneur's tasks are more complex (Simon 1969). In order to obtain a more realistic model it is necessary to represent the external and internal environment more precisely: a representation of the external environment which takes into consideration available technology and other firms' behaviour; a representation of the internal environment in organizational as well as objective terms. One might think that the levels of aspiration of a firm coincide with given profit expectations, that are raised or lowered depending on whether the economic and institutional environment is more or less favourable.

Still, reality is more complex. Organizations' internal dynamics will be better understood when I integrate *satisficing* analyses with *problem-solving* analyses, connected with procedural rationality (see the two following chapters). Now I wish to mention an aspect (which I will deal with in detail below) concerning the limits of a *satisficing* approach based only on the variation of the profit levels.

In 1950, Alchian put forward the hypothesis of *satisficing* behaviour on the part of firms (satisfaction of profit levels), on the grounds that competition sets in motion mechanisms that are similar to natural selection: those who make profits survive, those who do not are driven out of the market.[11]

Milton Friedman (1953), sharing Alchian's evolutionary theory of the firm, has maintained that the decision-making process (whether it is optimizing or satisfying) is irrelevant, since market is a mechanism selecting the firms which act (sometimes unwittingly) "as if" they were maximizing. Nevertheless, according to Simon, the evolutionary approach does not necessarily imply optimizing results; adjusting can be conceived as an optimizing process only by assuming a priori that the environment the species

the firm is not relevant for economic analysis, since people, in spite of all appearances, actually maximize. This opinion is similar to those expressed in Friedman 1953 (see the following pages).

[11] In this article, Alchian tries to abandon the maximizing outcome, by proposing an evolutionary approach (Alchian 1950). Nevertheless, Enke (1951), and later, with a critical approach, Penrose (1952) demonstrated that, in a condition of wide competition, the outcome of the evolutionary approach is necessarily a maximizing process. This opinion is shared by Friedman (1953), though with a critical approach. Alchian accepted these remarks (1953), but he maintained that, even if the outcome is the same as the neoclassical one, the evolutionary approach is to be preferred, since it is based on realistic assumptions, while in traditional models the assumptions are completely unrealistic. Winter (1964) puts an end to this debate, by demonstrating that the outcome of evolutionary models does not necessarily coincide with maximizing.

is adjusting to, is not changing. If environment evolves, as species do, the variation-selection mechanism will not lead to a definitive optimal state, but it will improve the preceding state; this is a local optimum: it is not a global optimum, as asserted by Friedman. Moreover, if individuals and firms work in an environment characterized by a high number of local maxima, it is impossible to predict their behaviour, without knowing their methods and their evolutionary history (Simon 1983).

In the light of the above-mentioned considerations, it is important to underline that the information process within organizations, according to the *satisficing* approach, is a very important field of research. For this reason, it is developing in the following directions: management theory; issues connected with the problems arising from information-flow handling; development of the techniques aimed at studying the *decision-making process*; use of computer software as an instrument of analysis of complex systems.

5.5 Concluding remarks

From the issues dealt with in this chapter, the following considerations arise: optimizing is replaced by satisfying; the alternatives of action, and the resulting scenarios, are discovered by decision-makers in successive moments by means of processes of research; both individuals and organizations develop plans of action, which are alternative choices in recurrent situations; every specific plan of action refers to a limited number of situations and a limited number of consequences; each plan can be carried out enjoying relative independence from the others (March-Simon 1958).

As above mentioned, Simon developed the satisficing approach, referring to both individuals and organizations. The most important message we can draw from this approach is that the neoclassical model is practically impossible to implement. People are not endowed with the rational abilities necessary to accomplish the aims described in the theory of marginal subjective utility. The *satisficing* approach, instead, is consistent with the assumption of bounded rationality and better fits real processes.

I will now examine decision-making processes in detail, starting from *problem-solving*.

6. Problem-solving

Organisms are problem solvers and explorers of their world.

(K. Popper, in Popper-Eccles 1977, p. 138)

6.1 Introduction

After the assumption of the bounded-rationality criterion and the criticism of the *optimizing* approach, the next step consists in the analysis of the decision-making process, with reference to both individuals and organizations. My premise will be the following assumption: choice is not determined by objective characteristics of the situation, but by information processing. In other words, the heart of the analysis is shifted from "what" is decided to "how" a decision is made (from object to process),[1] and the representation of the decision-making mechanism is shifted from a context of choices among alternatives to a context of formal representation of human symbol-manipulating processes. Thus, decisions become actions consisting in a process of assessment and analysis of problematic situations. The implications of the assumption of bounded rationality in the theory of *problem-solving*, refer to information-processing mechanisms, which are selective and heuristic and stop working long before all the available alternatives are explored.[2] Human information processing is serial. It can

---

[1] Reason can only help us find the means to achieve given aims, but it can tell us nothing as to the aims themselves (Simon 1983, p. 37).

[2] March and Simon credited Hayek with the merit of having implicitly shed light on the importance of a problem-solving approach, by realistically assuming that human capacities are limited, as concerns computing activities and the acquisition of knowledge. Nevertheless, this analysis is limited to a specific phenomenon: the workings of the market (March-Simon 1958). More specifically, according to the Austrian economist, this is the demonstration that a decentralized system is to be preferred to a centralized one. Yet, according to the two authors of *Organizations*, this approach could be generalized and include other mechanisms, which are not directly connected with market, such as the analysis of the procedures carried out in order to make decisions in complex situations (March-Simon 1958). In his arguments against planning, Hayek implicitly designs a mechanism of action with limited information, which Simon and March consider applicable to every decision-making process in conditions of limited information.

handle few symbols at a time or store them into memory structures, whose content can be rapidly changed (Giva 1985).

Problem-solving has been studied not only with reference to individuals, but also with reference to organizations, since also in organizations planned decisions are carried out and unplanned decisions are coped with (Cyert-Simon-Trow 1956). While the former are routines, the latter stir the working out of solutions, making goals explicit and adjusting them to the means available within the organization. An attempt is made to develop a series of procedures to reduce complexity: it may be accomplished, in a strategic context, by means of mechanisms of procedural rationality. Looking for new strategies is part of the general activity of problem-solving.[3]

In this chapter, I will take into consideration individuals, while in the next chapter I will deal with organizations. Now, before illustrating the problem-solving process, let us consider the psychological (J. Dewey's influence) and philosophical (Gestalt's influence)[4] background in Simon's works.

6.2 The philosophical background of problem-solving: J. Dewey

J. Dewey has studied the function of intelligence and thought in developing the cognitive instruments necessary to work out solutions, every time individuals face problematic situations.

A preliminary aspect is the rejection of any a priori distinction - typical of idealism as well as of empiricism - between subject and object. Dewey thinks that subject and object are strictly interdependent. Their interdependence is not fortuitous, as it is, instead, in the approach of deterministic materialism; it is based on an active relation between individuals and nature and between individuals and society.[5] On the one hand, environmental influences affect and set limits to individuals; on the other hand, they urge them to act so as to transform the environment itself. For this reason, it is necessary to refer to the strict relation between man and his world as "interaction".

---

[3] Egidi 1991, pp. 10-11. With reference to the link between innovation and problem-solving, see also Dosi-Egidi 1991. This aspect is dealt with in detail in Chapter 7.

[4] As to the characteristics of Gestalt psychology, see Chapter 8. Simon explicitly refers to Gestalt psychology, while his reference to Dewey is not as explicit. The American philosopher is quite frequently cited in *Administrative Behaviour* (Simon 1947), but only with reference to administration science. With reference to problem solving, instead, as far as I know, Dewey is cited twice only in short notes (March-Simon 1958, and Simon 1965). Yet, if one reads Dewey's works carefully, one can realize that his precise and exact illustration of problem-solving is quite similar to Simon's. This aspect, concerning Dewey's influence on Simon, has probably never been dealt with in the literature. However, it is not only a philological curiosity: it is also important because it shows the pragmatic roots of Simon's sources, which have addressed future developments towards this direction since the very beginning.

[5] By environment, Dewey (1946) means both natural and social environment.

Later on, Dewey replaced the word "interaction" with the word "transaction", since the former is too dependent on a causal view on the interconnection between objects, of Galilean origin. But within a view, which man himself is referred to rather as natural member of a disclosing universe than as a superior creature, whose superior capacities make him able to look down on that universe (Dewey-Bentley 1949, p. 207), the most suitable word is transaction, implying the presence of two active contracting parties.[6]

The last remark is especially important as regards the process of knowledge acquisition. Knowledge means restoring an interrupted interaction. When a problematic situation interrupts a normal routine action, it is knowledge that restores the relation, either changing or widening the context of preceding experience. Or, more precisely, it is knowledge acquisition, which, according to Dewey, consists in a process divided into phases. In *How We Think* (1993), he illustrates this process clearly and in detail. I will now outline its content, which is strictly connected with Simon's *problem-solving*.

The starting point is the emergence of a problematic situation. It brings about a phase of doubts, during which attempts are made to formulate a plan of action. The effectiveness of this plan is checked by means of the data, obtained - in turn - by observing facts. If new difficulties arise from this control, new solutions are developed as soon as new data are gathered. These two factors are developed respectively by means of observation (including - to simplify the concept - the memory of preceding observation of similar events) and of inference (Dewey 1993).

In this approach, two aspects are especially interesting. The first aspect regards environmental influence in the process of choice. The second one refers to the individual, as an active agent. The result is that the process of choice is linked to external environmental constraints (observing the facts that influence the individual) and to internal constraints (individual ability to work out solutions). It is also linked to the continuous inferential check of worked-out solutions and to the continuous reformulation of such solutions, until satisfactory adjusting is reached.[7]

Two more aspects are worth considering. The first one concerns the perception of the problematic situation, which, once more, underlines that the individual is active. In the first phase, the problem is not completely given. In fact, it is necessary to make an individual effort, in order to formulate it precisely and clearly. The individual perceives nothing but a difficult, doubtful and vague situation. The problematic representation itself is the

---

[6] The concept of transaction refers to a fact, none of whose constituent parts can be specified as a fact, unless all the other constituent parts of the subject as a whole are also specified (Dewey-Bentley 1949, p. 122).

[7] Dewey 1933. Dewey does not use the word satisfaction directly. Nevertheless it is implicit in his reasoning. Individual research comes to an end when a solution solves (meets the requirements of) the problematic situation setting off that research.

result of an intellectualizing action (Dewey 1933). This process - or, more precisely, the mechanism through which it is performed - is the other relevant aspect.

Here, better than in other passages, it is possible to comprehend the bases of constructivistic subjectivism. As mentioned above, it is the cornerstone of Hayek's methodological assumptions. In the intellectualizing process "the stretch of links brought to light by reasoning depends, of course, upon the store of knowledge that the mind is already in possession of. And this depends not only upon the prior experience and special education of the individual who is carrying on the inquiry, but also upon the state of culture and science of the age and place" (Dewey 1933, p. 111).

The individual has a stock of relevant knowledge at his disposal, and he draws from it spontaneously. He works out his plans of action on the basis of his past experiences and acquired knowledge, which he takes from this stock.

As you see, the main traits of Simon's *problem-solving process* as well as elements recalling Hayek's constructivistic subjectivism are clearly visible in Dewey's thought.

6.3 The psychological background of problem-solving: Gestalt's influence

A crucial moment in the history of psychology is the emergence of Gestalt psychology, which influenced Simon's thought deeply.[8] Max Wertheimer was the forerunner of cognitivism. He influenced Simon especially as regards the learning process. Wertheimer thinks that the psychologist should no longer wonder: "What did the individual learn?", but: " How did he learn to perceive the situation?" (Wertheimer 1945). This is a fundamental principle, shifting the analysis from object to process, and it is crucial for the development of the concept of procedural rationality.

Other aspects have be underlined, concerning Gestalt's influence on Simon's thought. Among them, the principle of psychophysical isomorphism. It consists in the correlation between perception of order in space and time and mind processes[9]. This is an extremely important principle, since it asserts that there is structural identity between physiological processes and lived experience. The latter is the faithful representation of the former.

---

[8] Among Simon's reference points, we can certainly mention: Tolman 1932, who refers to people and mice as goal-seeking organisms, and therefore as decision-makers, who adjust their behaviour to the environment; Katona 1940; Wertheimer 1945; Dunker 1945. Also Broadbent influences Simon in his studies on information processing, though Broadbent is closer to traditional experimental psychology, which subordinates theory to experiments and does not use computer simulation.
As to the influence of Gestalt psychology on Simon see also Legrenzi 1984.

[9] "All experienced order in space is a true representation of a corresponding order in the underlying dynamical context of physiological processes (...) experienced order in time is a true representation of the corresponding concrete order in the underlying dynamical context" (Kohler 1947, pp. 48 - 49).

Processes of thought, choice, and action are influenced, in turn, by their interactive relation (Kohler 1947). This is where Simon finds the roots for his studies on environmental influences (adjustment of the Self) in learning process, processes of decision and choice (Simon 1956). The active role of the individual, or, better, the active role of his mind, is underlined. In particular, Katona (1940) demonstrates that the individual tends to find rules and characterizing elements in the perceived situation, and if he manages to, it becomes much easier for him to memorize things. Memory works on the basis of criteria concerning the internal organization of stimuli, by means of rules and strategies developed by the individual and by means of checking processes.

This principle is at the basis of the subjective theory of perception and stimuli grouping. This aspect, as mentioned above, is connected with Simon's works as well as Hayek's model of the mind.

6.4 Simon's contribution

6.4.1 Links with "Gestalt psychology" and computer science

Simon's first works on this topic are in the wake of the results achieved by Gestalt psychology; he also tries to find new instruments. In his 1958 article (Newell-Shaw-Simon 1958a) similarities are underlined between *logic theory* and *human problem-solving theory*. Behaviour is described in terms of primitive information-processing programs, that can be run by computers. Information-processing theory is compared with neurological, associationalistic and Gestaltist explanations.

In an article of 1959, Simon and Newell illustrate the parallelism between mental processes and artificial intelligence, in detail. Since the phenomena regarding human thought are more complex than physical phenomena (Simon-Newell 1959), it is necessary to formulate a new theory of human behaviour. Up to a decade before, only those instruments borrowed from physics and natural sciences - like operationalism and classical mathematics - could be used. Now, thanks first of all to personal computers, a new instrument is available to study the processes of symbolic manipulation and to simulate the decision-making processes typical of human beings. The turning point was the development of the first computer program (Simon 1991). More specifically, through the development and structural analysis of a program, the authors had at their disposal an instrument which was, at the same time, less complex than behavioural phenomena, and more complex (better describing the real functioning) than the simple interaction mechanisms (neural events), which are the prime elements this phenomenon can be divided into. Simon draws an analogy between interaction mechanisms and the structure of artificial-intelligence programs, consisting in long sequences of elementary processes. In the process, each point is selected according to criteria of identity or difference (Boolean logic), through mechanisms of symbol identification. In other words, in order to understand the functioning of these processes, it is necessary to study the functioning of human mind, since it shows analogies with the software used in computer programs.

6.4.2 Simon's model of mind

As regards his model of mind, Simon moves along a path which is different but convergent on Hayek's. Simon thinks that the brain is a symbol manipulator, working like a computer.[10] The development of the first artificial-intelligence program by Simon and Newell, laid the foundations of a new view on brain functioning. One of the main innovations was the distinction, at an analysis level, between hardware and software. Thinking models (software) can be described independently of the peculiar structure of the nervous system (brain).

Another result of Newell's and Simon's studies, is the demonstration that any intelligent system uses symbols and manipulates them.[11] Simon thinks that human beings and computers are systems of the same kind. After discovering memory limits, Simon realizes that man produces "out-of-the-brain" symbols (writing etc.) to make up for memory limits. Brain is an information processor. A human thinker is a memory structure combined with a basic information system, using memory, along with new information, to solve problems (Simon 1967).

---

[10] Both the computer and human mind are symbolic systems: physical entities which process, develop, and handle different kinds of symbols in many different ways (Simon 1969).

[11] Therefore, it was important to focus attention on semantics, representation and learning (Simon-Siklòssy 1972). Yet, the decisive impulse for the new studies was the new approach to computers, whose use was radically changed by Newell, Cliff, Shaw, and Simon. They tried to use it as a general symbol-processor (which means thought-processor), rather than a fast instrument useful for solving arithmetical problems. Thus, the computer became a model of the brain. They developed a programme of non-numeric thinking, and in this way they solved the venerable mind/body problem, by explaining how a system made up of matter may own the properties of the mind. In order to implement this project, these scholars drew on manifold disciplines, such as logic, psychology and economics. Formal logic, by considering symbols as material models, shows that ideas can be represented by means of symbols, and that such symbols can be significantly altered by precisely definable processes (Simon 1991, p.193). This idea was adopted by Simon as a structure for the way of thinking in administrative decision-making. By applying this new idea to psychology, symbols may be used for everyday, metaphorical, and even illogical thinking. Thus the foundations were laid of a new formal theory of the economic decision-maker. This explicitly urged economics to focus its attention on "reasoning on the action". The orthodox economists' approach, instead, according to which reasoning could not be other than logical, correct, and deductive, delayed the acknowledgement of the common interests of economics and psychology (Simon 1991).

According to Simon, brain is a symbolic system. Any intelligent system (brain or computers) is a symbolic system. Symbolic structures are portraits of that environment these systems try to adjust to. There is an important interactive level: they create a more or less truthful model of the environment, thanks to instruments that gather information from the environment and codify it (Simon 1969).

To sum up, the complex phenomenon of *human thinking* can be explained on the basis of simple mechanisms of elementary information processes, which are organized into complex thinking and *problem-solving* processes. Computers use (combine) symbols similarly to what happens in human processes of memory and association (Simon-Newell 1959). Programs, in turn, are long sequences of elementary processes. In the process, each point is selected according to criteria of identity or difference (Boolean logic)[12] (Simon 1991).

The innovation in Simon's approach consists in his comparison between the results of Gestalt psychology and those of "computer science". Newell and Simon do not support the idea of a downright analogy between nervous system and hardware. They try to find an explanation of *thinking* in terms of information systems, which could apply to both computer and brain.[13] They do not assume a structural identity between logical and mental operation, yet they are quite close to it (structural identity between logical and mental

---

[12] Several steps forward in the development of artificial intelligence are due to particular applications of Boole's algebra, which was developed in the last century. These applications were quite relevant for the assumption of certain models of mind, which I will introduce further on. Boolean logic is based on a two-value whole: true or false. In the first half of 1900, it became clear that the whole human mind could be reduced to a series of questions with a yes/no answer. Shannon (1938) made a further step in this direction. He demonstrated that circuitries and relays could work as on/off switches, expressed in terms of Boolean equations true/false (Gardner 1985; Aspray 1985). Following his trails, Simon developed two concentric issues: mind/computer relationship, and the issue of the mind producing and processing symbols. Just like Hayek's model of mind, the development of Simon's model (carried out with A. Newell) takes into account the results achieved by Gestalt psychology (Newell-Shaw-Simon 1958a); the authors Simon directly refers to are: Dunker 1945; Wertheimer 1945; Katona 1940. Simon was remarkably influenced also by: Bartlett 1932; Boring 1933 and Broadbent 1954 and the results achieved in the field of cybernetics (see Richardson 1991 and Aspray 1985).
[13] Actually, other scholars had already discovered this path. Among them, A. Turing proposed, in 1950, the twing test. This is a comparison between human answers and answers given by a computer, aimed at assessing the computer's ability in this field. The astonishing result was that it was impossible to tell computer's answers from human ones. Ashby (1960), by applying the concept of feedback, describes the computer as a metaphor of the brain, just as Walter (1953) and, from his own point of view, von Neumann (1958) had done; von Neumann, more exactly, assumes that there is an analogy between the neurological organization of human brain and the electronic structure of the computer.

operation has been asserted by Piaget 1967 and 1969). These models of the world are not faithful portraits of reality; they are rather networks aimed at rationalizing and explaining the world. Simon thinks that, when individuals face a problematic situation, procedures are started by means of neurobiological mechanisms; they solve that problematic situation and generate a routine, which is somehow applied every time individuals face an identical situation. As you see, Simon moves along a path similar to Marshall's.

Let us now take into consideration the consequences of what I said, in a strictly economic dimension. The individual is seen as an agent, who processes and manipulates symbols and who, by doing so, portrays his reality, creates his "beliefs" and develops and assesses possible alternatives. Economic decision is seen as the result of symbol processing, rather than as a mere choice among alternatives. Symbol processing consists in gathering and assessing the information and knowledge which the individual needs to comprehend the relevant data of problems; rationality is bounded since symbol processing is subject to constraints in terms of time, costs and energy; it is well-known that the comprehending and learning process is extremely slow and demanding: usually only *a few* alternatives of choice are examined (Egidi 1991).

6.4.3 Problematic situations and generation of alternatives

Simon's contribution on problem-solving is mostly found, again, in his articles of 1955 and 1956. In the first one, he laid the foundations of the analysis of choosing processes, and he proposed substituting a choosing organism with limited knowledge and abilities for the *homo oeconomicus* (Simon 1955). In the second article, Simon (1956) assessed the role of environmental constraints and uncertainty. The starting point is the analysis of subjective behaviour, which is limited by human nature. Constraints consist in human computational, information-processing and problem-solving abilities. Thanks to the contribution of cognitivism, this analysis is extended from the procedures used by agents to the procedures which might generate possible courses of action (generation of alternatives).[14] A relevant aspect is the empirical proof that it is impossible to assess all the possible options. Actually, the mental process of generation of alternatives is very demanding, in terms of time and energy. It is a heuristic[15] process, and - as mentioned above - it tends to generate only satisfying alternatives.

---

[14] Newell-Simon 1972. In *Human Problem Solving*, a series of research studies are described concerning problem-solving, which the two scholars carried out with people as well as by means of computer simulation.
[15] Heuristics: thumb-rule strategy, suggesting a solution for a problem without guaranteeing that it works. According to Tamborini (1991, p. 26), heuristic operations are present in the whole cognitive process, from input processing to output

The different scenarios of action in the decision-making process, are not given: it is necessary to "discover" them, and the process of discovering or generating such scenarios is a very important aspect. There is more to it: one more issue, connected with the preceding one and just as important, i.e. the generation of the scenarios arising from every single choice, made on the basis of planned and unplanned decisions.

This approach sheds light on the fact that looking for alternative courses of action is a major phase of the *decision-making process*. This phase is absent in the classical theory of choice, while it ought to be duly included in a decision-making theory (Cyert-Simon-Trow 1956).

Thus, the starting point is not a mere choice among alternatives. This is a decision-making context. It is while seeking the solution of a problematic situation, instead, that the problem-solving process is generated, as Dewey maintains. In other words, the individual has to develop a strategy allowing him to shift from the "existing situation" to the "desired situation" (Pounds 1969). The crucial problem consists in tracking down the path, leading to the accomplishment of one's goal. Solving this problem means developing the sequence of operations that guide the individual from the starting to the final point. Structuring the problems and representing the final stage, though, is often difficult. A problem is well-structured only when it can be defined in an explicit and quantitative way and can be solved by means of computing operations (Newell-Shaw-Simon 1958b). The final stage can often be defined only when it is reached (Simon 1973).

A famous example of a not-properly-structured problem, refers to a chess-player, who faces the problem that the possible chessboard configurations are too numerous to be assessed (as mentioned above, 10 raised to the 120th power!). An algorithm (developed by von Neumann) by which the problem is solved does exist, but it is too complicated for the player to carry out (Simon 1973). In this case, the agent makes use of a procedure enabling him to decompose the problem into sub-problems he can deal with. Of course, the structuring process is strictly subjective and is influenced by the cognitive development and the knowledge at the disposal of every *problem-solver*. In more general terms, it is important to underline that the problem structure

---

processing. When an individual is faced with a problematic situation and he/she does not know an already-experienced procedure to solve it with certainty, he/she adopts heuristic strategies. This heuristic capacity is typical of human mind. It can help develop the strategies necessary to solve problems. According to Tamborini (1991), it is a development of Kant's idea of a priori categories. Yet, the heuristic capacity, unlike Kant's thought, is historically conditioned and is ever-developing. The fact that the heuristic procedures of relation with visible reality are common to all individuals, does not imply that the results are the same for all of them. The differences in the results are due to two characteristics of the initial cognitive phase: (i) the complexity, which is an external characteristic of the individual; (ii) the interchangeability, which is an internal characteristic of the subject (p. 33).

depends on the interaction between agent and problem and cannot be defined in the abstract, leaving the agent out of consideration.

6.4.4 The method of problem decomposition

Let us go back to problem decomposition as a method of solution (Simon 1973). By decomposing problems into a finite set of simpler sub-problems, it is possible to find a solution. This is also due to the characteristics of the human mind. The system works in a serial way. It can process only few symbols at a time, which are later stored into a limited space. Short-term memory makes use of extremely limited space (it can handle only four pieces at a time), while the time necessary to transfer data from short-term to long-term memory is five seconds (Simon 1969). Decomposing occurs in a sequence of phases. After identifying the problem, its constitutive elements are turned into brain-developed symbols (Newell-Simon 1981). Then, the constraints and conditions that might reduce the number of states are explicated. Solution procedures are developed and finally an empirical check is carried out, to spot the methodologies which may actually be performed. The sequence of steps that are necessary to solve the problems is not known a priori. Such sequence is to be determined by means of a tentative exploration of possible alternatives in the environment where the research is carried out (space of the problems) (Newell-Simon 1972). Each solution leads the individual to analyse new problems - which are often nest-built - that arise at a subsequent level. Of course, in such circumstances, it is necessary to take into account the trade-off in "time" and "labour" resource allocation, with an inverse relation between the cost of handling and the number of alternatives the individual can examine in detail (Egidi 1991).

6.4.5 The interactive relation with the environment

As regards environmental constraints, the individual-environment relation is interactive. The individual has his level of aspiration, towards which he conveys his efforts. He continuously adjusts his action, by means of feedback. Environmental constraints are here taken into consideration within a dynamic relation with the agent. In orthodox approaches, instead, they are given once and for all and are considered exogenous.[16]

Simon thinks that solving a problem means seeking in a labyrinth, i.e. the environment. Human behaviour is simple, while his environment is complex. Behaviour adjusts to goals and is consequently artificial. Computer and brain

---

[16] The importance of this interactive relationship is underlined by Simon 1969; see also Giva 1985, pp. 197 and 199.

are adjusting systems, which tend to adjust to the shape of the environment-task (Simon 1967).[17]

---

[17] Following these discoveries, the tools improve. Computer simulation and a description of the adopted strategies are used to solve jigsaw puzzles. Simon deals with this subject also in his later works with Hayes (see Hayes-Simon 1974; Hayes-Simon 1976a; Hayes-Simon 1976b; and Hayes-Simon 1977). In the following years, other generalizations are carried out concerning the simulation of a scientific discovery. In their studies based on the simulation of creativity, a few authors maintain that scientific discoveries are achieved by means of the normal problem-solving process, which has been observed in less relevant problematic situations (Langley-Simon-Bradshaw-Zytkow 1987; see also Egidi 1991). Thus, the scientist is a researching problem-solver inside a labyrinth, and the discovery theory is a reflex of the problem-solving theory (Kulkarni-Simon 1988).

7. Decision-making Process: Procedural Rationality and Learning

Most human brains are also constantly scanning for possible new experiences.

(R. Marris 1964, p. 137)

7.1 Introduction

Along the path leading us to defining the characteristics of procedural rationality and learning processes, an interesting stage is the analysis of the *decision-making process*, which is an aspect of the wider issue of *problem-solving*.

Choices are decisions that make sense for the individual who carries them out (Cagliozzi 1990). They belong to the wider class of decisions, which may be defined as psychic approval of a given action. In its most elementary form, a choice is a simple reaction to stimuli (Cagliozzi 1990).

The underlying problem is understanding how, in a situation of ignorance and complexity, decision-makers act (effectively). On the basis of what has been said in the section concerning problem-solving, we now know that the individual is constantly active and interactive in perceiving problematic situations, in developing and formulating alternatives and also in decision-making.[1]

In a problematic situation, a choice is made with reference to actions, after taking into consideration all the possible alternatives and after assessing their possible consequences. After making a choice, the decision-maker carries it out and controls whether what had been decided has been achieved. If it was not achieved, he goes back to the beginning round in a circle, and studies the problematic situation again.

In his works on theory of administration,[2] Simon maintains that the traditional theory is ineffective and he puts forward an approach based on

---

[1] Among the forerunners of this approach, we find, once again, J. Dewey. As early as 1910 he had proposed an approach based on the decision-making process, in contrast with the neoclassical theory of the choice. A clear synthesis can be found in Earl (1983).

[2] Two of his most important works on the subject are Simon 1944; Simon 1946.

decision-making, which he later implements in a more specifically economic and administrative field.[3]

As mentioned in the preceding chapter, the individual is a planner. When he acts in unplanned conditions, he tries to turn the existing situation into the desired situation (Simon 1969); seeking new courses of action is a significant part of the decision-making process.

7.2 The influences of the psychology of behaviour

While neoclassical theory was sticking to its positions, behaviourism developed following those psychological theories which were achieving interesting and encouraging results. As Simon remembers, studies were carried out to verify empirically whether, when facing a choice, individuals maximize expected utility. The results showed that they do not.[4]

Other studies were carried out on the microprocesses occurring in individuals when they make decisions and solve problems (Newell-Simon 1972). These studies concerned directly decision-making mechanisms in difficult situations and the issue of how complex problems are solved. Thus, research entered the vast field of the "psychology of information processing", thanks to computers and artificial intelligence. By means of computer simulation, the theories were tested. The major results showed that choice depends not only on objective characteristics, but also on the specific heuristic process through which the decision is made.

Progress was made in the studies on decision-making within organizations (March-Simon 1958). It implied a new formulation of the theory of the firm (Marris 1964). Most of the models developed in this field abandon the *optimizing* approach and shift to the *satisficing* approach, with relevant consequences on macroeconomic analysis.[5]

The outcome of this intellectual toil showed that man, when facing difficulties exceeding his capacities, uses his information-processing ability to find alternatives, to assess consequences, to cope with situations of uncertainty and to find new satisfying ways of behaving (Simon 1979a).

---

[3] Simon 1964a; Simon 1965. As concerns the theory of the organization, see Cyert-March 1964.

[4] Simon 1979a. Simon refers to the work by Kahneman and Tversky 1973. On this subject, see Chapter 9.

[5] An important application of the decision-making theory is in the theory of the firm. According to Simon (1962), this theory had to be reconsidered, by shifting the centre of the analysis to the processes by which information is acquired and conveyed. In the by-now classic work by Marris (1964), you can find one of the best analyses of the implications for the theory of the firm, of the results achieved in the development of the models of choice.

7.3 A systematic picture

Two aspects in the description of the decision-making process are worth underlining: the fact that one of the qualities of a choice is being the least expensive;[6] the interactive relation between decision-maker and environment. The individual, by means of his cognitive mechanisms, pictures the real system to himself and conceptualizes it. He develops one or several plans of action which may lead him to the desired situation; then he acts. The action may be carried out by means of innovatory or non-innovatory steps. The former modify the constraints and representation of the system; the latter are routines and therefore they do not modify the existing constraints. Innovatory steps are the most interesting ones, since they include mechanisms of authentic generation of solutions. Innovatory steps are subdivided into steps with learning or without learning.

To explicate this point, it is necessary to better specify the relation individual/environment. Each individual has an environment of possible choices at his disposal. When he works out his plans of action, though, he can also draw on other individuals' environments: there is a super-environment, in fact, which is defined as the possibility to modify one's environment, by drawing on others, which have already been tested and belong to the set of all the subjective environments. This way, new possibilities are added to the pre-existing scenario and its constraints are loosened.

The activity aimed at "widening" one's environment is again characterized in substantive terms. After innovating and modifying the system, the individual begins storing new experiences. An innovatory dimension becomes, step by step, a routine (Cagliozzi 1990).

In this first phase, environmental constraints compel the individual to make a choice by means of the mechanisms of substantive rationality; the choice becomes a routine.[7] The second possibility is choice without learning. In this case, every innovatory step is an original solution, with reference to the solutions which have already been experienced by the whole system. The crucial part is the creative action of the choosing individual. It occurs within the context of procedural rationality; developed procedures are innovatory sequences for the whole system. This process is characterized by structural uncertainty, defined as lack of information, hindering the individual from

---

[6] The behaviour of an individual is economic when he/she makes that/those decisions which guarantee a level of satisfaction which cannot be increased more than the cost of the research necessary to achieve such increase (Cagliozzi 1990, p. 11).

[7] With reference to the meaning of the word "apprendimento" (learning) used by Cagliozzi - though it might seem wrong from a linguistic point of view - it is necessary to draw the reader's attention to the existing correspondence between innovation without learning and Hayek's mechanism of learning through imitation, on the part of both agents and firms.

seeing and assessing - at least quantitatively - what is in front of him and he would like to grasp.[8]

Acknowledging such undefined dimension, necessarily implies a new view on mental processes, which used to be considered logical and are now considered analogical. The individual can go through structural uncertainty passively, if it pre-exists action. Otherwise, he can cope with it actively, when he reaches unexplored fields, looking for innovations. In the first case, decisions are made unawares, without planning them or thinking them over, spontaneously. They are routine decisions and are parts of tactical goals. In the second case, choices are aimed at specific tactical goals, arising from general strategical goals. For a choice to be made, margins of indeterminacy, of freedom and free will are required. This is true for both conscious and unconscious choices and, referring to the theory of knowledge in general, it presupposes Popper's or Lakatos' active subjectivism.[9]

From a social point of view, the issue includes also another very interesting aspect: it is the core of the remaining part of this work and concerns the very nature of economic theory, whose original subject is never nature; it is the functioning of man's creations, which can be referred to as institutions (Cagliozzi 1990).

---

[8] Cagliozzi 1990, p. 34. The author takes this definition from Langlois (1986), who distinguishes between structural and parametric uncertainty. The latter is defined as the possibility for well-defined events to occur (Langlois 1986).

[9] Lakatos-Worral-Currie (1978), following Popper (1965), distinguish three theories of knowledge: passivist (classical empiricism), conservative activist (Kant), and revolutionary activist (Lakatos, Popper; and I would add Hayek). The third theory is today known as sophisticated methodological falsificationism. According to this theory, the book of nature can only be read by means of a mental activity, with interpreting patterns that are created by the mind and that, unlike Kant's pre-existing and unchangeable patterns, are ever-developing. Shackle's contribution is to be studied starting from these considerations. He refers to an active mind, which imagines, creates, and determines, behaving like an arbiter. Mind cannot be explained only at a rational level: it is interlinked with the biological, historical, and psychological components of each individual.

According to Shackle, from this point of view every choice is initiative. It aims at compensating the lack of knowledge by means of imagination, analogy, supposition, undertaking, risk. The active mind keeps shifting from the psychic to the egological (considering one's own self-interest) level and vice versa, on the basis of the interaction with the others. Thus, we face the important issue of social/individual interaction. This aspect is dealt with further on in this book, but I deem it useful to mention now two points directly concerning the decision-making process. The first aspect is the role of subjectivity. It is not possible to refer to a super-environment in objectively defined terms. Learning is a subjective phenomenon, which cannot be perfectly controlled: it keeps creating new and original situations and changing the super-environment.

7.4 Procedural rationality

It is now necessary to introduce the concept of procedural rationality, which differs from both substantive and bounded rationality. The latter has developed as a criticism of Olympian or neoclassical rationality and it can be considered as the "destruens" part of such criticism. Procedural rationality, instead, may be considered as its "construens" part. It is the cornerstone on which an alternative approach to the traditional theory can be developed. This is why the last part of this work deals with the development of models based on procedural rationality.[10]

Unlike substantive rationality, a theory of procedural rationality is consistent with a world in which human beings keep thinking and inventing things. Defining a decision as "determined by the situation" is an illusion, since a part of the situation affecting the decison is inside the decision-maker's mind (Simon 1976).

Substantive rationality was developed within economics, while procedural rationality within psychology. According to the first approach, to understand whether behaviour is rational or not, it is sufficient to know the agent's goals and the objective characteristics of the situation. If goals are given, rational behaviour is completely determined by the characteristics of the agent's environment. These assumptions make economics completely independent of psychology. There is no point in studying cognitive or psychological aspects. If, instead, margins of indeterminacy do exist, then analogical processes become worth studying along with *procedural* rationality, which differs from *bounded* rationality. Bounded rationality remains within the sphere of what Simon calls substantive rationality and it has nothing to do with a non-defined situation, typical of procedural rationality (Cagliozzi 1990). Bounded rationality is still characterized by the decision-maker's environmental constraints and goals: it is sufficient to know the agent's goals and the objective characteristics of the environment, to define rational behaviour.

In a context of procedural rationality, instead, it is essential to know the procedures of conceptualization of the reality perceived by the individual, and his ability to infer from the information he owns.[11] Rational behaviour, in a procedural context, concerns the result of a convenient choice. Rationality concerns the process of generation of such choice. This process is irrational if it consists in an impulsive response on the part of a mechanism working

---

[10] Individuals and organizations are endowed with scarce memory and time resources and limited computing capacities. The main issue is not the rational choice; it is rather the way by which relevant information and knowledge is acquired and the individual capacity of formulating and solving problems (Egidi 1991).

[11] According to Simon (1969), an intelligent system can adjust to the external environment (substantive rationality) (external environment: technology, other markets, other economies, behaviour of the other agents) according to its capability of finding a way of acting that can be properly adjusted (procedural rationality).

independently of mind. Therefore, it is not useful to know the agent's "objective" conditions. It is important, instead, to study the mechanisms allowing him to picture the problem to himself and his abilities to solve it.

The *"search and satisficing"* theory showed how choices may be made by means of reasonable computational activities and on the basis of incomplete information; it is no longer necessary to assume unreal behaviour, i.e. optimizing. Today we know that man - when he faces problems that exceed his abilities to cope with them - makes use of his ability to process information, in order to find alternatives, predict their consequences, tackle uncertainty and discover satisfying behaviour.

7.5 Uncertainty

Thus the link between rational behaviour and uncertainty, with reference to future events, becomes evident.[12] Nevertheless, it is worth specifying what I am referring to, when I use the word uncertainty.

F. Knight was the first author to shed light on the difference between risk (which sometimes can be estimated by means of calculus of probability) and uncertainty, which cannot be estimated. There is a crucial character of the distinction between measurable risk and unmeasurable uncertainty (Knight 1921, p. 20).[13] Uncertainty may be defined as lack of information, regarding the objective probability of future events, which matter as to the choices that economic agents are to make. On the contrary, economic agents run a risk, when: i) assuming that the possible states of the world do not exclude each other, every single action is associated with a series of consequences and each consequence implies that a specific state of the world has been accomplished;

---

[12] We live in a world full of uncertainty, and we have only imprecise ideas about the future. This is true for every sphere of human activity. The information we own is incomplete and imperfect and our knowledge is partial. If we want to understand the workings of the economic system, we need to investigate the principle and the meaning of uncertainty (Knight 1921, p. 199).

[13] Knight (1921), p. 19; see also Chapter 7, pp. 197-232. Dosi-Egidi (1988 and 1991) have recently given a new definition of Knight's procedural uncertainty. These authors have studied situations characterized by endogenous changes of taste or technology, and they describe innovators as agents, who carry out their activities by pursuing their own self-interest and on the basis of incomplete information and knowledge. With reference to Knight's distinction between risk and uncertainty, see also Egidi 1989a. In this article there is also a good definition of procedural uncertainty: if the agents are not able to reach a "constructive" definition of all the events which would be considered relevant, if they were known, we can define their uncertainty as procedural (ibid. p. 90). Knight's substantive uncertainty, instead, can be considered similar to the concept of risk (all the events are known and their probability can be estimated) (ibid. p. 97).
With reference to the difference between risk and uncertainty in the psychological field, see Deaton-Muellbauer 1980.

ii) the economic agents credit the possible states of the world with given probabilities.[14]

Demaria has dealt with this issue systematically. Reality is characterized by ever-changing facts (entelechian facts) that we cannot determine a-priori, because of the limits of human mind. When observing facts, we encounter two limits. The first limit refers to our observation being imprecise, since facts are too numerous (uncertainty in induction); or else, even if facts could be taken into account one at a time, yet they could not be observed with perfect precision. The concept of imprecision can be considered similar to Knight's idea of risk, while the concept of indeterminacy to Knight's uncertainty.[15]

Allowing for uncertainty, economists have developed two different approaches. It is possible to decide not to take uncertainty into consideration and study only those situations concerning risk, assuming that it is impossible to analyse situations of uncertainty.[16] Another possibility is to consider uncertainty a predominant condition in economic analysis and, as a consequence, make efforts to develop new instruments of analysis: H. Simon's procedural rationality is a major instrument to study and understand this world.

Simon acknowledges that, in reality, uncertainty has deeper roots.

A situation of uncertainty is the necessary prerequisite to generate alternatives of choice and especially to generate procedures for solving problematic situations. It is reasonable to believe that substantive rationality is to be found only in situations which are easy to understand and simple enough for our mind. In any other situations, mind acts on the basis of imperfect information, simplifies and pictures the situation to itself and performs computing operations within its capacity.

7.6 Learning

Learning plays a key role with reference to procedural rationality. By means of learning, agent's knowledge as well as the whole array of choices at his disposal are enriched with innovations.

---

[14] In the probabilistic theories, a distinction is made between the concept of subjective probability and that of objective or frequentist probability. The latter refers to how frequently an event occurs within an experiment that is repeated several times, and it reveals objective aspects of the real world. Subjective probability, instead, refers to the state of individual knowledge, to how probable an individual considers a given event. Among the major theorists of calculus of probability see De Finetti 1974.

[15] Demaria 1962, Chapter 1. More specifically, with reference to entelechian facts, pp. 39-40; with reference to the limits of intelligence, p. 48; as to the concepts of indeterminateness and inexactness, p. 46.

[16] "In situations of risk, the hypothesis of rational behavior may be explainable in terms of economic theory. (...) in cases of uncertainty, economic reasoning will be of no value" (Lucas 1981, p. 224).

Learning may be defined as the human ability to modify one's behaviour on the basis of experience, in a more or less permanent way and beyond instinctive reactions. This implies that organisms have a "plastic base" allowing them to respond to environmental variations (Droz 1977).

This definition is open to a two twofold view on learning. According to the first view, of associationalistic origin, learning is an aspect of the natural world. In this case, learning is a phenomenon consisting in associating stimuli and responses. The second one is the cognitivistic view. It is focused on individual cognition of the environment (perceptions, interpretations) and on how these cognitions affect behaviour. The cognitivistic approach, therefore, is more involved with understanding mind processes (Hill 1963). Both (associationalistic and cognitivistic) mechanisms are present in individual behaviour, according to the type of action that is being performed. Yet, I think that - beyond this differentiation - the learning process, at an individual and organizational level, is a very interesting issue. As mentioned above, any problematic situation stirs a problem-solving process, through which the agent finds a solution. This process occurs in a situation of strategical interdependence among decision-makers, which is the cause of incomplete knowledge and procedural uncertainty (Egidi 1991). Individual action may be the result of deduction, only if it is part of an array of already solved problems. In this case, an already acquired and experimented routine is implemented. The routine is stored into memory, by means of a set of records in the brain, and is retrieved every time the individual encounters the same problematic situation, which generated that routine (Gregory 1987).

If the problem does not belong to a class of already solved problems, then the individual is supposed to generate new routines by means of induction (Egidi 1991), making use of heuristic procedures. Where can he obtain useful data from? The interactive relation with the environment plays a major role. Simon, for example, points out that learning also means *adjusting* already known programs (routines) to new problems, arising from an ever-changing environment. Knowledge is often obtained by rearranging data rather than by adding or multiplying them (Simon 1967). The subject conceptualizes his environment by picturing it to himself. When he performs non-innovatory, routine actions, he modifies neither his representation of the environment, nor the existing constraints. Modification takes place, instead, when the individual takes an innovatory step, which is worked out, either drawing on other environments (other individuals' behaviour), or through an authentic process of discovery.

With reference to firms, in the first case other firms' more efficient routines are implemented (copied); in the second case, absolutely new routines are developed. In the latter situation, learning is a new method of environmental planning, which differs from the already tested ones and is carried out through the mechanism of procedural rationality (Simon 1978).

In organizations, this process occurs because of their hierarchical structure, based on the division of competence-knowledge and on control. Firms, as well as individuals, cope with an extremely complex situation of strategical interdependence. Their survival depends on their ability to adjust to an ever-changing environment. Hierarchy and division of labour - organized by means of the mechanism of power - give way to a better process of procedure coordination. This process - once again - consists in making use of already tested routines or in organizational and inductive learning processes, aimed at developing new routines.

According to Egidi, the structure of the firm itself (internal definition of roles) is based on this internal microinnovating process. It is so organized as to carry out routines, whose variation implies a structural change.[17] Within organizations, every problematic situation is creatively solved by means of *problem-solving* and division of problems and is then turned into a routine (the same happens with the implementation of a program on a machine). Therefore, technology is defined as a set of effective solutions of a production problem, which can be implemented mechanically, without using induction (Egidi 1991). The technology of a firm is made up of the whole set of its implemented routines.

All this affects the role of competencies remarkably. At the highest levels of an organization open and general plans are developed. At the lower levels, work consists not only in carrying out routines mechanically; the general ideas are interpreted and adjusted, in order to solve problems.

7.7 Concluding remarks

Procedural rationality is a very significant achievement. It is an important methodological instrument, allowing us to understand the mechanisms of choice in conditions of uncertainty. Now my goal is proposing new models of individual choice and of institutional and organizational-technological change. These issues belong - directly or indirectly - to the neoinstitutionalist school, of which I will give a preliminary outline. Before that, let me put forward for consideration a short digression or interlude. I have already mentioned the important role played by psychology in formulating criticisms of the traditional theory and alternative methodological approaches, especially with reference to Hayek and Simon. Now I would like to examine this subject closely: I will deal with the relation between economics and psychology and I will try to outline the cultural background, in which Hayek's and Simon's ideas were developed. This is the content of the next chapter: I call it "Interlude" and put it between two quite different parts of the book: criticism and constructive proposals.

INTERLUDE

8. Economics and Psychology

> Economics will progress as we deepen our understanding of human thought processes.
>
> (H. Simon 1976, p. 146)

8.1 Introduction

The relationship between economics and psychology has been discontinuous. An exhaustive study might disclose interesting nuances. In this context and referring only to this century, it is possible to outline this relationship as follows. After a phase of cooperation - which reached its height in the neoclassical theory of the consumer - and since the 1950s, economics and psychology have had no common ground until only recently.[1]

As mentioned above, Simon insisted on the necessity of an osmosis between them. According to him, economics concerns choices, and choosing is basically a psychological process; the *role theory* is the common ground linking the economic and the psychological theories of decision-making (Simon 1959).

In neoclassical economics, consumers and firms are considered selfish and individualistic rational maximizers. Empirical data, though, show that this assumption on human behaviour is "naive" (Legrenzi 1991) and should be replaced with an alternative approach, connected with the psychological theory of perception and cognition (descriptive theory) (Simon 1957).[2]

---

[1] Tarde (1902) is the first author who stated that it was necessary for the explanations of economic processes and the results of psychological analyses to be in agreement. He emphasized the need to give due consideration to developing models of choice, the principle of imitation and interaction of social processes. As regards the last twenty years, Scitovsky (1977) introduced the principles developed by psychological theory into economic theory; Katona (1975) introduced the results achieved by Gestalt psychology, as we shall see further on; Strumpel-Morgan-Zahan (1972) the results of motivational psychology; Newcomb (1972) the results of social learning. Yet, among the authors who offered the major contributions to a "psychological" approach to economic theory, there are certainly Kahneman and Tversky (see below), whose debts to Simon are both evident and acknowledged.

[2] With reference to Simon's criticism of neoclassical methodological assumptions, especially M. Friedman's ones, contradicting psychological empirical tests, see also

In order to avoid a possible misunderstanding, I would like to underline that I do not think that between psychology and economics there has never been an exchange of ideas. I think that while psychology was going through its cognitivistic "revolution", standard economy has been sticking to its behaviouristic assumptions. The transition from behaviourism (the prevailing theory until the 1950s) to cognitivism has a remarkable importance. While in the past, in a behaviouristic context, there had been agreement between economics and psychology, with the emergence of cognitivism a gap appears between them. What were the causes of this gap?

According to Katona,[3] the responsibilities of psychology lie in its focusing its attention on pathological aspects, while the responsibilities of economics are to be found in its attempt to become an exact science, by eliminating psychological variables. Thus, the mechanistic theory of economic behaviour has been applied also to problems concerning dynamic situations (choice in a situation of uncertainty and of incomplete knowledge, choice aimed at goals other than profit maximization, etc.). Examples of mechanistic economic theory are the following: expenditure in consumption, considered as a mere function of income, and expenditure in investments as a function of profits (Katona 1951). In reality, choosing processes are much more complex than how traditional theory describes them.

Katona had a brilliant yet simple idea, in the 1950s: interviewing people on their aims, reasons and opinions. These data became more and more precise and sophisticated and showed the wide gap existing between real behaviour and economists' assumptions (Legrenzi 1991).

Economic agents are intelligent individuals; they are aware of their actions and goals and should not be considered as robots, merely reacting to the mechanism of demand/supply. Instead of formulating general principles, applicable only to ideal circumstances, economists should study consumers' and firms' real behaviour. Therefore, it is incorrect to assume that an ex-ante *rational* behaviour exists and that this is the fundamental subject of economic analysis. On the contrary, it is necessary to describe real behaviour and only afterwards, ex-post, is it possible to try to understand which behavioural acts may be considered rational (Katona 1951).

A classical example of psychological theories applied to economics is the theory of the consumer.[4] It will be dealt with in the next chapter.

Filippi, "Introduzione" to Simon 1985. As regards the need to adopt a psychological approach in economics, see also Van Raaij, Introduction to Antonides (1991) and Scitovsky (1977).

[3] George Katona is a very important author with reference to the psychological approach in economics. He founded a school of this kind. He wrote several works on economics and psychology.

[4] Another interesting and more recent example of the application of results achieved by psychology to economics is the "cognitive dissonance". Following the works by Festinger (1957) and Brehm-Cohen (1962), Hirschman (1965) applied this theory to economics. According to the theory of cognitive dissonance, an individual who, for

I will now outline the cultural context in which Hayek's and Simon's ideas developed, especially with reference to cognitive psychology and contemporary neurobiology, examining the transition from behaviourism to cognitivism in detail. Behaviourism had been the prevailing approach until the 1950s, then it was replaced by cognitivism. I will then underline the features of Cognitivism, especially those aspects (such as the models of memory) that contributed to formulating the microfoundations of economics and that influenced Hayek's and Simon's ideas.

For the last decade an alternative approach to cognitivism in social sciences has been emerging: connexionism. I will refer to this approach when I illustrate the "neural network" models, that are being developed also in an economic context.

In this chapter one more topic is examined. In the preceding chapter I underlined that also neurobiology - along with cognitivism - exerted a great influence, especially on Hayek's thought. In the final part of the book I will examine this topic in detail, starting from this chapter, where the differences

given reasons, induces himself/herself to behave in a way contrasting with his/her own beliefs (or what he/she considers his/her own beliefs) is in a state of dissonance. This is a rather unpleasant feeling. Generally, that individual aims at reducing such dissonance by adjusting beliefs to behaviour. Actions, being concrete acts, cannot be cancelled, once they have been performed. Beliefs, instead, can be - and usually are - adjusted to the contrasting behaviour, in order to mitigate that unpleasant feeling (Hirschman 1965, p. 392). Hirschman is the first author to use this theory to describe the change in the approach to modernization in the course of development. Hirschman's analysis, aimed at studying the hindrances to development, finds effective tools in the theory of cognitive dissonance (Akerlof-Dickens 1982). Akerlof and Dickens further extend the application of this theory in economics, and offer a new view on irrational behaviour. Unlike sociologists, anthropologists, and psychologists, economists have adopted different principles to develop their own analyses. According to these two authors, psychology can and must be incorporated with economic theory, and this is proved by cognitive dissonance. It can explain irrational behaviour. Individual preferences concern not only the state of the world, but also the individual views on the state of the world. Individuals control their beliefs, which, once they have been chosen, are persistent. According to Becker (1962), irrational behaviour is characterized by casual deviations of economic rationality; on the contrary, these two authors, in agreement with the results of psychological tests, think that such behaviour is predictable and therefore it is not completely casual (Akerlof-Dickens 1982, p. 307, note 1). The implications of this assumption are quite relevant in developing a decision-making model; in fact it is deeply modified as compared to the traditional rational decision-making model. Still, it is necessary to specify what follows: according to Akerlof and Dickens, the limits of cognitive dissonance consist in the fact that it seldom occurs in reality. It does not characterize every economic transaction. In fact, it plays a major role only in few and peculiar circumstances. Nevertheless, in such circumstances this theory can explain certain phenomena better than the standard approach. It is necessary to point out that not all psychologists agree on these results. For a critical approach to the theory of cognitive dissonance, see Chapanis-Chapanis (1964).

with the cognitivistic approach are briefly outlined. I believe that the limits of contemporary analysis lie mostly in the renewed assumption of the old dualism mind-brain. I will refer to this problem in the last paragraph, concerning the results achieved by Soviet neuropsychology; I will also propose an integration between cognitivistic and neurobiological approaches. This is the methodological path that I am following: a unification of Simon's and Hayek's ideas. This will be the subject of the third part of this book.

8.2 From behaviourism to cognitivism

> I regard the view that our perceptions are "given" to us as a mistake: they are "made" by us, they are the result of active work.
>
> (K. Popper in Popper-Eccles 1977, p. 49)

Around the 1950s a so-called *"mind's new science"* developed through the convergence of several disciplines. The highest point of this integration process consists in the development - in cybernetics[5] - of the concept of feedback[6] and its use in psychology.

---

[5] The word "cybernetics" was introduced by N. Wiener, who in 1948 published *Cybernetics*. This word has a Greek origin; it means "steersman" and refers to a theory of self-regulating systems, applicable to both machines and living beings.

[6] Generally speaking, feedback can be defined as a control system continuously adjusting (offsetting) the action that is being carried out to its goals, on the basis of the information it receives from outside. Feedback acquires a crucial role in Hayek's and Simon's analyses. Hayek used the concept of feedback and the results of the theory of systems; Simon directly applied feedback to economics (for a clear synthesis of the concept of feedback, see Gregory 1987).

It is interesting to point out what happened immediately before the 1950s. In the decade 1943/1953 the concept of feedback, developed by Wiener and McCulloch, is for the first time directly applied to social sciences by N. Wiener, K. Lewin, K. Deutsch, A. Tustin, and H. Simon. The fusion of different traditions gave rise to two different fields of application. In the first line of research, attention was focused on the role of feedback with reference to communication, and on the analysis of the control mechanisms in the social context (cybernetic line of research). The second one emphasized the role of feedback within the concept of dynamic behaviour (line of research of servomechanism). The latter was developed by economists who were familiar with engineering and the theory of the servomechanism. They were especially interested in economic fluctuations, and therefore they focused their attention on the dynamic aspects of economic cycles. The role of feedback, in this case, is studied by means of formal models, first of all because it can create patterns and movement in the dynamic systems. Richardson (1991) is, as far as I know, the most systematic illustration of the origin and development of these lines of research, with interesting historical explanations. With reference to the history of the scientific conceptualization of information (also this is due to the development and application of the concept of feedback in the first decade of the second post-war period), see Aspray (1985).

When the concept of feedback was introduced into psychological theories (Miller-Frick 1949), behaviourism was abandoned and cognitivism replaced it. Behaviourism supported the idea of a completely objective psychology, interested in behavioural acts, which may be described in terms of stimulus-response; as a consequence, all the words and concepts referring to mind had to be rejected. Words such as imagine, mind and conscience were meaningless in that context (Schultz 1974). In this perspective, environment played a central role in determining individual action. The individual did not act on the basis of his own ideas or goals: he passively responded to environmental stimuli. Several scholars gave their contribution to this approach.[7]

In the 1960s, the transition had already been completed and the behaviouristic theories of reflected arc had been replaced by a cybernetic approach. In 1967, Neisser published *Cognitive Psychology,* one of the fundamental works on cognitive psychology, in which he put forward a clearly constructivistic view on human activity (Gardner 1985).

8.2.1 The features of cognitivism

According to cognitivism, every individual is endowed with cognitive functions, allowing him/her to interact with his/her environment. An organism adjusts to its environment and *modifies* it according to its needs. Attention is focused on the information-gathering processes, carried out by means of perception, processing and interpretation of the surrounding environment. The individual is active and he/she continuously adjusts his/her behaviour to the information he/she receives from outside. The behaviouristic model does not take into consideration retroactive round systems and multiple proactive

---

[7] In 1948 in the U.S.A. an important conference was held on "the brain mechanisms of behaviour". It was aimed at explaining the workings of the brain and also at contrasting the predominance of behaviourism (Gardner 1985) and for both aims the foundations were actually laid. First of all, it was demonstrated that behavioural sequences are planned and organized before the action is carried out. They are not mere connections of stimuli and responses. Form precedes and determines behaviour and it arises inside the organism rather than outside. The new approach spread quickly and cognitive science was officially acknowledged in 1956. The same year, in September many experts in the field of science of communications and human sciences participated in the Symposium on Information Theory, held at MIT. Newell and Simon illustrated for the first time a theorem of logic performed by a computer. Chomsky presented his studies on language and Miller the ones on the limited capacity of short-term human memory (see the paragraph on the models of memory, below). Another important innovation was the distinction made between hardware and software. Thought models (software) could be described independently of the particular structure of the nervous system (hardware): this affected the development of artificial intelligence. In 1975, Putnam introduced the use of software into philosophy to solve identity problems.

systems. The heart of the cognitivistic theory, instead, is the concept of *feedback*. The immediate and direct relation between two variables (like in a Cartesian context) is replaced by a a model in which action is continuously adjusted to stimuli, which, in turn, are modified by the individual patterns of interpretation (Gardner 1985).

The most important aspect regards this interactive process between perception and "adjustment" of individual patterns, which, in turn, are modified according to external stimuli. Every individual is endowed with inborn patterns of interpretation. Being pre-programmed and hereditary, they allow the individual to adjust to the surrounding environment from the moment of birth. Piaget (1969) thinks that inborn reflexes improve and develop by means of two opposite and complementary mechanisms: adjustment and assimilation. Individuals discover new aspects along with already known ones, in their perception of the world. In the case of already known events, a process of recognitive assimilation is started, by means of which a pattern is applied to the already known situation. If, instead, that action or situation is new, then a process of generalizing assimilation takes place, through which the new situation is perceived by applying (associating) it to one of the experimented patterns. If the new situation is complex, the pattern is adjusted every time. By means of *feedback,* patterns are modified and adjusted to the new experience the individual is perceiving. Besides, patterns supplement each other, thus generating new ones (Droz 1978).[8]

To sum up, the peculiar features of cognitivism are the following:

1) individuals are endowed with practical abilities (practical intelligence) enabling them to find a rapid solution of their problems. These abilities develop spontaneously and naturally from the moment of birth. Also the superior species of animals are endowed with such abilities;
2) individuals develop abilities, allowing them to understand their surrounding environment;
3) man owns a behavioural wealth, which grows richer thanks to adjusting or assimilating processes;
4) by means of more sophisticated inferential reasoning, a representation of the world is developed, consisting of a model rather than a reflex (Droz 1978).

---

[8] Moreover, according to Droz (1978, p. 322), Piaget's empirical observations may confute the logic of Popper's scientific discovery. When trying to verify an empirically formulated law, an adult or a researcher looks for new examples confirming it, rather than for facts contradicting it. From this point of view, the knowledge of the world is not a reflection of the surrounding world; it is rather an internal picture of it, obtained through processes of abstraction, categorization, comparison, inferential reasoning, etc.

8.2.2 Models of memory

The development of cognitivism gave a substantial impulse to studies on memory. The processes through which the patterns of interpretation are developed are directly linked to mnemonic processes. I will refer to the subject for this reason as well as because these processes affected the development of the theory of bounded rationality, one of the major topics of this book.

As mentioned above, cognitivism considers man as an information-processing system, i.e. an individual who processes the information he/she receives from the outside world, coding and decoding it. Man is also described according to his structural limits.[9] Human activity is carried out by means of continuous corrections of the plan of action, resulting from the comparison with the outcome of preceding actions (*feedback*). Every external impulse undergoes a checking process, on the basis of phenomena, that are not permanent features of memory, but depend on factors such as individual instructions, tasks and past history (Atkinson-Shiffrin 1968).

The bounded capacities of short-term memory are described by Atkinson and Shiffrin through the concept of a buffer. A buffer is defined as a metaphorical container with a limited capacity. Once its capacity has been determined and a strategy of reiteration has been chosen, it is filled with a number of items. When a new item is introduced, an old one is necessarily expelled.

Broadbent (1958) suggested using the theory of memory as a filter, to describe how the message selection is carried out. In this case, too, the individual makes a choice. He/she selects messages' physical features and examines their meaning. This occurs before he/she perceives and acknowledges the message.

Norman (1969) further develops this model: the stimulus is acknowledged as a result of a complex interaction between the information received from the outside world and the information stored in the long-term memory (see also Norman-Bobrow 1976). The difference between short-term and long-term memory consists in the fact that the former is limited, while the latter is unlimited and is measured in chunks.[10] Our forgetting something does not mean that we lost that piece of information, but that, in that very moment, we

---

[9] The new model of memory develops along with the theory of human information processing, distinguishing short-term and long-term memory. Miller (1956) underlined the limited capacity of short-term memory and later (with other authors: Miller-Galanter-Pribam, 1960) emphasized the importance of the concept of feedback in behavioural processes.

[10] A chunk is the unit of measure of capacity limits. It is a psychological unit, referring to the pieces of information that can be integrated. It does not always contain the same number of pieces of information, since that number depends on how the system is organized.

do not manage to retrieve it from the long-term stock.

Another model of memory that is useful for my analysis and has been even more affected by cognitivism is the constructivistic model. The basic idea of the model is that memory consists in a series of processes by means of which the raw information received from the outside world is selected, organized and processed. The same recollection seldom occurs identically. Information is recorded according to its original context and the knowledge which the individual has already acquired. This aspect is connected to perception rather than to memory. From this point of view, these authors are in the wake of Gestalt psychology.

Katona (1940) demonstrates that the individual tends to find rules and characterizing elements in the perceived situation, and if he manages to, it becomes much easier for him to memorize things. Memory works on the basis of criteria concerning the internal organization of stimuli, by means of rules and strategies developed by the individual and by means of checking processes. This is a central aspect of the whole model. The individual interprets reality and develops his/her recollections on the basis of patterns. Recollections are not copies of the outside world; with the passing of time they are selected and processed along with cognitive development (Bartlett 1932; Piaget-Inhelder 1968).

This digression has a double purpose: specifying the psychological concepts from which the theoretical foundations of unorthodox theories have developed; and outlining the framework within which Hayek's and Simon's ideas developed, especially as regards the models of mind that are at the basis of their theories. In those same years, other models of mind have been developed. I will now outline them, too, since a few of them are influencing contemporary economics. Once again, they are connected to Hayek and Simon.

8.3 Alternative models of mind: neural networks[11]

8.3.1 Cognitivism and connectionism

In the second half of the 1980s, as the new connectionistic paradigm emerged, cognitivism began to be disputed. Cognitivism has its roots in the humanities and it is not interested in physical and biological elements. Connectionism, instead, is very interested in elementary mind activities and artificial intelligence. Cognitivism is criticized for explaining complex behaviour as a development of simple behaviour. Connectionism goes back to pre-cognitivistic approaches, whose attention is focused on the dynamic development of systems; rather than individuals, the centre of analysis consists in the relations between them (Parisi 1991).

---

[11] In the literature, the word neural and neuronal are used interchangeably, with reference to the same phenomenon I have illustrated here.

The development of connectionism is linked to the attempt to develop behavioural patterns which simulate - in associationalistic terms - the existing relations between man's most elementary nervous units: the neurons. The studies on associationism[12] date back to W. James and to the last century (Schultz 1974); McCulloch and Pitts laid the foundations for the recent development of this approach (Gardner 1985; Richardson 1991).

The most important aspect of their thought was that they did not consider neurons as the unit of their analysis, the unit of analysis was the relation and interconnection among them (synapsis, i.e. the connection between two nerve endings).[13] Nevertheless, their models and the ones developed later, have little to do with neurons and neural networks. There are remarkable differences and it is not possible to examine them here in detail. In this context, the major difference regards one of neurons' characteristics: their plasticity. Neural networks can modify their structure, since - as Maturana and Varela maintain - neurons are not linked to each other like cables plugged in sockets; they set up delicate dynamic balances that are continuously adjusted by an infinite number of elements. Artificial networks, instead, are characterized by rigid interlinking lines, connecting the elementary units, which consist of neurons or knots, endowed with one input and one output line. Units communicate by means of numerical rather than symbolic signals (Pessa 1992).

This problem is now being coped with in the most recent models, where the learning process carried out by agents (who are represented by means of neural networks) can be simultaneous to action (see Beltratti-Margarita-Terna 1996).

8.3.2 Boolean analysis of neural networks

This line of research has its beginnings in the 1940s, with W. Pitts' and W. McCulloch's studies (Aspray 1985). They demonstrate that human brain works on the basis of logic principles, like a powerful computer. The work of a nerve cell (neuron) and its connection with other neurons (neural networks) can be represented in logical terms. The work of a neuron is conceived as a logical sequence, within which a proposition may imply another proposition. The analogy between neurons and logic is explained in electrical terms:

---

[12] This theory was developed in the psychological field at the end of the last century. According to it, learning and the development of superior processes basically consist in combining irreducible mental elements.

[13] At the basis of this approach lies the idea that, also in human brain, the most relevant feature is not the single neuron, but the enormous bundle of synapses that are created among them (Minsky 1975, p. 203). Another fundamental idea of this approach is that neural connections are not created by chance, but systematically, and that organized connections are related to the function of the system (Gregory 1987, p.173).

signals that are - or are not - carried through a circuit. Connectionists assume that, at a synapsis level, logical-mathematical formulae and neural processes are structurally identical (McCulloch-Pitts 1943).

This approach follows von Neumann's thought: any logical operation can be reduced to a set of elementary operations. McCulloch and Pitts conceived little neural systems as networks of logical gates. There are two possible states of a neuron's output: discharge/no discharge. When it discharges, it transmits a wave of inhibitory or exciting potential to the neurons it is connected with: also in this case the possible states are only two. Therefore, it is possible to conceive of neural systems that are capable of carrying out - as precisely as a computer's CPU - any operation of formal logic and any program structured like a system of simple logical operations (Gallino 1984).

McCulloch's and Pitts' approach was further developed by Piaget (1967). According to Piaget, logical-mathematical truths are objectified in the inmost fibres of organic structure; mathematical formulae are not only linguistic instruments: they are, first of all, a photography or reproduction of the rational structure of physical reality (Marhaba 1976).

According to Pitts and McCulloch, the nervous system works as an algebraic structure; the whole organism - of which the nervous system is a reflex as well as a regulator - may then be conceived in logical-mathematical terms. Piaget thinks that immanent ideas share the nature of those used in an electronic system. It is an isomorphic causal mechanism of conscious implications (Piaget 1967). McCulloch's and Pitts' well-known analyses underline the isomorphism between the transformations concerning synaptic links and logical operators; certainly, this "logic of neurons" does not contain in advance the logic of propositions at a thought level, since 11/12 years are necessary to reach this stage through constructions arising from reflecting abstractions (Piaget 1970). This statement refers to Hayek's mechanism of neural network formation, when the evolutionary and experiential aspect of this formation is underlined.

In the 1980s, the neoassociationalistic or neoconnectionistic[14] line of research - strictly linked to McCulloch's and Pitts' works - had developed. In Italy it includes important scholars.[15] Its major applications to economic theory regard, above all, the development of *decision-making* models in conditions of uncertainty (of consumption or investment). Applications exist also in the context of industrial economics.[16]

---

[14] McClelland-Rumelhart 1988; Anderson-Rosenfeld 1988; Aleksander-Morton 1990; Holland-Miller 1991; Gallant 1993.

[15] Parisi-Cecconi-Nolfi 1990; Cammarata 1990; Terna 1991 and 1995; Beltratti-Margarita-Terna 1996; Fabbri-Orsini 1991 and 1993.

[16] Actually, the concept of net used in this field is quite different. In this case, "a network is an organized set of partially separable productive units, with increasing overall returns which can be attributed not so much to economies of scale as to an overall 'subadditive' cost function which reflects the contribuition of relevant

8.3.3 Beyond Piaget

As mentioned above, Piaget develops McCulloch's and Pitt's approach. I have also referred to the "constructivistic" aspect of his thought: like Hayek, Piaget thinks that mind categories are not always present and are not always the same, they develop with the passing of time. He studied such development in the various stages of mind development in a child, assuming that developed human beings reason by applying logic principles.

According to Piaget, the activity of the mind is similar to a coordinating process. Developing Pitts' and McCulloch's approach, he writes about lower patterns that become more advanced structures, through transformation and coordination. This cognitive activity, conceived as coordination, has a social as well as an individual nature. In Piaget's thought this is a secondary aspect (unlike Hayek). Nevertheless it has been the major interest of two of the authors who followed his teachings (Doise-Mugny 1981).[17] They try to give an answer to the following question: can an individual alone organize (read by means of his/her intelligence) the surrounding experience? Several lines of research, including Piaget's, tend to isolate the single individual from his/her context, conceiving cognitive processes as the fruit of the activity of his/her mind. Yet, intelligence is not only individual property, it is also a process of relations among individuals, who design and organize their actions on the physical and social environment together (Doise-Mugny 1981). Cognitive processes are not independent of culture and do not concern only the single individual. On the contrary, intelligence and culture interact. Coordination among individuals is at the basis of coordination within individuals, it *"precedes it and it is its source"*. Yet this idea should not be carried to extremes, maintaining that individuals develop their knowledge passively, according to external rules. These two scholars' approach is interactionistic and constructivistic; it is not confined to the relation individual-object, it takes into consideration more complex interactions among a number of individuals and the object. Thus they propose to shift from an ego-object bipolar psychology to an ego-alter-object tripolar psychology (Doise-Mugny 1981).

This socio-cognitive approach is in sharp contrast to epistemological individualism as well as to those theories assuming only imitative mechanisms. It is a socio-interactionistic and socio-constructivistic approach. The action does not take place only between individual and object, since the

---

technical, pecuniary and technological exernalities, as well as the effects of important demand externalities" (Antonelli 1995a, p. 128). In this approach, attention is focused first of all on the relationships and the effects of interdependence (externalities) between single-plant businesses and major businesses.

[17] A central aspect of the book by Doise and Mugny is the demonstration that the cognitive process of intelligence-building is not a mere individual fact, concerning the subject (as it still is in Piaget): the social context has a decisive influence on it.

relation between them is influenced by the relation between that individual and the others. Every function first appears at a social level, between agents (interpsychological level), and later at an individual level (intrapsychological level) (Doise-Mugny 1981).

8.3.4 Some remarks on artificial neural networks

As above mentioned, artificial neural networks show a few limits if compared to other models. As Gardner remarked (1985), the unmethodical statistical aspect of these models, along with the evident lack of control "executive processes" contradict the logical programmes aimed at a gradual reduction of the difference, which were developed within Newell's and Simon's problem-solving models. I think that the most remarkable limit consists in the characteristics of the artificial neurons used in simulations, as specified in the following considerations:

i)   artificial neurons are not endowed with natural neurons' plasticity;
ii) the developments of contemporary neurobiology show that decision-making processes can be described on the basis of natural neurons' real work and their interconnections.

As Hayek knew by intuition, and as contemporary neurobiology is confirming (Patterson-Nawa 1993, Calissano 1992, Damasio 1995, Berns-Sejnowsky 1995), in order to act, an individual forms his/her knowledge according to his/her genetic characteristics and to his/her specific and personal experience. These two factors work simultaneously and, with the passing of years, they continuously re-create the neurobiological state by means of learning (Hayek 1952a).

I have already mentioned above (and I will examine it closely below) that learning is the keystone to understanding individual, organizational and institutional processes of change and market dynamics. Understanding learning processes depends on the ability of neurons to rearrange themselves continuously (plasticity), thus generating new synaptic structures, according to the processes described in the paragraphs dealing with Hayek's model of mind.

New models have recently been developed, which use artificial neural networks (Beltratti-Margarita-Terna 1996) in which it is possible to fix the experience of the whole experiment ex-post, thus allowing the simulated individual to act on the basis of acquired experience. It is also possible to obtain memorizing processes permitting more or less rapid network variations. In this field a new path is thus taking shape: it can bring a relevant contribution to the comprehension of learning processes. Generally speaking, an important contribution given by connexionism was underlining the importance of neurons (though I would rather speak of neurobiology) in order to understand how thinking and "*decision-making*" work. I think that the most correct methodological approach for economic theory is to be found in the elimination of the dichotomy between micro (individual cognitive processes) and macro (social and inter-individual relations), a dichotomy reproposing the old mind-brain dualism.

8.4 Mind/brain

Before concluding this chapter, it is important to refer to Soviet neurological studies,[18] from Pavlov[19] on, because there we find a synthesis of preceding approaches. In particular, there are several analogies with Simon's thought and, even more so, with Hayek's.

The heart of these studies is both social constructivism and the individual-environment interactive relation, aimed at determining mind development. As for post-Piaget scholars, according to Soviet neurophysiology, in order to understand the highest forms of human psychic activity it is necessary to go beyond an analysis focused only on the organism and study also the experiential, social and historical dimension; man is subject to the laws of nature but he also changes it, by means of his "extracortical functions". Brain is concrete, it is an instrument, an active bahavioural system. As compared to Western theories, the Soviet approach gave an overall and more dynamic interpretation of brain's functions, underlining their philogenetic and ontogenetic evolution, aimed at adjusting species and individuals to their environment (Mecacci 1977). Therefore brain, being an active and plastic instrument, has a dynamic and historical dimension, on which Pavlov shed light. He maintained that a behavioural pattern is characterized not only by the inborn qualities of the nervous system: it is also influenced by the training and education received (Pavlov 1928).

This idea of a social dimension of brain development is quite close to Hayek's approach, while another important aspect, regarding the interactive individual-environment relation reminds us of Simon's thought.

A Soviet tradition in physiology - related to Bernstein's studies[20] and referred to as "physiology of reaction" - assumed a continuous balance between individual and environment, due to appropriate individual responses to changes in the environment. But, after the emergence of the concept of feedback, Soviet research follows a new path and tries to demonstrate the active role of brain and psychic activity in adjusting an organism to its

---

[18] With reference to the features and history of the Soviet neurophysiological school, see Mecacci 1977.

[19] I. P. Pavlov (1849-1936) was one of the major Russian physiologists, who studied conditioned reflexes in animal behaviour and influenced the following studies on learning (Gregory 1987).

[20] N. A. Bernstejn (1896-1966) was the founder of the school of physiology of co-ordination and physiology of activity. As a scholar, he devoted his life to understanding the mechanisms of human movements and of motor activities.

environment. The heart of the research becomes the "functional meaning of the nervous system in adjusting an animal to its environment" (Mecacci 1977). The so-called new physiology of "activity" is thus started. The assumption is opposite to Bernstein's. The starting point is not balance, but imbalance. An animal lives in a state of continuous imbalance with its environment. It continuously assesses environmental conditions and coordinates, rules and re-adjusts its actions actively, according to the responses it receives, in order to better adjust to its environment. Action arises from an association between new data and past experience (as for Hayek); and also from a representation of future scenarios, predicting possible future events (as for Simon). By means of *feedback*, brain centres are constantly informed about the success or failure of an action. If necessary a correcting mechanism is started (Mecacci 1977). The correspondence between present state and pursued goal is constantly checked. Every time a discrepancy is revealed, new steps are taken towards a new afferent synthesis.[21]

Once again, this analysis seems to confirm the existence of subjective neurobiological differences. The main task of brain is planning, checking and ruling behaviour so that the individual adjusts to his/her environment, grows and survives, and the species is preserved (Mecacci 1977). Brain is a necessary condition for the development of higher psychic functions, but it is not sufficient. It is necessary to take into account also the interaction between the genetically-inborn brain and the environment. Yet, higher psychic functions are a functional reorganization of brain structures. Such reorganization is not genetically predetermined, it takes shape according to the individual-environment interaction and on the basis of the relations with other individuals, which are conditioned by history and society.[22]

Every individual has his/her own cytoarchitectonic structure,[23] different from anybody else's. This is confirmed by empirical data. Examining a number of brains, a difference in their organization emerges (Mecacci 1977) which proves that individual diversity at a cognitive and perceptive level has a biological and genetic origin.

Let us examine this aspect closely. I think that neurobiological diversity carries important implications. It is by now beyond doubt that brain is the

---

[21] In particular, P. Anokhin (1974), in developing his neurocybernetic model, introduced a concept which is similar to the concept of feedback. The "afferent synthesis" is the moment when organic needs are compared with the environmental situation and with similar preceding experiences that are stored in memory. The environmental situation reaches the brain thanks to environmental afference (defined as the series of stimuli coming from the environment), with a constant variation of the intermediate moments of the action, on the basis of a comparison between achieved result and pursued goal.

[22] Lurija 1976, Chapter 1.

[23] Layout of the various kinds of cells in a tissue and especially in the cerebellar cortex.

organ of the mind (Gregory 1987); mind is probably produced by brain in order to perform activities it may not perform on its own. Mind, in turn, when performing these activities (imagining, wishing, speaking, etc.), cooperates with, and is influenced by brain. As above mentioned, studies on mind have been carried out mostly in the psychological field, while studies on brain in the neurobiological field. The above considerations, along with the latest developments in contemporary neurobiology, suggest that the dichotomy mind/brain is to be cancelled in order to explain choosing processes.[24]

A new common element has emerged between the two lines of research that are, in my opinion, at the origin of neoinstitutionalism. Along with the macro aspects (convergence between the analyses on organizations and institutions), I mean to put forward also at a macro level an integration of Hayek's model of mind with Simon's. The resulting model - we might refer to it as neurobiological - includes all the major aspects of cognitivism and has (natural) neurons as its basic analytical unit. The next chapter has as its subject this link and the relation mind-brain: I will try to highlight the innovatory implications for the decision-making process. Moreover, what is to be examined in detail, in the light of the analysis of learning mechanisms, is the process by which knowledge is "built" and its implication for economic theory. I also believe that this methodological approach may help to shed light on the mechanism through which (individual, organizational and institutional) rules emerge, and on their nature and development. This is the purpose I will pursue in Part Three, starting from the innovations this approach brings to the *decision-making* process.

---

[24] Epistemological dualism does not imply ontological dualism. The fact that knowledge is organized in a dualistic way basically depends on the circumstance that mind and brain have different ways of being and of being known; this does not imply that they are separated and independent entities, as in metaphysical dualism or in spiritualism (Civita 1993, p. 13).

PART THREE

NEOINSTITUTIONALISM: RULES, LEARNING AND EVOLUTION

> Understanding the economic institutions of capitalism poses deep and enduring challenges to law, economics, and organization.

> (Williamson 1986, p. 1)

Part Two and the Interlude completed the picture of the neurobiological approach and the survey of the microfoundations of the unorthodox approach. My purposes, in this last Part Three, are the following: (i) examining in detail the implications, for economic theory, of the neurobiological approach; (ii) illustrating the main achievements of neoinstitutionalism.

As regards the second objective, I would like to point out the following. The neoinstitutionalist paradigm emerged between the second half of the 1970s and the first half of the 1980s. It is often associated with its major exponent, O. Williamson, who, in those years, published his more important works (Williamson 1975; 1986). The main feature of neoinstitutionalism is the express belief that, in order to understand economic relations, it is necessary to examine them in their own context. In other words, the theoreticians of this School think that transactions are necessarily carried out in an institutional context and are always governed by rules. A part of these transactions occur within hierarchical organizations, another part of them on the market.

The main questions this School tries to find an answer to, are the following:

a) what are institutions? how do they emerge?
b) what are organizations? how do they emerge?
c) what kind of relation is created between institutions and organizations?

Important considerations, that are central in and peculiar to the neoinstitutionalist analysis, arise from these issues. The first one regards the nature of (especially economic) institutions, affecting the relevant microeconomic issues of individual rationality and information acquisition/processing. The latter is at the basis of the analyses of market failures, externalities, and, above all, transaction costs.

The macro level of this approach affects directly the nature of firms, conceived as hierarchical organizations that are alternative to market.

In brief, after acknowledging that institutions are necessary, neoinstitutionalism aims at understanding the phenomenon of the emergence of rules and their dynamics.

As mentioned above, I believe that neoinstitutionalism is a synthesis of the neo-Austrian approach (in particular Hayek's ideas on the emergence of institutions) and Simon's approach on bounded rationality and the development of cognitivism. Moreover, in the preceding chapters, when dealing with the issues of microfoundations, we took into account basic elements of the neurobiological approach that may help to widen the neoinstitutionalist analysis. This paradigm yielded the best results in developing the theory of the firm and the models with positive transaction costs. This is the subject of Chapter 12. Other important issues of this model are dealt with in all the chapters of this part. They concern the theory of choice (Chapter 9), the models with asymmetrical information (Chapter 10) and the path-dependent models of technological and institutional change (Chapter 11).

The last chapter has as its subject some crucial aspects that are open issues in contemporary theory: the emergence of rules and the relation between organizations and institutions.

9. The Implications of the Neurobiological Approach for Economic Theory (I): The Decision-making Process

9.1 Introduction

As mentioned above, economic theory makes use of various decision-making models, in order to explain agents' behaviour. Optimizing behaviour is the cornerstone of standard economics, yet its main limitation lies in the lack of empirical evidence of its psychological axioms (self-interest, perfect knowledge, substantive rationality, etc.). This criticism has spurred economists to assume hypotheses that are more consistent with behavioural psychology, in order to explain agents' economic behaviour. On the one hand, this effort has led to the formulation of the theory of expected utility, an improvement of the method of maximization under constraints. On the other hand, a minority of authors have attempted - as an alternative to the preceding approach - a strong integration between economics and modern cognitive psychology, by developing a decision-making theory with a *satisficing* outcome. While the expected utility is within the orthodox paradigm, in the cognitive approach individual behaviour is examined in a context characterized by uncertainty (*à la* Knight) and imperfect information.[1]

Both the *optimizing* and the *satisficing* approaches refer to agents' rational behaviour, though in different models the notion of rationality is also different: substantive, strategic, bounded and procedural. The general idea is fairly clear: behaviour is "intentionally rational" when an aim (be it global optimizing, local optimizing or, simply, *satisficing)* is pursued through appropriate and coherent procedures and actions.

Let us imagine an individual who is to make a decision. He could examine all the possible alternatives and choose the most profitable one. However, as already pointed out by many authors, this possibility is thwarted by the cognitive and computational limits of human mind. Thus, in reality, that individual will act after assessing costs and benefits of the alternatives he knows. In this case, the outcome coincides with the maximization of expected

---

[1] According to Rachlin (1980, p. 214), microeconomics and behavioural psychology belong to the same field of studies. To the reader who finds this statement too radical, I propose, as an alternative, the assumption that the microfoundations of economic theory should - at least - not contradict the results of behavioural economics.

utility. Economic theory has worked out other tools for a context in which individuals need to take other individuals' behaviour into consideration before making their own decisions. Following a criterion that is similar to the preceding one, we may say that individuals decide after working out a strategy that takes into account the most probable behaviour of the other agents. Briefly stated, this is the approach used in the theory of games. Yet, also this criterion of behaviour is open to criticism, since it requires heroic assumptions about the possibility of the decision-maker knowing the distribution of the probabilities of the events produced by the possible reactions of the other agents (Simon 1979a).

As mentioned above, some authors propose a behavioural model based on the assumption that agents are endowed with bounded rationality. It is the model of bounded rationality which is at the basis of a great part of the unorthodox economic theory. Simon, in particular, has pointed out that, in the decision-making process, individuals "build up" the different alternatives by copying or generating routines of behaviour. In this approach the attention is focused on the individual ability to build up an adequate representation of the problem and to modify it according to heuristic criteria.

The preceding considerations point out that the criterion of procedural rationality developed by Simon is quite different from the traditional neoclassical model. Yet, also in the models of procedural rationality, individuals, in spite of the limits and potentialities that are typical of cognitive reason, base their reasoning on personal experience, on the information and on the knowledge they own. In these three cases agents are considered as decision-makers whose reasoning is more or less consistent with the principles of cognitive psychology and is certainly more typical of scientists than normal economic agents. In reality, seldom do the latter make a decision through "cold" and "deliberate" processes like those described in economic theory. Still, models keep describing decision-making processes based on a peculiar view of the work of mind: it is seen as a cold and computational instrument, maybe bounded, but in a way "pure".

This specification introduces the core of our topic: the difference between pure reason and practical reason. All rational models of behaviour used in economic theory (including procedural rationality) are based on the concept of pure rationality, while common behaviour belongs to the realm of practical reason. Explaining such common behaviour is more complex than the (interesting and mostly valid) answers given by the *decision-making* theory based on procedural rationality. Let us first consider the "original error" of these analytical limitations. In my opinion - as mentioned in the last part of the preceding chapter - it is to be found in the explicit or implicit assumption, in these models, of the dichotomy mind/brain: the efficient work of the mind is independent of the brain. Better, it is usually believed that there is, between the two, a relationship which may be effectively described by means of a metaphor: mind is the software and brain is the hardware.

However, the most recent studies in neurobiology have questioned this idea. The starting point is simple: if rational behaviour reflects the criteria that have been assumed so far in behavioural models, then it is not realistic enough. Under the best circumstances (*satisficing approach*) the time necessary is still very long and the decision-making process is still very complex. Under the worst circumstances (*maximizing approach*), the agent would get lost in an intricate and - in reality - unsolvable maze of calculations.

Contemporary neurobiology questions both the idea of the mind as software and the idea of "cold rationality", since such states of mind occur only in pathological situations. Yet, people are able to make fast decisions even when they are complex, and they often turn out to be correct and profitable. This happens because individual behaviour follows more complex and effective criteria than the ones so far applied in *decision-making* models. Before examining how it happens and its implications for economic theory, I shall deal with the major field of application of *decision-making*.

9.2 A glance to the past

9.2.1 Consumer theory

The traditional neoclassical consumer theory developed in perfect symbiosis with the neobehavioural assumptions.[2] Psychology in the behavioural age - characterized by an attempt to reduce mental activity to visible behaviour - tried to explain consumers' decisions by "translating" what is subjective (tastes) into something objective (choices concerning consumption) (Legrenzi 1991). This brought about an elegant theory, which fascinated economists. The concept of "pattern of revealed preferences" was linked to the idea of "utility", since preference axioms are equivalent to the axioms relative to utility functions (Legrenzi 1991). But, as Simon pointed out, such a sophisticated mechanism finds its natural place in Plato's sky of ideas; the number and nature of the difficulties it contains makes its use in mankind's daily decision-making process impossible (Simon 1983).

The choosing process is more complex than its behavioural simplified representation. It is characterized by routine actions and innovatory actions. There are expenses that are due to consolidated usage and custom and arise from advertising or from one's social status. Choices are almost always subject to social and cultural conditioning. One of the premises of the traditional theory, on the contrary, was that the behaviour of every individual is independent of everyone else's. Behavioural patterns are sometimes imitations of patterns that have already been experienced by parents or friends or are influenced by advertising. The individual keeps following these

---

[2] According to Legrenzi (1991, pp. 51-52) the attempts to "objectivize" economics had behavioural psychology as their most faithful ally, since psychologists had a deeper inferiority complex towards social sciences than economists.

patterns until something hinders his/her usual behaviour; new behavioural procedures are then developed (Katona 1951; Duesenberry 1949).

Over the years, this new approach has developed - becoming more and more sophisticated[3] - into a consumer theory that is more and more consistent with psychological postulates and cultural and environmental conditioning. These results have been achieved also thanks to the development of *experimental economics* (see next paragraph), based on the acquisition of the methods of experimental psychology. The most debated subject has been the theory of expected utility, developed within the neoclassical theory.

In 1944 von Neumann and Morgenstern formulated a normative theory of decision, according to which an action is rational if it maximizes the utility which derives from the outcome of a choice (von Neumann-Morgenstern 1944). One of the goals that these two scholars achieved successfully was to formulate in new and more realistic terms the heroic assumptions of the standard theory of Walrasian conception. The models of expected utility (Savage 1954) have given noteworthy advantages to the economic analysis of individual choice, thanks also to the inner characteristics of these models: axiomatic basis, independence from the decision-maker's constraints, formal elegance.

Nevertheless, this theory has been the object of a great deal of criticism. Part of this criticism concerns the actual individual ability to solve complex problems. In the light of the results reached by cognitive psychology on the computational limits of human mind, it is unreasonable to maintain that individuals are able to imagine all the possible outcomes of the various alternatives of action and consequently choose the alternative that maximizes expected utility. Furthermore, also the axiomatic assumptions of this theory have been criticized, particularly the principles of transitivity, dominance, and procedure invariance (Allais 1952; Luce-Raiffa 1957; Tversky 1969; Arrow 1972; Schoemaker 1982; Machina 1982; Fishburn 1983; Luce-Narens 1985; Kreps 1988).

More recently Kahneman and Tversky have unified the two criticisms of the theory of expected utility; first, the criticism of the idea that the psychological principles concerning computational abilities are inconsistent; and, second, the criticism of the systematic violation of the principles of procedure invariance. They have gone beyond criticism. Through a series of experiments, the two authors developed a new model to describe economic behaviour, the *prospect theory* (Kahneman-Tversky 1979). This theory represents an alternative to the theory of expected utility and has given a strong impulse to *experimental economics*, a rather successful branch of economics which has developed particularly in recent years. In extreme synthesis, Kahneman and Tversky hold that human reasoning is studded with weak points and, as a consequence, with continuous failures of rationality, as it is conceived in the *maximizing* approach. This is due to the limits of the

---

[3] For a survey of contemporary consumer theory, see Zamagni 1986.

computing skills of human mind, but also and above all to the fact that *biological impulses, which often manifest themselves as emotions, are active* in the process of choice. One of the most famous outcomes of the experiments of Kahneman and Tversky is the demonstration of the invalidity of the principle of procedure invariance. According to this principle, if a result is preferred to another, the order of preference cannot be modified or upset by the way in which options are compared. In other words, the decision-maker is not influenced by the type of representation of the decision-making problem. Yet, empirical reality shows a constant violation of the principle of procedure invariance, because individuals tend to handle profits and losses differently. The chosen options vary according to whether the emphasis is put on profits or on losses, even if the final results are the same.

Prospect theory has the merit of emphasizing the way outcomes are codified and the extent to which such codification is responsible for the different individual attitudes towards risk.

The fundamental passage from the theory of expected utility to *prospect theory* consists in the definitive abandoning of the unrealistic assumptions of the individual ability to assess the outcome of every known alternative. However, the most important concept in the works of Kahneman and Tversky is that rationality failures are due not only to the computing limits of human mind, but also to the influence of biological impulses. As we shall see, this aspect holds a noteworthy analytical relevance.

9.2.2 Experimental economics

For more than a decade, experimental economics has been quickly developing. An observer might receive the impression that economists aim at empiricism excessively. For a long time economic science has been accused of being exclusively deductive, lacking in empirical check data. In the economic literature (apart from a few examples I have referred or shall refer to) the validity of models is checked by means of statistics, whose reliability has often been disputed. Nevertheless, especially after Kahneman's and Tversky's works became widely known, a new method has been spreading: experimental economics.

From a methodological point of view, this method is based on two kinds of experiments: with or without the use of computers. When computers are not used, a selected sample of individuals is usually asked to choose among various alternatives. The selection of the sample, and of the place where the experiment is carried out, and the data processing must be carried out following the rules of experimental psychology closely. Thanks to the development of hardware and software, a new kind of experiment is nowadays performed, in which the selected individuals interact directly with a special partner, i.e. a computer or a person using a computer. Experiments have been performed with single individuals or groups (in this case computers need to be interlinked in a net by means of a server controlling the experiment). Through this kind of experiment, goals that used to be considered unattainable are being achieved, also thanks to the number of variables a computer program can handle. However one should not underestimate the main difficulty encountered in carrying out such experiments, that is "inventing" and developing the necessary software. Usually people who take part in these experiments (with or without the use of computers) are paid.[4]

This method of experimental check was developed long before the 1970s. Moreover, Kahneman and Tversky deal with only one of the branches of this composite line of research. We can distinguish at least three of them.

The first branch, whose major exponent is V. Smith, has developed since the middle of the 1950s uninterruptedly (Smith 1990). Here the object of empirical check is the consistency of market mechanisms. In other words, by means of laboratory tests, the assumptions concerning the behaviour of individuals who carry out exchanges on the market are confirmed or refuted. The forerunner for this kind of experiment was Chamberlin, who, in his famous article of 1948, described a laboratory experiment aimed at demonstrating the extent to which the theory of prices can actually predict real events. However, Smith himself confuted Chamberlain's conclusions in a series of experiments carried out at the end of the 1950s. Smith showed how important the role of institutions may be in price forming (an aspect that Chamberlain had neglected). This approach has been further developed by several authors who have studied oligopoly, market stability, market types and practices, the role of institutions, *sunk costs*, etc.[5]

Also the second branch (which I have already referred to in detail) took its first steps in the 1950s. However, unlike the first branch, this one had a real boom at the beginning of the 1980s, when Kahneman's and Tversky's works became widely known. Tversky, in particular, described *decision-making* in a situation of uncertainty, with specific reference to the consumer theory. This second branch is connected with both the first experiments carried out by Katona in the United States, starting from the 1940s, and Allais' criticism of the theory of expected utility.

I have already referred to Katona in the preceding chapter. As regards Allais, in the 1950s he confuted the theory of expected utility, demonstrating that the function of utility of an individual is different from the cardinal function of utility of the same individual. The French economist, introducing the experimental method into the consumer theory, confuted Savage's principle of independence, according to which consumers' preferences are

---

[4] With reference to experimental methodology and, in general, for a systematic illustration of the decision making line of research in experimental economics, see Hey 1991.

[5] An excellent survey of this line of research can be found in the book edited by V. Smith himself in 1990.

independent of the way options are compared. Allais' criticism was followed, several years later, by the development of *prospect theory* by Kahneman and Tversky, who accepted and developed the ideas of the French Nobel prize-winner.

This is the branch of experimental economics that has drawn more attention. Nowadays several centres for experimental economics exist where economists and psychologists cooperate,[6] and in several works this cooperation goes beyond the boundaries of the consumer theory.

A third, more recent - and probably less studied, though it is extremely interesting - branch, is concerned with experimental works on the nature and emergence of routines (Cohen 1991). It has developed only recently, thanks to the development of very sophisticated software, and it deals with the process of emergence of rules (Egidi 1991). This is the subject of Chapter 13.

In this Section I have tried to organize the complex world of experimental economics systematically. However, this cannot be considered a thorough description, since there are authors whose works deal with aspects belonging to each of these three branches and because experimentalism is quickly spreading throughout all the fields of economic theory. An especially important field is the theory of games.

9.2.3 The theory of games

The application of the theory of games in economics has developed within the decision-making theory, in a probabilistic context and in strict connection with the theory of expected utility.[6] In this case, too, rationality operates by estimating costs and benefits and by taking into account the probable behaviour of the opponent. The main innovation introduced into the theory of games seems to me the concept of strategic behaviour. It is well known that the theory of games has developed from a simple and very famous example: the dilemma of the prisoner, in which two individuals must decide whether to cooperate or defect in a situation of uncertainty.[7] If each individual has a dominant strategy, calculated with the minimax criterion, this strategy will determine individual behaviour. If there is no dominant strategy, every individual defines his own strategy according to his opponent's expected behaviour. It is well known that the most probable result of non-cooperative

---

[6] With reference to the introduction of the theory of games into economic theory and for a systematic historical picture, see Innocenti 1995.

[7] In my opinion, Axelrod (1984, pp. 7-8) offers the shortest and at the same time the clearest and most complete description of this game. "In the Prisoner's Dilemma game, there are two players. Each has two choices, namely cooperate or defect. Each must make the choice without knowing what the other will do. No matter what the other does, defection yields a higher payoff than cooperation. The dilemma is that if both defect, both do worse than if both had cooperated."

games is a Nash equilibrium,[8] that is a failure of standard rational behaviour. However, Axelrod (1984) has held that, in the case of repeated games, it is possible to reach a Pareto equilibrium, thanks to the learning processes of the individuals involved in the game.[9] According to Axelrod, Nash equilibrium is due to the fact that in games like "the dilemma of the prisoner" individuals are involved in such a situation only once. If, instead, the game is repeated a sufficient number of times, or even if there is only a theoretical possibility of repeating it, individuals tend to cooperate, spontaneously reaching a Pareto optimum.

What are the criteria lying at the basis of the strategic behaviour assumed by the theory of games? Several problematic issues might be discussed and I believe that Rapoport (1962) has already pointed them out several years ago. In my opinion, the weakest point of this theory is the assumption that every individual has a payoff function, which presupposes a scale of values that can be given to events. This assumption is once again inconsistent with the limited cognitive skills of human mind. Furthermore, in most models including the theory of games, the qualifying element consists in the fact that individuals act only on the basis of calculated personal interest. In the case of repeated games, however, behaviour expectations arise from individual learning processes, which resume categories such as trust, non-belligerence, etc. As Rapoport (1962) pointed out, people - in this case - follow their wisdom, rather than their knowledge.

In brief, the rational behaviour assumed in the theory of games undergoes the same criticism as that assumed in the theory of expected utility, with the important addition that, in repeated games, learning plays such an important role that it leads to Pareto-efficient results. However, I believe that, in the light of the most recent neurobiological discoveries, also this conclusion ought to be reconsidered. I shall return to the subject later on.

9.2.4 A few critical considerations on procedural rationality

As mentioned above, Simon conceived one of the most convincing models of rational behaviour. He started from identifying human cognitive skills with the individuals' ability to make symbolic representations of reality, by means of which they form their own beliefs and shape and assess the possible alternatives. This model is consistent with the psychological theories of behaviour and choice and with the cognitive and computational limits of the

---

[8] This is a non-Pareto outcome, since Nash equilibrium is dominated by another equilibrium, i.e. Pareto equilibrium, which nevertheless can be reached only if the two individuals cooperate

[9] Axelrod (1984) carried out an interesting experiment with a computer and a number of people who were invited to participate in the experiment several times. The result achieved is very interesting, since it predicts the emergence of cooperation in repeated games.

human mind. Besides, it is at the basis of both individual and organizational behaviour.

Two aspects of this theoretical-methodological approach appear particularly relevant. The first one concerns, once again, the fundamental role played by learning in imitating other individuals' routines, as well as in generating new ones. The second one concerns the explicit use of the above-mentioned metaphor of human mind conceived as software and human brain as hardware. According to this metaphor, the models of thought (software) can be taken into account independently of the structure of the nervous system (Simon 1969).

The picture emerging from Simon's models represents individuals and organizations acting rationally, in order to reach *satisficing* goals. This approach includes neither traditional cost-benefit analyses, nor strategic rationality. Nevertheless, it shares with other models the following idea: rational behaviour means assessing the alternatives and this is obtained exclusively by means of mental operations. At this point a dichotomy appears between reason and emotions; emotions are excluded from decision-making.

In brief, behavioural theories in which individuals are characterized by procedural rationality have proved valid when applied, and have been widely confirmed by empirical data. Nevertheless, they fail to give a full explanation of individual behaviour and need to be supplemented with new elements that are normally excluded from this approach.

9.3 Hayek's sensory order and the decision-making process

As mentioned above, the knowledge used by individuals is the outcome of mostly tacit processes that are based on genetic differences and preceding experiences. Every individual acts after carrying out a process of "interpretation" of the external (objective) information, which he/she turns into subjective knowledge; this is unique and original, since it arises from individual genetic traits and personal experiences. Through a learning process that takes place over the years, in turn, genetic traits and personal experiences recreate the neurobiological condition (Hayek 1952a).[10]

Contemporary neurobiology is confirming Hayek's intuition: "as we develop from infancy to adulthood, the design of brain circuitries that represent our evolving body and its interaction with the world seems to depend on the activities in which the organism engages, and on the action of innate bioregulatory circuitries" (Damasio 1995; see also Hayek 1952a; Patterson-Nawa 1993). "The unpredictable profile of experiences of each individual does have a say in circuit design, both directly and indirectly, via the reaction it sets off the innate circuitries, and the consequences that such

---

[10] U. Witt (1992, p. 402) shares the idea that the process of knowledge generation is a highly individual process, in which new concepts emerge from the specific processes of data interpretation on the basis of individual experience.

reactions have in the overall process of circuit shaping" (Damasio 1995; see also Hayek 1952a). However some cerebral circuitries remain stable and the brain builds up its balance between stable and unstable circuitries.

Hayek has thus laid the foundations for a neurobiological understanding of subjective diversity. At any given point in an individual's life, a great part of his/her cerebral circuits *is personal and unique, since it reflects the history and events of that particular organism*, which is also the result of the interactive process which takes place with his/her cultural and social context.

Therefore, insisting on the creative dimension of individuals, Hayek portrays subjective perception as the primary source of the dynamics of social processes, including the economic ones. Differentiated perceptions obviously affect also individual learning, characterized as heterogeneous. This is the cornerstone of economic change (Rizzello 1995).

Moreover, the perception process is also the source of the unpredictability of behaviour, since individual patterns of experience are unique. Even in the simple case of a transaction between agents with equal distribution of information, it is impossible to predict the outcome, since it depends on how individuals build their own knowledge - subjectively and unpredictably - starting from the same data (see the next chapter).

Before moving on to describe in a somewhat more systematic way the results achieved by contemporary neurobiology, let me underline some important aspects. I believe that so far two different and well-founded approaches have emerged, with respect to the problem of how knowledge is acquired: on the one hand, the psychological approach - mostly developed by Simon - which highlights the mechanical (and bounded) aspect of the processing of complex information; on the other hand, the neurobiological or subjectivistic approach of the Austrian school - mostly developed by Hayek[11] - which emphasizes the creative aspect of decision. At this point, I would like to anticipate one of the conclusions of this chapter: the two aspects are complementary and both of them should be taken into account in order to understand the *decision-making* process. As a consequence, rationality is bounded not only by individual cognitive and computational skills, but also by unintentional and unexpected aspects, such as the ones appearing in the process of formation of our perceptions.

9.4 The neurobiological dimension

A. Damasio, one of the most prominent contemporary neurologists and author of *Descartes' Error* (Damasio 1995), has achieved extremely interesting results, starting from the distinction between pure and practical reason. The decision to get married, to enrol in a university, or to make an investment, are

---

[11] Kirzner (1979) is a qualified follower of Hayek. He maintains that the solution of problems entirely depends on the creative aspect of our decision: the process of environmental perception.

influenced by the social context an individual belongs to. Solving a complex physics theorem, or deciding whether an appeal should be presented to the Supreme Court, involves choices that reach further than the immediate personal dominion. Practical reason is exerted in the first case, in the second one, theoretic or even pure reason.

Undoubtedly, if we face the analysis of the decision-making processes at a positive rather than normative level, and if we refer to the behaviour of a common man rather than to the behaviour of a scientist, the object of our analysis is practical reason. Up to now, we could avail ourselves of a theory of choice derived from cognitive psychology and based upon criteria of procedural rationality, which has proved to be rather satisfactory. However, this theory makes no distinction between theoretical and practical reason, or at least it does not do so explicitly.

Neurobiology teaches us that practical reason has two aspects, which directly concern the *decision-making process*. They have not been considered, so far, by traditional theories. I would sum them up as follows:

1. The ability to predict and plan one's future depends not only on psychosocial aspects, but also on cerebral aspects, without which the action does not take place.
2. Normally, the individual ability to plan one's economic actions depends on the so-called "somatic markers". These are cerebral mechanisms that have *a biological nature*; whenever they register a danger in any of the options they are assessing, they signal it to the prefrontal cortex, the seat of rational planning, urging the individual to be cautious.

Let us now examine the characteristics of these two aspects more closely.

9.4.1 The influence of neurobiological processes on decision-making

Up to now, authors have felt that the decision-making process of economic agents depended exclusively on psychological characteristics. Now it is possible to assert that it is necessary to integrate this analysis with research into the neurobiological aspects. It has been proved, in fact, that there are individuals with specific neurobiological characteristics, who are not able to perform common actions, such as being cautious when circumstances require it. This phenomenon has been observed in individuals (the so-called prefrontal individuals) characterized by a particular cerebral structure, i.e. a slight lesion in the brain: it does not allow them to be "cautious" and, above all, to foresee future events, especially with reference to risks connected with economic decisions. Let us consider an example. Let us imagine that someone invites us to take part in an extremely risky game, which we have not known before, and which is likely to make us go bankrupt (but we do not know it). After a few moves we are likely to realize the risk we are running and decide to stop. If we are prefrontal individuals, on the contrary, we will quite probably continue to play until we are bankrupt. In the first case, the somatic markers after a few moves signal the danger and the player is induced to quit the action. In the case of individuals with a prefrontal lesion, the somatic markers (see the next chapter) are activated and signal the danger in a part of the brain, but they are unable to convey this signal to the area of the brain that is responsible for rational planning, since some kind of switch hinders the transmission of the message.

Unlike others, these individuals are unable to learn from the game and, in general, from their own mistakes, because at some point the interaction between brain and mind is interrupted. This situation is not due to those traditional psychological mechanisms, typical of individuals who are in favour of or against taking risks, it is due to innate neurological causes (Damasio 1995). A particularly interesting aspect is that there can be relevant consequences also for those people who have slight and not immediately evident inborn prefrontal lesions.

I shall assess the importance of these discoveries for economic theory, further on. Now let us examine the second aspect, synthetically described above in point 2.

9.4.2 The importance of feelings in decision-making

Contemporary neurobiology is giving evidence that feelings have a powerful influence on reason (Damasio 1995). When an individual faces a problematic situation, he can feel unpleasant physical sensations preventing him/her from choosing certain alternatives or, conversely, inducing him/her to choose others.

There is something in our body that, in a natural and unconscious way, compels us to focus our attention on the negative outcome a certain action might yield, thus acting as an automatic alarm device warning us: "beware the danger that is awaiting you, if you choose the option that leads to such results". This signal induces us to abandon that option, decreasing the number of possible alternatives. The "signallers" are the "somatic markers" which make an immediate screening of the alternatives we are building up (Damasio 1995). Somatic markers are generated by secondary emotions and *have been connected through learning to foreseen future outcomes of some settings.* They are impulse leading our reasoning in the form of a feeling or unconscious tendency (Damasio 1995).

In order to avoid the risk of giving the reader a wrong idea, it is nevertheless necessary to specify that in the decision-making process we do not use only somatic markers. As already stated, they make an initial screening and are then connected with the reasoning process. These markers simply make the decision-making process more efficient and precise, while their absence reduces efficiency and precision (Damasio 1995).

Most somatic markers, that we use to make rational decisions, are formed within our brain during the educational and socializing process, through the connection of specific classes of stimuli with specific classes of somatic states (Damasio 1995). They are acquired through experience in a system of internal preferences, under the influence of an external system, which includes not only entities and events one interacts with, but also social conventions and ethical rules (Damasio 1995). Prefrontal cortices represent categorizations of situations the individual has been previously involved in, during his/her life experience.

9.4.3 A few considerations

At this point there seem to be two relevant aspects to emphasize: (i) the subjective nature of neurobiological processes and (ii) the role of somatic markers in the *decision-making process.*

This teaches us that explaining and predicting behaviour is a more complicated task than what has so far been believed, and that it is necessary to begin giving serious consideration to the hypothesis that prediction may be altogether impossible. This hypothesis arises from the following considerations.

As far as the first aspect is concerned (i), we now know that everyone, when facing a problematic situation, actuates a continuous series of events, according to his/her previously categorized knowledge.   Consequently, individual uniqueness is a very important criterion for defining the processes of choice and action, especially when trying to develop homogeneous models of action. This is due to the unpredictable pattern of individual experiences, pointed out by Hayek.

As concerns the second aspect (ii), the presence of somatic markers adds one more element to the already satisfactory theory of procedural rationality. This theory is enriched and completed by the idea that somatic markers act to reduce the need for sifting; this helps to describe the decision-making process in an even more realistic way.

9.5 A few economic consequences

If we accept the validity of the above considerations, there is no point in engaging in optimizing analyses any longer. For this reason, my remarks on the economic consequences of the neurobiological approach will deal only with those theories which abandoned the strong hypothesis of optimization: . prospect theory, theory of games, asymmetrical information and path-dependence.

9.5.1 Prospect theory

I believe that few words are enough to assert that what has so far emerged corroborates the hypothesis of Kahneman and Tversky on the invalidity of the principle of procedure invariance. The important influence of somatic markers in the processes of choice and, in particular, their emotional dimension explain why there are rationality failures when the way in which options are compared is modified. These failures occur not only because of the computational limits of human mind, but also because of the influence of such emotional stimuli, whose nature and role in decision-making processes is finally known.

9.5.2 The consequences of the neurobiological approach on the theory of games

In Section 9.2.3. I have already mentioned the limits of the criteria of strategic rationality, as assumed by the theory of games. However one point is still pending: the hypothesis that, in repeated games, learning leads to Pareto-efficient solutions. I believe that also this idea should be looked over in the light of what has emerged so far.

What has emerged is that the traditional processes of "learning by doing" work in a different way than what is widely accepted today. The theory of games, for instance, assumes that agents are characterized by homogeneous learning criteria. Yet, if we pay attention to the outcome of recent neurobiological studies (learning criteria differ - from a neurological point of view - from individual to individual) we can hardly assert the validity of the outcome of repeated games. In these games, in fact, agent A creates his expectations on the behaviour of agent B, according to his/her own perception and learning criteria, and vice versa; but, if perception and learning are strongly influenced by subjective criteria, the uncertainty about the behaviour of other individuals increases. Standard models are based on the homogeneous presupposition that agents follow their own self-interest. Now we know that between the two extremes - on the one hand individuals who are absolutely unable to pursue their own self-interest (prefrontal individuals) and, on the other hand, the pure economic man (non existing) - there are individuals with personal characteristics that are unpredictable beforehand, being highly subjective. It is especially important that learning processes are diversified and not homogeneous. This diversity - based on neural structural differences and on the subjective traits of somatic markers -, even if it is a slight diversity, may have an exceptional influence on the final results of decision-making processes.

This conclusion affects not only the theory of games, but also all the models based on learning processes. If we abandon the simplifying idea, which has not found full empirical evidence, of the homogeneity of learning processes among agents, it becomes necessary to reconsider also all the models based on procedural rationality.[12]

---

[12]Nevertheless the validity of this idea is still to be verified empirically.

9.5.3 Asymmetrical information

In the model of choice with asymmetrical information, developed by Akerlof in 1970, the concept of equal distribution of quality may only be admitted in theory if - as in the Walrasian model of exchange - one assumes the traditional axioms of equal distribution of information and of substantive rationality.

This assumption, however, becomes now inconsistent, because we know that the differences in the neural structure and in somatic markers induce individuals to interpret the same data differently. This means that even if information is objective - as in the case of equal distribution among agents - the knowledge used in the processes of choice is subjective, idiosyncratic and personal. Thus, the only element supporting the validity of the traditional transaction model - though only in theory - is refuted (I shall deal with this subject in detail in the next chapter).

9.5.4 Path-dependency

Path-dependency has been introduced into economic theory in the last decade. In general terms, at the basis of path-dependency there is the idea that relevant consequences may follow small historical events, and economic action may modify such consequences only in part (David 1985; Arthur 1988). David (1985) shows that the adoption and spreading of new technologies may depend on the existence of externalities on the demand side. The traditional mechanism through which more advanced technologies replace pre-existing ones may not be set off.

Neurobiological analysis seems to confirm and corroborate the idea that small and fortuitous events may turn out to be irreversible and relevant. It should be clear by now that the shaping of neural circuitries and the somatic markers, which lie under the construction of the knowledge used in the decision-making process, are strongly path-dependent, since they depend on the subjectivity of the innate circuits and on the uniqueness of the experience of every individual (this subject is dealt with in detail in Chapter 11).

9.6 Concluding remarks

The central idea in this chapter is that neurobiological processes matter in decision-making. Starting from this statement, I have tried to explain the main characteristics of neural processes and some of their implications for economic processes.

The idea of bounded rationality has weakened the neoclassical hypothesis of substantive rationality, giving birth to new models of behaviour based on procedural rationality; I am now trying to enrich these models, by introducing neurobiological concepts.

In this chapter I have asserted that pointing out individual limits (bounded rationality) or the potentialities of human rationality (procedural rationality) is not enough to infer, on a psychological basis, an explanation of common behaviour and thus support the full validity of individual learning processes. If neurobiological differences are taken into consideration, the picture becomes more complex. In order to achieve the results that are typical of the approaches where learning matters, such as Simon's, Akerlof's, Nelson's, Winter's, etc., one should assume that individuals are endowed with procedural rationality, and also that they have an identical or very similar neural structure. Since neural structures are different, as empirical evidence is showing, behaviour cannot be foreseen and it turns out to be significantly different from its description in procedural models.

In short, taking into account the achievements of contemporary psychology, knowledge can be conceived as the result of an interaction between information and mental patterns, which, in turn, are the result of an endogenous process. Taking into account the achievements of contemporary neurobiology, instead, action can be conceived as the result of a process of interaction between mind and brain. For economic theory, it is important to know the mechanisms generating individual knowledge and it is still more important to understand the mechanisms which, making use of that knowledge, generate action.

The outcome is a theory assuming the complementarity of the subjectivistic and the procedural approaches, and supplementing it with the hypothesis of somatic markers.

The most immediate consequences on economic theory seem to be the following:

i) the idea that failures of traditional rationality are at the basis of the economic behaviour is further corroborated at an empirical level;
ii) the neurobiological approach to decision-making corroborates the criticism of the optimizing approach;
iii) the heterogeneous character of learning processes seems to exclude the Pareto optimum outcome of repeated games;
iv) the validity of the models based on agents' procedural rationality is enriched and extended;
v) the validity and relevance of path-dependent processes, with respect to economic theory, is confirmed.

10. The Implications of the Neuro-biological Approach for Economic Theory (II): the Process of Exchange with Asymmetrical Information

10.1 Introduction

In "The Market for 'Lemons'", George Akerlof (1970) dealt with one of the most interesting issues in economic theory: the process of interaction between information, uncertainty, and difference in the quality of goods. According to Akerlof, it is very difficult for both parties to have the same information about the goods exchanged when the transaction occurs. One party is likely to be better informed than the other. This factor allows the better informed party to operate with an advantage which, if exploited, leads to dishonesty.

This situation is characterized by asymmetrical information, whose consequences have been clearly pointed out by Akerlof. In such conditions, market failures[1] come about, since pricing is influenced by dishonesty. Prices do not contain all the information concerning the quality of goods. The seller, who is better informed about the actual quality of the goods, could sell low-quality goods to the unaware buyer at the same price as better goods, thus giving way to a process in which the bad "drives out" the good. The consequence of this situation is a non-market clearing equilibrium, since demand curves may, under quite plausible conditions, not be downward sloping and market equilibria may be characterized by demand not equalling supply (Stiglitz 1987a).

A second consequence of asymmetrical information is the birth of economic institutions. They arise spontaneously to reduce the risks of dishonesty and to make exchange easier. In other words, as we shall see in detail further on, one of the roles of institutions would be discouraging opportunistic behaviour (Ricketts 1987).

One of the most important implications of Akerlof's formulation is the demonstration that the neoclassical theory of exchange in the Walrasian conception is not valid in the case of asymmetrical information. It is valid only when quality is evenly distributed. In every other case, the exchange

---

[1] In this case, the failure is due to the presence of imperfect information.

occurs according to different criteria. Therefore, competition cannot always allow a fair play that favourably selects the firms with the best products and the individuals with the best skills. Akerlof demonstrates that, in the presence of asymmetrical information, a process of adverse selection[2] comes about. The market may fail and may not be able to allocate resources according to a virtuous selection of the best technology, behaviour and organizational forms.

Still, how widespread are the situations characterized by asymmetrical information? According to Akerlof, those situations are inherent in the whole business world, because every transaction is characterized by uncertainty, and success is measured according to the individual ability to recognize good quality from bad quality. Akerlof holds that all transactions are characterized by asymmetrical information. The concept of equal distribution of information can only be admitted in theory if, as in the Walrasian model of exchange, one assumes the traditional axioms of equal distribution of information and of substantive rationality, that are consistent with the principle of maximization. Thus, at a practical level, Akerlof seems to exclude what he holds still valid at a theoretical level. In other words, he rules out the possibility that situations characterized by an even distribution of quality may actually occur. And since the business world is different from theoretical assumptions, it follows that, for a more realistic understanding of exchange processes, it is necessary to take into consideration the role of asymmetrical information.

10.1.1 A new concept of asymmetrical information

The theory of asymmetrical information has influenced subsequent research deeply, not only with reference to the problems of information and market failures, but also as regards the emergence of rules, the transaction costs and, more generally, the theory of the firm. However, I think that some aspects which carry important implications have not been fully developed: situations of asymmetrical information characterize every form of economic interaction and there is no situation, *not even at a theoretical level*, allowing exchange to occur according to the assumptions of the traditional theory. I am putting forward the idea of generalized asymmetrical information, in an attempt to bring new elements in support of Akerlof's thesis.

However, my approach differs on a fundamental point. I believe that

---

[2] The situations characterized by adverse selection have been mostly studied with reference to the insurance market. Usually, the individuals who take out insurance are those who are more at risk. Nevertheless, if insurance companies make insurance premiums too expensive, they risk losing their best customers, i.e. those who are less at risk. If they do so, they increase their earnings, but they also select their worst customers; therefore they will have to pay higher compensations. In Akerlof's model, adverse selection refers to the fact that there might be fewer buyers and sellers than in the case of perfect information (Stiglitz 1987a).

asymmetrical information has an endogenous nature, while in Akerlof's formulation it is exogenous. My approach derives from the firm belief that every form of exchange takes place between individuals, who are always asymmetrically informed, even in those situations when they receive the same kind of information, as in the traditional case of perfect knowledge or, to say it with Akerlof, of even distribution of quality. In practice it is possible to demonstrate that the field in which the traditional theory may still be considered valid shrinks until it disappears. This carries important consequences for the understanding of economic processes in dynamic terms, such as the functioning of the mechanism of competition, the nature of organizations, the role of institutions and their evolution.

The fundamental point lies in the interaction between information and uncertainty. In other words, it is necessary to understand which microfoundations are at the basis of the process by which asymmetries are formed. In this perspective, it is necessary to refer to the processes of learning in conditions of procedural uncertainty (Dosi-Egidi 1991).

As mentioned above, since 1937 Hayek has clearly shown that the main unsolved problem in economic theory is the acquisition and use of knowledge in an individual (Hayek 1937) as well as in a social context (Hayek 1945). Later, Simon pointed out that individuals are characterized by bounded rationality and act according to criteria of procedural rationality. Akerlof suggested a model of exchange consistent with these theories. My purpose is now generalizing Akerlof's model according to Hayek's and Simon's theories.

In short, our objective is to demonstrate the following three statements:

i)   asymmetrical information has an endogenous nature rather than an exogenous nature, as in Akerlof's theory;
ii) this supports and extends Akerlof's criticism of the process of choice, as conceived in the traditional theory;
iii) not only is generalized asymmetrical information at the basis of the process of exchange, but it may also help in developing the analysis of the nature of organizations and institutions and their evolution.

10.1.2 Exogenous information and endogenous knowledge

In Akerlof's model, information is conceived in quantitative terms. One party has more information than the other, with reference to the actual quality of the goods. In this case, the asymmetrical information between the two parties is exogenous, since these are external data which the parties do not own until they acquire them. Asymmetry arises when one party acquires the information without the other party knowing it.

Akerlof's problem (explaining how the exchange takes place in the presence of asymmetrical information) would not exist if both parties acquired the same amount and the same kind of information. The exchange would take place in the traditional terms, with prices being reliable indexes of the quality of goods and with no risks of dishonesty. The problems underlined by Akerlof, including the risks of dishonesty, would arise only in the opposite situation.

Unlike Akerlof, I consider asymmetrical information the result of an endogenous process. Information, in fact, is exogenous, but the knowledge built inside the individual is endogenous. The individual acquires information from the external world, but, in the decision-making process, he uses the knowledge he builds upon the acquired data. These data represent the exogenous and quantitative component. After the individual has perceived them, they are interpreted and their meaning is explained by means of subjective mechanisms varying from individual to individual. The final product the individual uses when choosing is specific and personal in terms of quality.

When the individual who has acquired this information transmits it to the external world by means of communication signals, it represents new data for another individual. He/she will build upon it, endogenously, his/her own knowledge, which, in turn, represents new data for a third individual, and so on. This means that the acquisition of quantitative data is only the beginning of the process through which individual knowledge is created. In order to obtain useful information, the individual needs to give these data a qualitative meaning, via an internal process. Therefore, the emergence of asymmetries in individual knowledge is an endogenous process, even when the individuals receive the same quantitative data from outside. Also in the traditional hypothesis of equally distributed information, individuals build up and use differentiated knowledge.

10.2 Neurobiology and asymmetrical information

In the light of these elements, let us now examine the relation between neurobiology and asymmetrical information. As already mentioned in the sections dealing with the models of mind, the different distribution of information is the final result of a very complex feedback process between neural structure and experience.

Research (Patterson-Nawa 1993; Calissano 1992) is confirming that in the synaptic contact, besides neurotransmitters which account for neural communication itself, other kinds of molecules are released. These molecules influence every nervous cell, modifying it; each cell, then, has the power to influence the surrounding cells, by operating much more in depth than the common synaptic structures, going all the way to their "heart", that is to their genes. These processes, taken in their specificity, vary from an individual to another.

In order to understand this process better, one needs to think of what happens in human society. Communication between individuals frequently involves a reciprocal influence on the personal beliefs of each. These influences settle on the already existing beliefs, setting up an individual's specificity of character. Similarly, every single neuron is unique. This characteristic is conferred on it by the molecules released through the influential relationship with the other neurons.

As mentioned above, Hayek had understood these phenomena by intuition and had made use of them in his research. At a methodological level, his works are characterized by extreme subjectivism. At the basis of the shaping of individual differences, of the mechanisms of interaction and of the emergence of rules, there are the mechanisms of acquisition and conveyance of knowledge. This is evident with reference to his model of mind. I think that now I can make explicit what, in my opinion, is only implicitly present in Hayek's works, by taking his analysis of the microfoundations of subjective diversity to its extreme consequences. The result is that asymmetrical information is typical of human nature and is therefore endogenous.

10.3 Implications for economic theory

It would certainly be impossible to analyse systematically here all the economic implications of the presence of endogenous asymmetrical information. In my opinion, it affects the exchange processes, the structure of organizations and the evolution of institutions. Moreover, from this point of view it is possible to analyse the processes of economic change and the microfoundations of path-dependence. I shall deal with these aspects later. Let us now take into consideration the issue of the exchange process.

10.3.1 Individuals

As above mentioned, individuals are characterized by limited rationality. They act in a context of uncertainty, as defined by Knight, and face problematic situations by means of the elaboration and application of routines, arising from the imitation or genuine generation of routines.

What is the role of generalized asymmetrical information in this kind of process? It certainly plays a very important role. If we refer to the microfoundations of asymmetrical information, we can see that, in accordance with his/her own individual and original neural processes, everyone can introduce small innovative elements, which could prove to be important, even in the simplest actions that imitate procedures. Such innovations become evident also in the case of the generation of new routines. This procedure always takes place in accordance with the mental mechanisms which produce diversification. The more the devised solution will be fitting for the problematic situation, the more it will have a probability of success and will tend to consolidate and spread within the system through a process of selection.

10.3.2 Competition

Traditionally, market is considered as a spontaneous institution, which makes the interindividual processes of production and exchange of goods and services much easier. It is based on the mechanism of competition, which emerges in a context of scarcity, and works on the basis of processes of acquisition and use of knowledge.

When individuals plan their choices, they codify all the signals at their disposal, starting from prices. In the case of traditional asymmetrical information, the party that has more or better information can take advantage of it in a dishonest way. In the case of generalized asymmetrical information, instead, the winner is the one who interprets external data in the most effective way and acts consistently. This is a very important characteristic, because it represents the impulse of change. As soon as they discover the most efficient solutions, individuals and firms try to imitate them. Seldom is imitation perfect. Most likely, environmental conditions are different and, above all, the imitation takes place according to processes of interpretation that are always differentiated. Therefore, during the process of imitation, individuals and firms are likely to introduce innovations, which, in turn, will involve other processes of imitation and innovation. As far as competition among firms is concerned, this mechanism has been pointed out by Alchian (1950). According to this author, imperfect imitation supplies opportunities for innovations, which, in turn, generate new organizing forms that are open to selective processes. Thanks to innovations, the uniformity brought about by natural economic selection has a dynamic, rather than static character; new forms are incorporated according to the efficiency they have shown.

These factors - that I have briefly illustrated - characterize the process of competition. It consists in the ability to respond to environmental variations as well as possible, in a world characterized by uncertainty. Those who find more efficient and adequate responses, survive and improve the system, those who find the least efficient responses may succumb. As far as firms are concerned, their hierarchical organization responds to the need to react in an effective way to environmental changes, by adopting mechanisms of knowledge division, on the basis of division of competencies, technological innovations and processes.[3]

As you can see, neural mechanisms preside over the different individual characterization of information. Small differences in the interpretation of external signals, derive from the particular architectural structure of each individual, that is built upon the single experiences; such differences represent the element which determines the success or failure of a process of

---

[3] This cannot certainly be considered as a full explanation of the origin and structure of organizations. Several other elements interact and several works have been written on this subject. Nevertheless, I think that this aspect should be considered one of the most important.

interaction with the environment.

10.3.3 The process of exchange

In Akerlof's hypothesis, whenever there is an even distribution of information, exchange takes place in traditional terms. When information is asymmetrical, instead, the problems pointed out in Section 10.1 arise. Akerlof has analyed a case of exchange between two asymmetrically informed individuals, a seller and a buyer. We assume, instead, a situation of asymmetry among three individuals: one seller and two buyers. The three of them own different information. The hypothesis is that of the purchase of a used car (which we assume to be a "lemon"). According to Akerlof's model, extended to two buyers, we have the following situation.

The supply is

$$S = S(p) \tag{1.1}$$

with the classic hypothesis, formulated by Akerlof and Stiglitz, that the seller fixes a higher price than the actual value, in order to hide the low quality of the car.

The demand of a is

$$Da = Da\,[p\,,m\,(p)] \tag{1.2}$$

where p is the price and m the quality that depends on price. And if the demand of b is

$$Db = Db\,[p,\,m(p)] \tag{1.3}$$

where i represents one extra piece of information owned by b. In this case, it is easy to predict that a will buy the car and b will get a good bargain since he does not purchase a lemon.

Let us now examine a case of equal distribution of information. According to the traditional theory of exchange the supply is (1.1) and the demands are respectively:

$$Da = Da(p) \tag{2.1}$$

$$Db = Db(p) \tag{2.2}$$

If the object of the exchange is only one, as assumed, in this case a process of competition similar to an auction is triggered off. The purchaser will be the individual who can bid the higher price.

According to my formulation of generalized asymmetrical information, the situation is different. Let us assume that the only piece of information the buyers have at their disposal is the price and that they estimate the value of the good on the basis of that piece of information.

The supply is again (1.1). The demands of the two individuals, instead, are respectively:

$$Da = Da[p, m(p), \gamma'(p)] \qquad\qquad (3.1)$$

$$Db = Db[p, m(p), \gamma''(p)] \qquad\qquad (3.2)$$

The factor γ represents the subjective meaning that each individual gives to the same kind of information, and depends on all the complex factors analysed in this chapter. In this case, it is not possible to say beforehand who will buy the good.

In conclusion, the result of the exchange in these three hypotheses is the following:

1) Traditional hypothesis, scarcity and equal distribution of information. As a result, an auction is triggered off.
2) Akerlof's asymmetry: scarcity, uncertainty and unequal distribution of information. As a result, those who are better informed can take advantage of it.
3) Endogenous asymmetry: scarcity, uncertainty and equal distribution of information. It is not possible to predict the result, because of factor γ, which cannot be determined beforehand.

10.4 Concluding remarks

We have seen that, in Akerlof's theory, asymmetrical information has an exogenous nature and arises from the combination of different distributions of information and uncertainty. This view involves the narrowing of the range in which it is possible to apply the traditional theory of exchange to those unique situations, admissible in theory, of even distribution of the quality of goods.

I began this analysis by trying to find the microfoundations of asymmetrical information, and I found out that they are strictly connected with human nature. Then I tried to demonstrate that asymmetrical information has an endogenous nature and arises from the individual neurobiological processes. As a consequence, the exchange cannot occur in traditional terms, not even in the presence of an even distribution of quality and information, since this conclusion would be inconsistent with the cognitive processes, through which knowledge is acquired and used. I carried out this analysis by drawing on the results of modern neurobiology and on Hayek's brilliant intuitions. I also mentioned the implications of this formulation for economic theory and, above all, for the understanding of the dynamic processes of competition, of organizations and institutions.

In conclusion, I would like to put forward a few final considerations about other consequences of generalized asymmetrical information. There is one more consequence at a microbehavioural level, which has not been pointed out, yet. In Akerlof's approach, the risk connected with asymmetrical information is the dishonesty of one of the parties. In my formulation, instead, the risk connected with asymmetrical information is opportunism. The difference is relevant. Dishonesty means unfair behaviour, through which one party consciously takes an advantage. Opportunistic behaviour means that everybody acts according to what he/she considers the most opportune criteria in order to achieve his/her goals and an unfair behavioural act does not necessarily take place. Opportunistic behaviour is typical of those who operate on the market and need to plan their line of action, according to their ability to acquire and make use of knowledge. Certainly, unfair behaviour does not disappear, but it represents only one possible component of opportunistic behaviour. More generally, opportunism includes every kind of behaviour that is rooted in the complex and diversified individual cognitive processes and it generates, all things considered, creativity.

11. The Implications of the Neuro-biological Approach for Economic Theory (III): "Path-dependency"[1]

11.1 Introduction

For a decade now, unorthodox economic theory has been using an analytical category that has proved to be quite fruitful. This category is *path-dependency*, which I have already mentioned and shall now examine in detail. It was first developed and used in natural sciences, in particular in the evolutionary theory, and it was later extended to economic theory by Paul David in 1985 (David 1985). Since then, a number of works on the subject have extended its application, especially in the fields of innovation economics and of institutional change.

In scientific research, the acquisition of new analytical tools is often due to the results achieved in different fields. The use of path-dependency in economic theory is, from this point of view, emblematic. Applications of this category can be found in several related disciplines: economic history, economic geography, industrial economics and policy, theory of the firm, history of technological development, neoinstitutionalist theory, etc. Most of the scholars of industrial economics and neoinstitutionalist economics, who have given the major contributions to the subject are Anglo-Saxon. Among them, there is also a distinguished Italian scholar, who died less than a decade ago, Franco Momigliano; his contribution has, till now, stayed in the background.[2] The goal of this chapter is to outline the use of this category in

---

[1] This chapter is the result of an integration and extension of a few parts of two already published works: "The Microfoundations of Path-dependency", in Magnusson-Ottosson 1997, and "La 'path-dependency' nella teoria economica e il contributo di F. Momigliano", in *Storia del pensiero economico*, n. 30, 1995.

[2] Some authors (among them Marchionatti-Silva 1994) acknowledge that Momigliano has had a great influence on the major Italian heterodox economists, who are now well-known at an international level in the field of economics of innovation: Amendola, Antonelli, Dosi, Archibugi, Pianta. Moreover, according to Malerba and Orsenigo (1990), Momigliano must be included - along with Nelson, Winter, Rosenberg, and Freeman - among those who have given a fundamental contribution to the development of economics of innovation (p. 52). Antonelli (1995b) acknowledges that the Italian tradition has its own peculiarity, and that it is pre-

economic theory and examine its outcomes.

Path-dependency was first observed in natural history, in the analysis of the evolution of species, as a characteristic trait which affects future development in a relevant way. In other words, this approach implies that every successive act in the development of an individual, an organization, or an institution, is strongly influenced by and dependent on the previously covered path (experience and evolution). Moreover, in the path-dependent approach, change is underlined as a mainly endogenous phenomenon.

It is some authors' belief that path-dependency is also present in human history, and that, consequently, it has a natural as well as a social dimension (Arrow 1994b). In general terms, at the basis of path-dependency lies the idea that trifling historical events may have relevant consequences and that economic action may change them only in part (David 1985; Arthur 1988). In this perspective, path-dependency implies the idea that history is very important.[3] With reference to this concept, it is necessary to make clear an aspect which might bring about misunderstanding. Path-dependency should not be conceived as *"past-dependency"*. If it were so conceived, it would only point out how, when passing from one state to another, the preceding structures are pervasive. A *"past-dependent"* model would describe the dynamics of transitions, referring exclusively to the conditions of the preceding state, on the basis of simple Markovian processes, with a probable deterministic-causal outcome.

Path-dependency, instead, combines *"past-dependency"* with agents' intentional behaviour. Agents are conceived as individuals, who are able to change and influence the probability of transition from one state to another, thanks to the actions they carry out within the mechanisms of local interaction (David 1988). Path-dependency implies that the actual outcome of change is intrinsically unpredictable. This is due, first, to the assumptions concerning the qualities of economic agents, who are not characterized by irreversibility, indivisibility, bounded rationality and imperfect knowledge rather than by traditional parametric behaviour. Moreover, if we refer in particular to

---

eminent above even the Anglo-Saxon tradition (p. 2) in the development of a dynamic structuralist approach based on a path-dependent analysis, in which Momigliano's contributions are explicitly, though briefly, mentioned (p. 12). It is also my opinion that several parts of his works should be reconsidered from this perspective.

[3] As mentioned above, David (1985) showed that the adoption and the spreading speed of new technologies may depend on the existence of externalities on the demand side. The traditional mechanism - i.e. improved technologies replace pre-existing ones - may not work. An example is the QWERTY keyboard for typewriters and computers. Though it is far less efficient ergonomically than other keyboards, it became widespread because it was the first one to be launched on the market. This brought about an abundant offer of labour that is used to this keyboard. As a consequence, only QWERTY keyboards have been requested on the market. This mechanism has slowed down and hindered the spreading of more advanced technology (ergonomically more efficient keyboards).

industrial economics, we can conclude that, thanks to these structural differences of individuals and firms, it is possible to explain ex post the high levels of heterogeneity that are present in several industries in terms of growth rate, and the gap among firms with reference to dimension, organization, behaviour on the market, and mechanisms of introduction of innovations. With the passing of time, these differences tend to persist and strengthen and they allow - or do not allow - the evolution in a certain direction.

The outcome of path-dependent models is especially relevant: trifling fortuitous events may lead to situations of multiple equilibria or of efficient equilibrium (David 1985; Arthur 1988). This idea is in evident contrast with the traditional idea that market forces reach a unique and efficient situation of equilibrium spontaneously.[4]

11.2 Path-dependency in economic theory

One of the purposes of this chapter is to outline the applications of this category.[5] The three main fields of application of path-dependent analyses are: industrial economics, economic geography and neoinstitutionalist economics. I shall examine the first field of application more specifically, as regards innovation economics. I shall also mention the other two fields of application, but not in detail. The main reason why I chose the area of innovation economics is that path-dependency was first introduced into industrial economics and later extended to other areas. Therefore this seems to me the natural field of interest.

At first, I would like to deal with a crucial element, present in both the approach of innovation economics and the approach of neoinstitutionalist economics: "change". I shall first refer to technological change, then to institutional change and, finally, to the analyses within economic geography.

11.2.1 Technological change

With David's (1985) and Arthur's (1988) works, innovation economics and, in particular, the models of technological change reached a turning point. I shall outline this development below; now it is enough to take into consideration what follows. The term technological change refers to what happens within an organization when an innovation is introduced. Every firm

---

[4] In the preceding chapter, I maintained that these phenomena take place also on the demand side.

[5] I am referring to the major applications, and in particular to the theoretical ones, since, starting from 1988 (Antonelli 1988), path-dependent analyses are spreading also at an empirical level, especially in the field of advanced telecommunications.

makes use of organizational and technological routines,[6] that are the result of previously acquired and codified knowledge which is used regularly. When a new problematic situation is faced, sequences of change of pre-existing routines are developed, by means of imitation and adjustment of mechanisms used by other firms, or by generating new routines (Rizzello 1996a). In this second case innovations are introduced. Understanding this process is fundamental, in order to develop effective dynamic models that may help analyse economic development.[7]

A large number of the economists who have studied these issues, have tried to understand whether technological changes have an endogenous or an exogenous nature. The introduction of path-dependent analysis emphasized the endogenous, idiosyncratic and specific character of technological change. In fact, it is strictly related to the specific conditions of the market within which the firm works, with its specific pre-existing structures, with the history, the dimension and the peculiarities of the markets it is linked with, and the specializations it acquired, that are often the results of knowledge that has been planned and developed in the firm's development and research laboratories. Apparently, what is assumed in the traditional models never occurs: exogenous technological development is conceived as the result of external research and it is at everyone's disposal. In this case, introducing an innovation becomes the act of a courageous and clever entrepreneur, who understands the potentialities of an exogenous innovation.

The application of path-dependency to innovation economics implied the development of models that have been defined "models of localized technological change". They have been corroborated by empirical data and are consistent with the assumptions of bounded rationality and agents' imperfect knowledge. These models play quite an important role, and therefore I shall take them into consideration further on. Before that, I shall examine the application of path-dependent analysis to the institutional field.

11.2.2 Institutional change

Recently, path-dependency has also been introduced into neoinstitutionalist literature (North 1990). There are several examples of path-dependency at a

---

[6] If one refers to the organizational structure as a specific aspect of the more general technological dimension of an organization, one can certainly use the concept of technological change with reference to any kind of restructuring activity, of process, or of product within the firm. Technology can therefore be defined as a series of effective solutions helping to solve a production problem, which can be carried out mechanically without using induction (Egidi 1991, p. 109).

[7] This process, which is here presented in general terms, is evidently related to Nelson's and Winter's idea that change is due, first of all, to a stochastic shock, and it leads to an adjustment to new environmental conditions. Yet, this is not always the case. There might be situations in which resistances of various kinds bring about periods of behavioural rigidity, followed by (more or less) minor variations.

social level (the development of language and culture). The consequences of stochastic events may determine situations which, once they have prevailed, can consolidate and establish a "set path". North (1991), in particular, has underlined the strong relationship between historical evolution and evolution of institutions. According to the recent Nobel prize-winner, institutional change has the same path-dependent nature as technological change, since in both cases "ideological beliefs influence the subjective construction of the models that determine choices" (North 1990, p. 103). Therefore, the evolution of behavioural explicit and implicit rules derives from a spontaneous interactive process. Institutions are spontaneously arisen rules, within which organizations and individuals act. Among them we can distinguish formal rules (constitutions, laws, regulations) and informal rules (behavioural rules, tacit conventions, etc.). An organization can be created which codifies these spontaneous rules, so as to allow institutions to work. As you see, the process through which material rules are turned into formal rules is sometimes implemented by creating hierarchical structures, whose task is to make the application of institutional rules effective. Therefore, institutions are not organizations, since institutions arise spontaneously while organizations are planned. Nevertheless, an organizational dimension of institutions may exist, aimed at carrying out the process of implementation of the latter.[8]

Organizations are the players (North 1992) and they have an instrumental character, distinguishing them from institutions. Both organizations and institutions have their own rules. The internal rules of organizations are binding only for their members and are subordinated to institutional rules, whose applicability is wider. Moreover, organizations must meet requirements of efficiency, while institutions must meet requirements of effectiveness. The rules of organizations are created within institutional constraints, and they are often the result of mediation between individual self-interest (power dynamics) and requirements of efficiency. It is now clear that organizational rules have their specific character, which makes them, at least theoretically, more subject to change than institutional ones. Organizational rules must be flexible, so as to adjust quickly to environmental and institutional innovatory impulses. They also play an active role, since they can influence the process of change of institutional rules. The continuous interaction between institutions and organizations, in a context characterized by scarcity and consequently by competition, is the key to institutional change.

In the literature, there are authors who prefer to consider the dynamic processes between institutions and organizations in a context characterized by "increasing returns", rather than by scarcity (Smith, Young, Schumpeter, Nelson-Winter, etc.). In my opinion, these two approaches are not

---

[8] In the literature, there are quite controversial views on the nature of institutions and organizations and on the relationship between them. This subject will be dealt with in one of the following chapters.

incompatible: competition is a unifying element, since we find it both in a context of scarcity and in a context of increasing returns. Once the context is defined, be it characterized by scarcity, increasing returns, or both of them, it becomes important to understand the dynamics that take place between organizations and institutions. It is possible to describe such interaction here, though in very broad terms.

Organizations, urged by competition in a context of uncertainty, keep investing in knowledge and skills, in order to respond to the problems arising from the environment as efficiently as possible. These choices, as well as the structure of organizations itself, are influenced by the institutional environment. Whenever institutional rules become too binding for organizations, a conflict starts and a request for a change of institutional rules is made.

However, one should always keep in mind the dynamics underlying the generation of new rules. I have already mentioned that individuals, organizations and institutions follow specific rules, with a few, important differences. Both individuals and organizations cope with problematic situations through learning and according to criteria of procedural rationality. Yet, individuals change their routines faster and in a less "bureaucratic" way, within the constraints arising from institutional rules and from the rules of the hierarchy they work within. Organizations, instead, carry out changes more slowly than individuals, within the constraints arising from institutional rules and the rules of competition.[9]

In short, the complex and changing environment urges organizations to reshape their structures and to adjust to changes. Whenever the institutional environment is too binding, with reference to the necessary changes, a process starts through which institutions are modified. This is usually a slower process than the one necessary to modify organizations, since they, by their own nature, need to be more flexible in responding to environmental changes.

In general, institutions can be thought of as routines. As a consequence, institutional and organizational change can be conceived as a process through which new routines try to take the place of old ones. Taking all this into consideration, what are the mechanisms that give rise to organizational or institutional change and that rule the dynamics taking place between organizations and institutions? It is my belief that these mechanisms have, first of all, an individual character. They can therefore be found in the subjective processes through which routines are generated, especially with

---

[9] The process of generation of rules, through the study of learning processes, is a flourishing line of research of the contemporary theory. One of its branches is based, above all, on the theory of games (Walliser 1989; Ullmann-Margalit 1977). Simon's studies on rationality and the achievements of cognitive psychology intermingle in the other branch, which has developed models of organizational learning (Egidi 1992a). The path-dependent approach is especially evident in this second case.

reference to underlying neurobiological, psychological and social processes. Before examining this subject thoroughly, it is necessary to refer to the use of path-dependency in economic geography and in industrial economics.

11.2.3 An outline of path-dependency in economic geography

In the 1990s path-dependency has been introduced not only into neoinstitutionalist literature, but also into the studies on the geography of industrial settlements. P. Krugman wrote the most important works on the subject. They share with similar works developed in other fields, the analysis of concrete historical events, used to enrich the theoretical models.

The core of Krugman's analyses are the concepts of territoriality and geographic influence on industrial development, starting from the belief that the allocation of production processes through geographical space occurs in "unmistakably" path-dependent terms (Krugman 1991b). In this way, he tries to explain the differentiations and specializations both within a country (Krugman 1991b, Krugman 1991c) and, at an international level, among countries (Krugman 1991a).

I shall now briefly examine the most relevant aspects. There are two crucial elements: increasing returns and externalities (as we shall see further on, these two aspects are present in most path-dependent models).   In studying industrial settlements, this approach takes into consideration a few factors that are considered endogenous. Among them, a reference is made to the attempt on the part of firms to obtain economies of scale, by minimizing the cost of transportation. Therefore, production activities tend to group where demand is concentrated; demand, in turn is concentrated according to the territorial allocation of manufacturing industries (Krugman 1991c). A well-known historical example of this phenomenon, that is consistent with the model I have illustrated, refers to the concentration of manufacturing industries in the United States (Krugman 1991b).

The conclusions of this approach further corroborate what we have noticed in other analytical contexts: fortuitous historical events, thanks to the externalities they can generate, often play a decisive role in the evolution of economic reality. By spotting them out within models, it is possible to explain more realistically both the processes of accumulation and production with increasing returns. This hypothesis is much more consistent with reality than the traditional assumptions of production with constant returns (Krugman 1991b).

In this chapter I am taking into consideration above all innovation economics and I am only briefly outlining the context of economic geography. Nevertheless, several elements that have been mentioned here, will be dealt with again, when examining the issue of the connection between industrial settlements and genesis of innovations. Externalities will be fully included in analytical models. This aspect permeates all the past and present literature we are referring to.

11.3. Applications in industrial economics

As mentioned above, the introduction of path-dependency into industrial economics has allowed economists to achieve remarkable results in the field of innovation economics. This implied the formalization of the models of localized technological change, no longer conceived as exogenous and perfectly flexible (according to the assumption of the standard economic theory), but as strongly localized and mainly endogenous (Antonelli 1995a).

That of technological change is one of the crucial aspects of industrial economics. In order to point out the development introduced into this literature by the "path-dependent" approach, let us trace back, in a very general way, the most relevant steps of innovation economics, starting from Schumpeter.[10]

11.3.1 Technological change in the first Schumpeter

Since the beginning of this century, Schumpeter has studied the characteristics of economic change and criticized the traditional approach. It is well-known that, according to classical economists, economic development is determined by three traditional factors of production: land, capital, labour. Technological change is considered a secondary and exogenous factor, equally affecting all agents and allowing an equal increase in productivity. As such, it is conceived as an external element in the formalization of models.[11]

Unlike these authors, Marx has studied systematically, at an aggregate level, the issue of the effects of technological progress on economic development.[12]

Neoclassical authors did not take into account the new concepts introduced by Marx and kept considering production methods as "given and exogenous".

---

[10] For a systematic history of the development of economics of innovation from Schumpeter on, with special reference to technological change, see Antonelli 1995a, in particular Chapter 7.

[11] With the important exception of C. Babbage (1832).

[12] It is well known that the new concept introduced by Marx consists in considering technical progress as a factor of development. In particular, he links competition with the origin of technical progress. This mechanism can be summarized as follows (with all the limits necessarily implied by any synthesis). The urge towards innovation arises from competition. In order to increase its own surplus value every single firm invests in new technology. The increase in profits is thus linked to competition dynamics, which, in turn, are based on the introduction of innovations. As a consequence, there is an increase in what Marx defines as the organic composition of capital: urged by competition and technical progress, the capital employed in production processes increases, while the employment of the workforce decreases. In this way, Marx fully grasps the "economic nature" of technical progress, arising from competition. This is a first important acknowledgement of the endogenous nature of innovation.

According to them, entrepreneurs acquire new technology at no cost and with no dimensional, technical, organizational or market asymmetry.[13]

Schumpeter, on the contrary, understood the importance of Marx's intuition and criticized neoclassical economists and, in particular, their statical models. It was his firm belief that the dynamic components of the process of technological change had to be underlined, thus emphasizing the link between economic development and the technological change itself. In this context, Schumpeter conceived the role of entrepreneurs as the engine of economic development, since they introduce innovations, working in an environment where such innovations are unequally distributed in space and time and are concentrated in cycles (Schumpeter 1912).

The change following the introduction of an innovation brings short-term advantages to the innovating firm and it is also a long-term growth factor for the whole system. These concepts are well known and are part of every economist's basic knowledge. Therefore, I shall not write at length about it. Nevertheless, I would like to highlight an important element. On the one hand, Schumpeter emphasizes an interesting perspective, thus helping towards the comprehension of economic development; on the other hand, however, he takes a backward step as compared to Marx. According to Schumpeter, innovation - that is the application of an invention to production processes[14] - is exogenous and it is the result of fortuitous and meta-economic factors. It consists in the combination of the results achieved by single inventors and of the personality and the psychological characteristics of single entrepreneurs. As you see, Schumpeter introduces a new and clear approach to the relationship between competition process and economic development, but he abandons Marx's relationship between innovation and accumulation, i.e. the endogenous character of innovation resulting from planned investments. Innovation in the first Schumpeter has an exogenous character, since it arises from mechanisms that are sometimes fortuitous and in any case are not a part of the direct relation between capital accumulation

---

[13] Neoclassical economists neglected not only Marx's thought, but also another important intuition, i.e. – as mentioned above - Marshall's idea of organization as the fourth production factor.

[14] The distinction introduced by Schumpeter between invention and innovation is well known: an invention is a discovery, the implementation of an idea; an innovation, instead, is the adoption of an invention within a production process. An invention has a fully exogenous dimension and is public domain, a kind of manna one can decide whether to use or not. Its adoption within production processes depends on the entrepreneur's ability to understand its potentialities and turn it into an innovation. "Economic leadership in particular must hence be distinguished from 'invention'. As long as they are not carried into practice, inventions are economically irrelevant. And to carry any improvement into effect is a task entirely different from the inventing of it (...) besides, the innovations which it is the function of entrepreneurs to carry out need not necessarily be any inventions at all" (Schumpeter 1912, Eng. tr., pp. 88 - 89).

and technological change (on this subject see also Momigliano, 1975).

11.3.2 Technical change in the second Schumpeter

Schumpeter, in a sense, later regained Marx's contribution. Starting from *Capitalism, Socialism, Democracy*, he acknowledged the endogenous nature of technological change. The Viennese economist pointed out the following virtuous circle: as the result of the introduction of successful innovations, "almost-monopolistic" returns are created, which can be used to fund research and development; these investments lead to other innovations, whose introduction yields more "almost-monopolistic" returns, which can be invested, and so on. If, on the one hand, he still retains the fundamental idea of the entrepreneur as the subject economic development depends on, on the other hand, he acknowledges the endogenous and planned nature of innovations (Schumpeter 1971). At a level of trustified capitalism, the real competititon is the competition among innovatory firms, i.e. the ones that carry out entrepreneurial activity, which, according to Schumpeter, coincides with the ability to generate innovations (Schumpeter 1943). In this way he regains, within his model, Marx's idea of the relation between accumulation and investments aimed at generating innovations (on this subject see also Egidi 1981).

11.3.3 The most recent approaches

Our purpose is not that of outlining the whole debate on technical change. This would require a longer book and very many authors should be taken into account (such as, for example, Keynes, all the Marxist authors who have dealt with this subject in this century, and other important authors, among which R. Marris, Baran-Sweezy, etc.). I am now examining only path-dependent analyses, and I have referred to the history of economic thought only in order to give the reader an outline of the development of theories, up to the introduction of the category that is the subject of this chapter. In this perspective, I shall now briefly illustrate the characteristics of the most recent models that somehow made the development of path-dependent analyses possible, within the theory of technological change.

Several authors think that the evolutionary theory (Nelson - Winter 1982) - that is directly derived from the Schumpeterian tradition - made further steps ahead towards the introduction of path-dependency. Taking into consideration the role of learning and externalities, Nelson and Winter underlined the highly specific and idiosyncratic nature of technological knowledge and the fact that, very often, it is not accessible to everybody. On the contrary, the impossibility of taking possession of innovations and the protection from free imitation are among the most important elements urging firms to invest in research and development and to introduce specific technological change. Conceiving organizations as structured into routines, is typical of the evolutionary theory. This concept gave rise to a series of works in microeconomics, which shed light on another aspect of organizations: their specificity. I have just now mentioned learning and externalities. The latter are specific characteristics of compared advantages or disadvantages influencing - as potentialities or as limits - the choices of the organization remarkably. Learning processes, instead, consist in those mechanisms of imitation or genuine generation of routines which I have already referred to. These dynamics, which play a major role in explaining technological change, arise from the specific characteristics of the organizational structure, from its history, and its tradition, from the previously acquired knowledge, and the ability of each of its components to develop innovations.

11.3.4 Localized technological change

It is not a long way to the results that have recently been achieved in the economics of innovation. The path-dependent nature of these dynamics is fully acknowledged: they can be defined in short by the words "processes of localized technological change". The word "localized", in this context, has two valences: its specific nature and the endogenous nature. In practice, all the sequences leading to an innovation are generated within the firm and depend on its specific dynamics. They do not derive from a succession of decision-making events, according to which the firm's managers simply decide whether to introduce an innovation which has been produced exogenously and which is accessible to everybody.[15] Localized technological change is the core of a theory formalizing the model "structure-behaviour-performance".[16] It is highly path-dependent and it is the result of the combination of manifold aspects, typical of the unorthodox approach. Out of these aspects, it is important to underline the fact that localized technological change is consistent with the theories of bounded and procedural rationality,

---

[15] Actually, this approach takes into account both kinds of adoption. In fact, the empirical evidence proves that innovation has mostly an endogenous origin, but the traditional Schumpeterian (the first Schumpeter) mechanism of the adoption of an exogenous innovation is still active. The path-dependent approach, nevertheless, mainly accounts for the first kind of process, since it is a more widespread mechanism and it can explain the most important structural dynamics of firms.

With reference to research within the firm, prevailing over exogenous research, Momigliano wrote in the 1970s: starting from 1920, individual applied research has become more and more difficult to carry out, while funded and promoted inventions and innovations - i.e. planned and intentionally carried out within large industrial business – have become more and more widespread (Momigliano 1975, p. 619).

[16] This definition (from Antonelli 1995b) helps us understand the existence of influences and links between the structure of a firm and its internal and external peculiarities, behaviour and performance. We use this definition referring to the analyses carried out before the introduction of path-dependency, which implicitly contained it.

and with the theories of organizational learning and of imperfect information. It is also consistent with the most recent literature on externalities (Coase 1960), asymmetrical information (including its application in the field of the theory of the firm) and, above all, with the sunk costs models.

Though it is not possible to go into all the various complex factors giving rise to technological change (price dynamics, cost trend, etc.), nevertheless it is possible to maintain that the recent literature on the subject emphasizes its endogenous and idiosyncratic character. This new model includes the path-dependent approach, in fact it is this approach (arising from wide empirical evidence) that corroborates hypotheses and conclusions.

11.4 The microfoundations of path-dependency

To sum up the aspects I have mentioned so far, we have seen that the framework of the path-dependency model is based on the following assumptions: a) agents are endowed with bounded rationality and act on the basis of criteria of procedural rationality; b) firms work within heterogeneous markets and are characterized by substantial diversity as to their use of methods, structures, and organization, and as to their market behaviour and innovating and learning capacities (Antonelli 1995a); c) information is imperfect; d) sunk and switching costs are especially relevant (Stiglitz 1987b; Sutton 1989; Schmalensee 1992).

By emphasizing specialization and diversification, the theory takes into account both competition advantage, characterizing each firm, and all the innovating or substituting processes, that are precisely highly path-dependent (as regards this aspect, see also Arthur 1988).

Yet, as I have repeatedly mentioned, path-dependency affects also the processes of institutional change. It is consistent with the methodological assumptions of this book (drawing on Hayek's subjectivism) to hold that path-dependency is present in the choosing processes, at the level of every agent, as well as at an organizational and institutional level.

Saying that individuals are characterized by path-dependency when they act, implies that they are influenced by their own specific characteristics, their experience, the specific feedback with their surrounding environment during decision-making processes, individual learning processes and, above all, by individual mechanisms of knowledge acquisition.

Let us once more take into account Hayek's and Simon's contributions. Hayek held that individuals, for their actions, make use of the knowledge they acquire through a mechanism (described above) that appears highly path-dependent. Simon developed a concept of rationality (described above) which sheds light on the fact that every individual is endowed with bounded rationality and acts according to criteria of procedural rationality. By combining their approaches, we obtain the microfoundations of the individual economic behaviour of the unorthodox approach. I shall now try to outline this approach and to explain why I consider it highly path-dependent.

The most important point now is understanding how individuals develop the routines they use to solve problematic situations. Let us now leave out the mechanisms of imitations, and focus our attention on the genuine generation of new routines. They arise from mental mechanisms of external data perception through a mechanism of association with already codified data. As Hayek underlined (1952a), individuals build up their knowledge by interpreting sensory data according to classifying criteria; these depend on inborn characteristics of the subject, on mental categories and, above all, on acquired experience, which changes from individual to individual.

Path-dependency in the processes of knowledge acquisition is evident. Knowledge acquisition, in fact, depends on the history, the upbringing and the experience, which the individual has acquired and keeps acquiring. Each perception of external data depends on subjective features, arising, in turn, from individual processes of data interpretation.

Let us see the implications in Simon's approach. As mentioned above, individuals face problem-solving, either through processes of imitation of already experienced procedures, or by generating new routines. Simplifying the issue, it is possible to state that also firms make use of - more or less - the same mechanisms. However, Hayek's thought, as well as cognitive psychology, demonstrate that agents interpret observed data subjectively also when they imitate other agents' procedures. Knowledge means adjusting situations that are not consistent with what has been learned. In other words, knowledge means continuously adjusting perceived data which do not coincide with preceding experience.

This accounts, in part, for the return differences in similar firms carrying out processes of imitation. This path-dependent approach also explains that innovation is, first of all, an individual act of data interpretation, whose specificity and possible effectiveness depends on the learning abilities of individuals or firms, which, in turn, depend on their histories.

Since the environment is complex and changes rapidly, organizations are urged to restructure themselves and adjust to change. When the institutional context is too binding, a process of institutional change is started, which is usually slower than organizational change, since organizations, by their own nature, need to be more flexible and respond to environmental change according to criteria of efficiency. Such criteria depend, in turn, on individual abilities to develop solutions and behavioural rules.

The path-dependent nature of these processes accounts for the assumptions and analyses on technological and institutional change at a micro level.

11.5 Implications for economic theory

11.5.1 The implications of path-dependency for the models of technological change

Following the approach of Nelson and Winter, the technology used by firms can be considered as routines, arising from previously experienced and codified knowledge, and applied always in the same way (Egidi 1991). On the basis of this definition, and taking into consideration the organization in general terms and not only with reference to its technological structure, routines can be located at every level: at an organizational, technological, commercial, or at a production level, etc. Let us now deal with the issue of how this change takes place and why it can be considered path-dependent, taking into due consideration what I have stated about microfoundations.

Let us start from the example of a firm or an organization using routines. As soon as a problematic situation occurs - e.g. an erosion of profits, losses of market share, an increase or decrease in costs, etc. - the firm must face it. As already stated above, it can either carry out processes of imitation, or it can generate new routines. In both cases, the change the firm will bring about is likely to be of a path-dependent kind, all the more so if the firm is characterized by constraints, such as the levels of sunk or switching costs, the specific market conditions, the presence - or absence - of available internal capital for investments in research and development, and the level of access to credit.

Growing empirical evidence (Antonelli 1988) has shown that these constraints are fundamental in the process of introduction of an innovation, from two different points of view: as constraints and as potentialities. The more a firm is characterized by high sunk and switching costs, by particular market structures, by particular plant dimensions, by the availability of capital for research and development, etc., the more, in the processes of imitation, it will tend to adopt an innovation by fitting its configuration (adjusting it) in the best possible way to its specific situation, holding back the costs of adoption as much as possible. This will allow the firm to produce changes in the innovation it is adopting-adjusting. Such changes will be specific and idiosyncratic and will become, in turn, the object of further imitation.

But in the case of genuine generation of new routines, the process is path-dependent and probably stronger. Also in this case, the spur towards change arises from a problematic situation (it could even be a very general problematic situation, such as keeping a leadership). The more the firm is characterized by the above-mentioned elements, the more specific and path-dependent the innovations will be.

Before moving on to the next Section, let us make a last but fundamental point. First of all, it is easy to see the analogy between individuals' processes of knowledge acquisition through the imitation or generation of new routines, and the firms' processes of innovation or genuine imitation. Yet, this is not the only relevant point. It is important to remember that, even though they are structured in teams, it is individuals who act within organizations. These individuals have the above-mentioned psychological and neurological characteristics, and their decisions arise from the process of feedback between problematic situations, existing constraints, environmental complexity, acquired experience, and learning ability. At this point, the path-dependent nature of the process becomes evident also in the framework of what we may define, in general terms, as technological change. The conclusion is the following: the more the markets are characterized by heterogeneous, specific, idiosyncratic, etc. firms, the more the processes of change are path.-dependent. As we can infer from the analysis of microfoundations, there is perfect coherence between individual and organizational learning processes. Such coherence is present also within the institutional context, though with a few differences.

11.5.2 Institutional change

I feel that many of the above statements concerning technological change are also valid for institutional change. For this reason, in this section I shall only point out the small, but significant, differences.

Institutions, too, can be thought of as routines. However, compared with the routines of organizations, they have a slightly different foundation. The rules adopted by firms must fulfil criteria of efficiency, since a competitive market punishes those who adopt inefficient innovations. Institutional rules, as mentioned above, must fulfil criteria of effectiveness. Every institution, in fact, will continue to exist as long as it is effective and in harmony with the other institutions. Therefore, it is possible to recognize two moments through which a set of rules can assert itself as an institution. In the first one, as we have seen, a behavioural model develops spontaneously; once it has proven effective, it spreads by means of imitation (Hayek 1963; Horwitz 1993). This is what North calls "informal constraints": it is the element introducing the predictability of the conduct of others and the simplification of environmental variables, thus allowing individuals' limitation to be surmounted. In this phase, the respect of "normal behaviour" is guaranteed through a network of informal sanctions.

In a second moment, these set rules, i.e. the informal institutions, need a sort of "protection" to defend them and guarantee their functioning. A process of institutionalization takes place: the spontaneous rules are now supported by other formal and planned rules, conceived in such a way as to allow the survival of the spontaneous ones and to enhance their effectiveness. However, the relationship between the two is not necessarily linear. Informal institutions usually have a spontaneous nature but their formalization is also the result of mediations and conflicts of interests. The context in which institutions are generated is substantially limited by two constraints: effectiveness and harmony with the other institutions. Within the scope of these two constraints, the conflicts of interests take place.

Between informal and formal institutions there is a relationship through which they affect each other (feedback). The effectiveness of formal institutions arises directly from the characteristics of the informal ones: the fact of being conventionally recognized and of being perceived as "right behaviour" (tacit conventions); at the same time, however, the purpose of formal rules is to stabilize and defend a mechanism that has proven effective. Informal institutions are, therefore, strongly influenced by the formal ones.

Although the effectiveness of the two kinds of rules has different sources and characteristics, there is a common element allowing us to apply the same concept of institution to both of them: their ordering function. If being a rule is a fact for informal institutions, it is an act for the formal ones, since it is the result of choices that are immediately and consciously directed towards the creation of rules.

As already stated above, I consider valid for institutional change, what has been said about the similarities between individual and organizational processes of imitations, of learning, and of generation of new routines. However, I believe that in the case of institutional change it is necessary to distinguish different path-dependent processes. In the spontaneous emergence of institutions (*à la* Hayek), path-dependency derives mainly from individual processes, by which problematic situations are perceived and knowledge is acquired and conveyed to other individuals; path dependency derives also, but a little less, from the history and the tradition of a country (North 1991). In this first case, I believe that the individual dimension prevails over the holistic one.

On the contrary, in the case of the processes by which institutions are formalized, the situation seems to be the opposite. Usually, in law-making processes, tradition and history prevail (just think, for instance, of the differences between common law and civil law) along with the solution of power conflicts, taking place in a path-dependent way. The spontaneous, individual dimension, which was prevailing in the first case, is here less relevant.

The conclusion on the subject of institutional change is the following: also here we find path-dependency in the processes of change, and a strong link with the above-described microfoundations. However, in this context it is necessary to distinguish between two kinds of path-dependence: the first one is tied to the spontaneous process of the emergence of rules and it is certainly linked to the processes of acquisition of knowledge and of adoption of routines on the part of individuals; the second one is more closely connected to the cultural tradition of the formalization of rules, which has a more holistic dimension and is more dependent on the society's history.

11.6 Concluding remarks

In this chapter I have pursued three goals. First of all, I have tried to point out the central and fruitful role of path-dependency in the whole heterodox literature. Second, I have systematically analysed its microfoundations, and from this analysis at least two important aspects have emerged: their neurobiological nature, and their connection with two heterogeneous trends of contemporary economic theory, that have been developed for the last fifty years on the basis of Hayek's and Simon's studies. Finally, as the third goal, I have tried to point out a few implications of the results achieved, that are relevant for economic theory, especially for the theory of innovation and the neoinstitutionalist theory.

In this context, I would like to point out what I consider the most significant result of these studies: at a neural level, path-dependency can be traced back to the very perception mechanisms, and as a consequence, to the mechanisms that underlie the use of information and the generation of knowledge. These processes can produce different interpretations of external data, thanks to each individual's genetic differences and experience. This consideration allows us to apply the concept of path-dependency to the above-mentioned theoretical contexts and it suggests its development along well-determined outlines. For instance, some recent path-dependent analyses (Arthur 1989 and Rizzello 1996b) question economic theory's predictive ability. There certainly is a great deal more to be explored in this field, but the right direction seems to have been pointed out.

I believe that in this chapter I have managed to show the unifying role of path-dependency, with reference to the various unorthodox theories. Moreover, the path-dependent nature of human creativeness, leads us to the conclusion that both technological innovation and the emergence of "rules" arise from one source: the neurobiological characteristics of economic agents.

In conclusion, I would like to underline briefly two aspects that are, in my opinion, of great moment for the subject dealt with: the endogenous nature of change and the neurobiological nature of the microfoundations of path-dependency.

The first idea is not new: endogenous change is a characteristic of the evolutionary tradition (Witt 1992). However, among the still open questions on the subject there is the problem of understanding how change is generated, trying to find an answer that goes beyond intuitive reference to human creativity (Witt 1992). It is my hope that this chapter may give at least a partial contribution to find the way to a more satisfactory answer.

As regards the idea of the psychological nature of microfoundations, it comes from the traditional theory of subjectivism. According to this theory, the generation of knowledge is a highly individual process, in which new notions emerge from the specific processes of data interpretation and from individual experience.[17] In this connection, this chapter asserts Hayek's central role, as the founder of the subjectivistic approach. His role is not always duly acknowledged; if it were, his thought would be the object of interpretations of more consequence.

In short, I have stated the following: i) path-dependency is a powerful analytical tool for the comprehension of the processes of change, studied in economic theory; ii) microfoundations have a neurobiological nature, which confirms the results of the tradition of subjectivism; iii) the achieved results

---

[17] Witt (1992, p. 408) emphasizes this aspect, drawing, in turn, on Shackle 1972 and Loasby 1976.

are the product of analyses that integrate Hayek's contributions on the generation of knowledge, conceived as a process of endogenous information processing, and Simon's contribution on the generation of innovation as a process of feedback between the individual (or the firm) and the environment, in an attempt to adapt the levels of aspiration, on the basis of tradition and past experience (satisficing approach).

Finally, I would like to state that: the source of human creativity and, therefore, of the process of change has been located in the neural perception processes and, in other words, in the imperfect predictability of human behaviour. Innovations may derive from processes of perception, planning and implementation, that are certainly path-dependent; yet they keep a certain degree of free will, arising from imperfect information and procedural rationality.

12. Transaction Costs and the New Theory of the Firm

An accurate assessment of the economic institutions of capitalism cannot, in my judgement, be reached if the central importance of transaction cost economizing is denied.

(Williamson 1986, p. 17)

The main reason why it is profitable to establish a firm would seem to be that there is a cost of using the price mechanism.

(Coase 1937, p. 390)

12.1 Introduction

Defining production costs is not simple. Williamson himself, in his several papers on the subject, has never given an all-encompassing definition. The closest definition to the concept of production costs - which he used in *The Economic Institutions of Capitalism* - is Arrow's definition: the cost one must meet to run an economic system (Arrow 1969).

The first author to introduce the concept of "cost of using the price mechanism", that is to say the market cost, was Coase, as early as 1937 (Coase 1937).[1] But, as Coase himself acknowledged (1988a, Chapter 1; 1988b), such a relevant aspect has remained in the background of standard economic theory. Apparently, the main reason is that this concept is not widespread among economists, who have developed models in which transaction costs equal zero.[2]

---

[1] Coase has repeatedly proposed this point of view. In particular, in 1960 he wrote: "In order to carry out a market transaction it is necessary to discover who it is that one wishes to deal with, to inform people that one wishes to deal and on what terms, to conduct negotiations leading up to a bargain, to draw up the contract, to undertake the inspection needed to make sure that the terms of the contract are being observed, and so on " (Coase 1960, p. 15).

[2] Actually, the concept that has become widespread among economists is the so-called Coase theorem, which was formulated on the basis of the assumption of zero transaction costs. According to Coase's theorem, in a system with zero transaction costs, a bargaining between the parties would maximize wealth, independently of the initially granted rights. Yet, this is not Coase's formulation, it is Stigler's (1966). As mentioned above, the standard theory accepted only this aspect, while Coase

Acknowledging the presence of positive costs of transaction means acknowledging also the presence of alternative coordination mechanisms to market. Moreover, these alternative mechanisms may, sometimes, be preferred to the price mechanism. Thus the idea gains ground that production planning in hierarchically structured units allows a more adequate reduction of such costs, which are due to the drafting of contracts, or, more generally, to negotiations (defined beforehand); and to the fulfilment (defined afterwards) (Williamson 1986).

Several transactions are carried out within the firm and planned according to a hierarchy aimed at making production relations efficient. This replacement of market relations with property relations is the mechanism by which transaction costs are reduced and production is made more efficient (Moe 1984). Market and firm are, therefore, two different ways of solving the problem of coordinating the diversified knowledge, which is scattered among individuals. The combination of these two different (spontaneous and planned) ways is a better form of economic organization, as compared to planning and market taken into consideration one at a time (Nelson 1981). The birth and development of firms take place on the basis of the ratio between transaction costs on the market and transaction costs within the firm's hierarchical structure (Coase 1937). In particular, the development continues "and expands up to the point where the cost of an additional transaction within the firm begins to exceed the cost of the same transaction in the market. In equilibrium, some transactions will therefore be internalized within firms of various kinds and sizes, and some will be left to the market" (Moe 1984, p. 743).

Organizations, therefore, play the same role as the market in reducing the complexity of information handling. Yet, there are relevant differences. Market coordinates the activity between individuals and organizations within a given "social" division of labour. Organizations coordinate the activity of a number of individuals and can therefore solve complex problems, by subdividing them into several sub-problems that will be handled by different functional sub-systems of the firm. This accounts for the hierarchical organization of the firm.

Entrepreneurs' activity consists in planning new forms of division of labour. This differentiation is due to the fact that firms exist in order to reach given aims that are, at the most, only partially deliberate, while market is a non-deliberate institution (according to Hayek's approach). Being a deliberate institution, the firm is able to plan the possible forms of co-ordination, in an attempt to pursue its aims best. We cannot credit the market with the same functional ability.

Yet, the real core of the theory of transaction costs consists in the existence of incomplete and unequally distributed information. These are the situations

---

considers it only as the first step towards a more interesting development of models with positive transaction costs.

characterized by asymmetrical information, which are - as mentioned above - the rule.[3] If information was free and exchange took place at no cost, the agent had nothing to worry about. The problems he/she has to cope with, arise from situations of ignorance. The agent keeps looking for new information until the time spent in this activity outweighs - in terms of alternatives to which he/she loses - the advantages in terms of the new opportunities that might be discovered. The preliminary problem of the lack of information (or only partial information) concerning the individual we are dealing with, urges us to insert a number of clauses in the contract, providing for penalties if the contract is not fulfilled (contractual costs) (Ricketts 1987).

The principal-agent model, which is at the basis of the theory of the agency,[4] is an analytical scheme explaining how the consequences of asymmetrical information may be reduced.

Along with Coase, Williamson also has given relevant contributions to the analysis of transaction costs.[5]

He has also introduced the two important concepts of bounded rationality and opportunism into this analysis. If individuals were endowed with substantive rationality, all exchanges might be efficiently organized by means of complete contracts. If bounded rationality is assumed, instead, coping with the complexity by means of contracts becomes impossible: as a consequence, an incomplete contract is the best agents can work out. An interesting aspect is that generalized, though incomplete, contracts might still be possible and presumably fulfilled by agents, if the individuals endowed with bounded rationality were fully reliable and if their behaviour were not opportunistic. But this does not happen, since reality is characterized by opportunistic behaviour, that is the extreme pursuit of egoistic aims. Williamson gives further explanations. By opportunism he means shrewdly pursuing egoistic aims, passively or actively, beforehand or afterwards. The author refers to

---

[3] Besides the above-mentioned Akerlof model of 1970, Arrow (1962) dealt with the problem of the presence of asymmetrical information in the insurance market. Beforehand, it might be very expensive for an insurance company to sign a health insurance contract, since the customer is certainly better informed on his/her health conditions (Ricketts 1987).

[4] In an agency contract, there are two parties, one of which (the agent) acts on behalf of the principal. The latter grants incentives to the agent, so that his/her actions coincide with his/her own self-interest. Such incentives are fixed beforehand in the so-called agency contract. Thus the principal faces his/her own problem by signing a kind of contract in which the agent's incentive wages are linked to the results he/she achieves. The agent, instead, has to take upon himself/herself a part of the risks connected with the results of his/her own work, which are due to his/her own skills, but also to exogenous and unpredictable events (Harris-Raviv 1978; Arrow 1984; Zeckhauser-Pratt 1984).

[5] Both of them draw on Commons' proposition (1934), according to which the transaction must be considered the base unit of analysis.

agents who disclose incomplete or wrong information and try to mislead or confuse the other agents. Opportunism is a particularly important aspect. Without it, every action might be governed by rules, and preliminary overall planning would not be necessary (Williamson 1986).

The behavioural assumptions of bounded rationality and opportunism, especially if combined, deeply influence economic organization. As a consequence of bounded rationality, all complex transactions are inevitably incomplete, and actions are based on sequential adjusting decisions. As a consequence of opportunism, contracts conceived as promises and supported by reliable commitment are naive hopes exposing the contracting parties to danger (Williamson 1988).

Another aspect that is connected with transaction costs concerns the emergence of institutions. According to Ricketts, it is due to a spontaneous mechanism that furthers exchanges by cutting their costs. Many institutions, such as firm, market, money and political institutions have developed in order to cut such costs and to further transactions, which, otherwise, would not take place (Ricketts 1987). Thanks to money, contracting parties, when there is a great number of them, are not compelled to reach simultaneous agreements, while this is necessary in a barter system. As regards political institutions, Hume had already assumed that they may emerge in order to overcome the hindrances in exchange processes. More recently Buchanan, following this assumption, has referred to the state as a manufacturer of goods, which individuals can take advantage of, thanks to added consumption and to the principle of non-excludability.[6]

12.2 The new role of the firm

When an agent makes agreements or contracts with other agents in a situation of asymmetrical information, he cannot make sure that they are actually interested in fulfilling that agreement. Opportunistic actions may be carried out and one of the firm's roles is reducing that risk (Brosio 1989). The firm is no longer defined as it used to be in the neoclassical approach, on the basis of mere technological characteristics; the entrepreneur determines its boundaries by comparing two possible forms of organization: either producing by integrating the cycles provided for in the production plan, or decentralizing intermediate production cycles on the market. The firm is structured according to a contract, in which external suppliers are replaced with internal suppliers, i.e. the employees, whose work is directly controlled by the manager. This reduces the entrepreneur's uncertainty remarkably, as he/she coordinates and controls their actions directly and thus he/she has more chances to carry out the actions he/she has undertaken (Brosio 1989).

---

[6] Ricketts 1987. This is a peculiar feature of the school of public choice, of which Buchanan is the major representative. There is an evident reference to the organic evolution of institutions, as in the Austrian tradition (Buchanan-Vanberg 1991).

Therefore firm and market belong to the same conceptual framework, being two different ways of handling transactions. Their boundaries are not rigid and are characterized by a high level of uncertainty.

The transaction-cost approach is much closer to the real model, characterized by asymmetrical information, conflicts arising during exchanges, bounded rationality, etc. Organizations have a contractual nature and they can be better understood if it is studied from this point of view (Moe 1984). The fact that a firm has better chances in negotiating can be easily demonstrated by means of an example. Outside the firm, every factor of production must reach agreements with all the others. Within the firm, instead, a central negotiator (coordinator) reaches agreements with each factor; therefore each factor makes only one contract. The advantages are evident. "In an extreme case where n individuals must all co-operate closely, a set of $n(n-1)/2$ bilateral contracts would be required to bind the parties together. For five individuals (...) ten agreements would be necessary (...). In the firm (...) one person would become the central contractual agent and a total of four contracts would be sufficient to link all the parties together" (Ricketts 1987, p. 40).

12.2.1 The firm according to Coase

Coase thinks that, in order to understand economic activities, it is necessary to analyse their institutional context systematically.[7] His major "task is to attempt to discover why a firm emerges at all in a specialised exchange economy" (Coase 1937, p. 390). As stated above, the answer is to be found in the fact that the price mechanism implies a cost, which can be eliminated or cut by an entrepreneur-manager. I want to underline now that there are two kinds of costs. The first one is the cost of gathering and assessing information, since market indexes, as mentioned above, do not contain all the relevant information. The second one is the cost of negotiating and making separate contracts for every transaction: it is possible to cut such costs by means of one contract that "is made for a long period, instead of several shorter ones" (Coase 1937, p. 391).[8] According to this approach, one of the firm's aspects consists in a bundle of long-term hiring contractual relations, which can remove the risk (Aoki 1984).

These two aspects already contain two guidelines of the development of the theory of the firm: in some circumstances firms handle information more efficiently than market; the division of labour within the structure of firms means subdividing information and competencies in order to reduce transaction costs. Thus, firms emerge in order to cut transaction costs and produce more efficiently, by means of an internal organization among agents.

---

[7] This approach is at the basis of classical institutionalism and the most recent neoinstitutionalism, of which Coase is considered one of the founders.

[8] Coase 1937, p. 391. See also Coase 1988b, pp. 40-41.

The major innovatory idea introduced by Coase as regards the firm consists in conceiving it as a way to guarantee a process of social co-ordination that is alternative to and works simultaneously with market.

In economic theory, firms and market are considered as two alternative ways of organizing economic activity: the first one has a hierarchical structure, the second one has a decentralized structure. Until the beginning of the 1960s, economists - with the exception of Coase and Knight - had not taken into account the issue of the compatibility of the two forms, since the prevailing (neoclassical) tradition had focused all its attention on the market. The firm had been considered as subordinated to market and as a mere "function of production". For the last thirty years, instead, several economists have tried to explain the true role of the firm, which is different from the role of the market in the solution of the different economic problem of information handling.[9] I will now outline the major theories of the firm.

12.2.2 The neoclassical theory of the firm (until the 1950s)

The neoclassical theory considers the firm as characterized by its technology, defined as a proportion of input to output. This is enough for Demsetz (1988, Part III) to state that the neoclassical theory of the firm is not a theory of the firm, but a theory of prices.

The firm is conceived as a black box, in which the factors of production are combined with its specific resources to obtain a market output. The coefficients of return on capital and labour are included in the model, but the assumption is that they are determined by market and *external* to the firm. The way input is turned into output is not analysed, with the exception of the assumption of perfect information and "Alchian's principle" (an urge to survive in a competitive environment). These assumptions imply maximizing behaviour. What is maximized is the profit, i.e. the return on capital of the most efficient entrepreneur (Arrow 1971). Profit, conceived as residue, is the core of the old-fashioned neoclassical analysis. Nevertheless, the entrepreneur's role is not clear, in a world where information is perfect and there are no innovations, no risks and organization.

Yet, the theory includes two definitions of the entrepreneur. In the first one, he is considered as a mere production manager, who assumes prices and production as "given" (Walras 1889). In the second one, he is defined as the owner of the resources (Arrow-Debreu 1954). In both cases, because of the assumptions concerning rationality and the existence of profit-maximizing rules, that are expressed in the assumption of perfect knowledge, the entrapreneur has no real choice as to the allocation of resources. That choice is made, on his behalf, by neoclassical rules and conditions (Kay 1984, p. 5).

---

[9] Among the most recent works on the evolution of the theory of the firm, see Grillo-Silva 1989; Williamson 1988; Milgrom-Roberts 1988; Holmstrom-Tirole 1989; Brosio 1995.

In the neoclassical world, given the prices, the only constraint is the scarcity of resources. There are no organizational problems. Information is public domain, it is free and accessible to everyone.[10]

12.2.3 Alternative proposals

As stated in the chapter dealing with bounded rationality, acknowledging the presence of limits in gathering and handling information in conditions of uncertainty, and the resulting presence of positive transaction costs, implies a new view on the firm.[11]

In the light of these assumptions, the criticism of the traditional theory of the firm has developed after the pioneering approaches of Coase, Simon and Alchian. I have already dealt with Coase's approach. As regards Simon, we know that his main goals were replacing the conventional model of the maximizing individual endowed with unbounded rationality with an empirically correct theory of individual choice, and using this new theory to develop a new general theory of the organization. These aspects have already been dealt with, but in this context I would like to underline that, according to Simon, organizations are useful in order to pursue human goals, precisely because human knowledge, prediction, capacities and time are bounded (Simon 1957). Thus, organizations are the tool, helping to carry out complex tasks by means of cooperation (which is obtained out of the market) and the division of labour and knowledge among a large number of individuals. Individuals show a tendency to simplify their tasks in an attempt to reduce information and decision complexity: on the one hand, if they can express their abilities, they tend to turn their behavioural acts into routines; on the other hand, the managers try to force their employees to carry out the same routines, in order to make their decisions uniform. By combining bounded rationality and managerial efforts to plan employee's behaviour, Simon explains the workings of most organizational structures.

Let us now examine the theory of the firm according to Alchian, who started one of the most successful lines of research of the contemporary

---

[10] "Orthodox economic theory has little to offer in terms of understanding how non market organizations, like firms, form and function. This is so because traditional theory pays little or no attention to the role of information, which evidently lies at the heart of organizations" (Holmstrom 1982, p. 324).

[11] The firm is, therefore, an alternative to market. It arises when, in an uncertain world, information becomes valuable and market is a less efficient tool than firms for gathering and checking information (Silva 1985, p. 106). In fact, if we assume that within the organization a process of synthesis and conveyance of the relevant information is carried out, and taking into account that the organization is intentionally established and it is the outcome of a choice and of a deliberate process, it becomes necessary to credit the individuals working within it with the ability to plan and design new organizational forms in order to handle information (Egidi 1989b, p. 65).

theory of the firm: the evolutionary theory.

12.2.4 Alchian's principle

Also Alchian's contribution is part of that line of research that aims at "the removal of the unrealistic postulates" (Alchian 1950, p. 211), that are at the basis of the traditional theory of the firm. The goal is a better comprehension of firms as organizations, by introducing the concepts of uncertainty and incomplete information. According to Alchian's approach, the existence and behaviour of economic organizations can be understood by applying Darwin's theory of evolution and natural selection, duly modified.

Alchian rejects the idea of profit-maximizing as such, since, in a condition of uncertainty, there is no reliable criterion to select the best decision, and, at any rate, it would not be necessary to understand the features of organizations and economic systems. In an economic system, the firms with positive profits survive, the ones with losses tend to disappear (Alchian 1950). The process of imperfect imitation offers chances of introducing innovations, which in turn lead to new organizational forms that will undergo a new selection process. Thanks to innovations, the regularity arising from natural economic selection becomes dynamic, rather than static; new forms are adopted after proving to be efficient.

Unlike Simon and Coase, Alchian rejects a model of individual choice. He explains emergence, structure and survival of firms at a system level.

12.3 The most recent approaches

12.3.1 The behaviouristic approach

This approach began with the contributions of March-Simon (1958) and Cyert-March (1963). They criticized the conventional models of the theory of the firm and rejected all their basic elements. Simon's concept of bounded rationality lies at the basis of this paradigm. According to these authors, a realistic theory of the firm should be based on the assumptions of individual and organizational limitations as to gathering and handling information. The main consequence is that actions take place in a context of incomplete knowledge of all the possible alternatives.

Information and goals are no longer reduced to simplified hypotheses, and become endogenous within the organization's dynamic decisional process. The only possible way to interpret reality is interpreting routine behaviour. Complex organizations (firms, first of all) retain knowledge by repeating "effective" behavioural acts. Information is gathered by means of a searching process (March 1991) and is adjusted to the individual and his/her history; the individual is replaced with a complex system including cybernetic mechanisms, which guarantee the stability of its structure.

12.3.2 The evolutionary approach

In the following years, behaviouristic theories have faced the issue of evolution, and models based on the theory of probabilities are developed following Alchian's example; the context is definitely Lamarckian: the firm's strategies aim at its own survival by adjusting to the environment. Nelson's and Winter's works[12] gave the major contribution in this field.

In Nelson's and Winter's evolutionary theory of the firm's behaviour, the concept of natural selection is applied to market conditions. The evolution, due to natural selection, is a kind of "organizational genetics", according to which every organization adopts survival strategies based on the individual selection of the information received from the surrounding environment.

In this case, as well, organizational, technological and economic knowledge is arranged in repetitive procedures, i.e. routines: rules emerging from the historical learning process (learning by doing). If an exogenous event changes a state of equilibrium, at least some firms will start modifying their routines, and the process of selection by competition will lead - through a sequence of phases that are analysed by means of Markov's stochastic processes - to a new state of market equilibrium.[13]

Nevertheless, the evolutionary theory has some problematic aspects, which were already present in the 1950's in Alchian's view. According to standard economics, economic change is not so relevant, since it is considered as the result of definitely exogenous forces, a "noise" upsetting the equilibrium and urging agents to adjust their parametric behaviour in terms of quantity or prices. On the contrary, in the evolutionary theory (Alchian 1950; Nelson-Winter 1982; Dosi-Nelson 1994; Nelson 1995) change is the fundamental element.

Every evolutionary theory, including those developed within economics, considers change as a regular and characteristic trait of social and natural systems. According to evolutionary economists, in particular, change consists in a process of alteration of an order (mutation), evolving into a new order by means of selection. Since this is considered as a continuous process, the result is an ever-evolving orderly gradation of states. Moreover, the analytical units, on which the interest of evolutionary economists is mainly focused, are likely to be the organizations. In other words, in order to understand such gradation of states, it is necessary to describe the evolution of organizations correctly. They are described as hierarchical structures, whose order is guaranteed by the dynamics of the routines used. Routines, in turn, consist in already

---

[12] Winter 1964, 1971, and 1975; Nelson and Winter 1982.

[13] By reading these statements, one can easily understand why Nelson and Winter are considered neo-Schumpeterian. One of their major merits is to have formalized the processes of destruction, innovation, and creations, which Schumpeter had pointed out.

experimented, codified and regularly used knowledge.[14] New routines are adopted (mutation) every time a stochastic shock takes place (Nelson-Winter 1982, pp. 36-38; Nelson 1987, p. 20).

This is a first relevant element, to which it is important to draw readers' attention: in evolutionary economics, the impulse (i) to change in organizations is due to exogenous stochastic shocks. In a situation of uncertainty, in particular, the process of industrial evolution is not deterministic, it shows a non-ergodic nature. The transition from a state *t* to a state *t*+1 depends on the conditions at time *t*, but also on the actions carried out to direct change towards one of the possible transition states.

Now we will try to understand what is the source (ii) of change in the evolutionary approach. It consists in the process of imperfect imitation, on which Alchian (1950) shed light for the first time and, more generally, in the individual and organizational learning process and problem-solving, carried out according to the criteria illustrated in the models of procedural rationality. These are the aspects (the analysis of individual and organizational learning, aimed at reaching results that might further corroborate the theory at a level of microfoundations) on which, for the last few years, a number of scholars have focused their attention (Holland-Holyoak-Nisbett-Thagard 1986; Goldberg 1989; Cohen 1991; Egidi 1992b; Egidi 1996).

Yet, if we try to give a contribution to the evolutionary approach, relevant difficulties emerge. One of them is the attempt to make evolutionary theory and the path-dependent approach coexist. In fact, in the presence of path-dependent processes, apparently economic change takes place in a different way, as compared to the assumptions of standard evolutionary economics.

Moreover, some major aspects of the evolutionary approach are ambiguous from a theoretical point of view or they are still unsolved problems. The first aspect concerns the assumed nature of economic change. As regards the second aspect, it will be the subject of the next section.

Why is the nature of economic change ambiguous in the evolutionary theory? The answer, in my opinion, is to be found in the fact that this theory makes use of biological analogies, which implies that:

(i) the market works like natural selection (Nelson - Winter 1982; Dosi-Nelson 1994).
(ii) the change/adjusting of routines is explained by describing genes' behaviour within DNA (Nelson-Winter 1982; Dosi-Nelson 1994; Nelson 1995).

The ambiguity is due to the assumption that change within organizations is the same as the in human body. Yet, as early as 1952, E. Penrose underlined

---

[14] In spite of its ambitions, such as that of developing dynamic analyses of economic phenomena in general, the evolutionary approach has given its most relevant contributions almost exclusively to the theory of the firm.

the presence of a sharp difference. Unlike genetic mutations, which are fortuitous, independent of human will, and have nothing to do with selection, the changes of routines arise from planned and conscious choices (Penrose 1952). Although Nelson and Winter accepted this criticism, they kept using biological analogies, considering them useful to explain the phenomenon of mutation and adjustment to the environment, which is generally considered valid also as regards firms.[15] Therefore, the ambiguity is still there.

In brief, the relevant points of Nelson and Winter's approach are the following: change is exogenous and arises from learning processes, which mostly occur through imperfect imitation; this theory is applied only in the context of industrial economics; dynamics processes are explained by means of mutation/selection mechanisms, directly drawn from biology.

Unlike the standard evolutionary approach, the considerations I propose here are based on the following preliminary hypotheses:

i) economic change has a mainly endogenous and strongly path-dependent nature (Antonelli 1995b);

ii) economic change is strictly connected to learning processes, in which unconscious mechanisms (tacit dimension) and conscious (intentional and interactive) mechanisms operate: these are more profound and extensive than the ones used in the standard approach;

iii) in spite of a few differences, economic change occurs on the basis of the same criteria and principles, both in the case of individuals, when they make choices, and in the case of organizations and institutions;

iv) any biological analogy is misleading, since its ambiguous assumptions "cage" the theory of change and limit its applicability to the theory of the firm;

v) instead of using biological analogies, it is necessary to base human behaviour on criteria that are consistent with cognitive psychology and contemporary neurobiology;

vi) finally, as a corollary of these hypotheses, I deem it useful to reconsider Nelson and Winter's concept of evolution by analyzing other evolutionary models.

---

[15] In 1950s, E. Penrose wrote a very interesting critical article on the use of biological analogies in economic theory. It stirred an immediate reaction by Alchian, who accepted such criticism only in part (Penrose 1952; Alchian 1953). The same happened in standard evolutionary economics: most of the remarks regarding the biological approach have been accepted (Dosi-Nelson 1994; Nelson 1995, p. 69), but others, which I consider relevant, have not been taken into consideration (see below). Also Schumpeter (1912; see also Schumpeter 1954, p. 789) had already criticized the use of biological analogies in economic theory.

12.3.3 Some unsolved problems in evolutionary economics

In my opinion, three unsolved problems are present in evolutionary economics; they regard: i) the causes of economic change, ii) the outcome of the evolutionary process, and iii) the reason why this theory is applied only in the context of the firm. We will now try to understand why these problems are still unsolved and why they should be considered relevant.

As regards the first problem, we know that, in Nelson and Winter's theory, firms are urged to change by an exogenous stochastic shock. Here the use of biological analogies is evident. Firms continuously face adjusting problems, just as organisms continuously face environmental mutations (Nelson-Winter 1982). Stochastic shocks arise from unpredictable environmental changes, and unpredictability is a relevant aspect of this analytical approach. If the environment did not change, firms would face the classical problem of optimization. But, as the environment does change, firms try to find a satisfactory level of adjustment.

Moreover, exogenous stochastic shocks and the causes of change themselves consist in the emergence of negative problematic situations, usually expressed by profit-share erosion. This theory does not explain possible adjustment, on the part of firms, to changes opening up new opportunities, without acting adversely on the old.[16] As this seems to me a relevant aspect, I will go back to it further on.

The second problem concerns the outcome of the selection-evolution process. Though in the evolutionary theory this outcome is not global maximization, in any case it seems to corroborate the cybernetic power of the market, since it "provides continuity of what survives the winnowing" (Nelson 1987, Nelson 1995). Unlike the evolutionary theories regarding the inorganic world, which usually take only change and order into account, several socio-biological evolutionary theories introduce the idea of progress and sometimes of perfectibility (Spencer 1857, Darwin 1859). The same happens with evolutionary economics. As early as the 1950s (Alchian 1950) the evolutionary approach described a process, whose outcome was likely to be maximization. Though later Winter (1964) showed that the outcome of an evolutionary process is not necessarily maximization, the idea that such process implies the passage from a worse to a better state is still widespread. Nevertheless, this approach is in contrast with other evolutionary theories used in economic theory, which avoid any finalist-teleological reference. These alternative theories only illustrate the mechanisms of change, whose outcome might be involution. Though this problem will be dealt with further

---

[16] E. Penrose (1952, p. 813) had shed light on the problem, by criticizing Alchian: "When changes in the environment opened up new opportunities without acting adversely on the old, then, on the assumptions of this analysis, firms would not respond at all to the new conditions since profits would already be positive and firms are assumed to be uninterested in increasing their profits."

on, it is important to underline now that the words evolution/progress or involution/regression have a high ideological content and should therefore be analysed from this point of view.

Let us now deal with the third problem: the theory of change did not go beyond the context of the firm. This aspect, too, is connected with the use of biological analogies. The inappropriate choice to explain how routines work as if they were genes, made the explanation easier but it also restricted the analysis of change and adjustment to an exogenous, uncontrollable and unconscious dimension, similar to genetic mutation. Apparently the difference between individuals and firms consists only in the fact that individuals' genes are rigid, while firms' routines are not (Nelson 1995). Nevertheless, if we take into consideration empirical evidence (especially in the neurobiological field) such difference between individuals and firms is not fully accounted for. As mentioned above, cognitive psychology and modern neurobiology show that change arises from processes that are part of individual learning processes (Gardner 1985; Patterson-Nawa 1993; Damasio 1995). Therefore, my methodological hypothesis is that the analysis should start from the above-mentioned learning processes. They seem to have a common source as regards both individuals and organizations (Rizzello 1996b).

12.3.4 The impulse to change

As regards the first problem, I think that the assumption that the causes of change are to be found only in stochastic shocks is too restrictive. In evolutionary economics, these shocks are induced by never-ending environmental changes, seen as the fuel of the evolutionary process. The role of the firm, therefore, consists only in carrying out procedures allowing it to adjust to such changes best. But, as I have already stated, there are approaches (and empirical corroboration), according to which change may also arise from non-problematic situations. Innovation, on the contrary, may be the result of continuous planning, inside firms, aimed at achieving leadership or simply at surviving.

Moreover, if organizations' endogenous dynamics are separated from exogenous environment - as, apparently, evolutionary theory does - it is not possible to say much about the process implemented by big firms in order to control and sometimes change environmental characteristics. This happens every time firms try to prevent and control the risks arising from stochastic shocks. In this second case, innovation seems to be the result of mainly endogenous, planned processes with a strong path-dependent nature (Antonelli 1995a; Antonelli 1997).

The major point of this approach is that one of the tasks of economic organizations is creating new needs (Momigliano 1975). This aspect changes the perspective of standard evolutionary theory radically: it can no longer be stated that individuals are adjusted to the environment; it is rather the environment that is adjusted to the individuals' needs, by means of deliberate and conscious choices. Change is due to the fact that organizations must keep creating reasons for their own existence, trying to be as influential as possible and, thus, to determine the future states of the world, so as to make it as favourable as possible for their development. Thus, the idea of a firm that is ready to adjust to the requirements of the demand in order to survive, loses its validity. Another hypothesis, on the contrary, gains ground: the supply is the result of an endogenous and path-dependent process, in which stochastic shocks play a less relevant role than what is credited to them in Nelson and Winter's models. The idea that innovation arises from path-dependent, endogenous processes and that its purpose is reducing the unpredictability of exogenous processes, moves along an opposite guideline, with reference to the idea that it is generated by stochastic shocks. Adjusting is, therefore, conceived as a continuous process, through which the environment and the internal structures of the firm are adjusted, in order to guarantee survival and control over the external world on the part of the firm. In fact, the reality shows that the rapid growth of a firm is not only due to a favourable change in the environment, or to peculiar, favourable environmental conditions; it is also due to the ability to remain in a specific condition or to direct it towards a certain target.

In conclusion, I would like to underline that the hypothesis I have put forward does not exclude Nelson and Winter's hypothesis. I believe that they are both valid. The fundamental idea is that it is very important to take these dynamics into account also, if we do not want to neglect a relevant part of our analysis.

I have mentioned two more aspects, which refer to the selection process, and to the fact that this theory is applied only in the field of industrial economics. This will be the subject of the next chapter. Let us now conclude this survey of the major theories of the firm.

12.3.5 The contractual approach: the team production function

In the 1970s, a few alternative theories were developed, in an effort to go beyond the dichotomy market/firm. These theories conceive the market as the fundamental organization, but they do take into due consideration the circumstance that specific subsystems are carried out more efficiently by firms (Alchian-Demsetz 1972; Jensen-Meckling 1976; Fama 1980; Holmstrom 1982).

The combined use of inputs in team production gives better results than the separated production of every single item. Formally this means that the firm uses a superadditive function of production: the combined use of inputs determines a higher level of production than the separate use of the same inputs. A consequence of superadditivity is that the effect of the variation of every single input cannot be separated from the variation of the output. Therefore, distinguishing the contribution of every single input becomes possible only by examining it carefully. Such control can be carried out only within organizations, since market does not own enough information to assess the contribution of every single input and to pay it according to the classical rules of productivity. Firms, instead, in order to use their resources efficiently, use the input until its cost, fixed on competitive markets, equals marginal productivity.

We have reached a paradox. On the one hand, team production is profitable, because it yields a surplus, as compared to separate production; on the other hand, it implies the risk of producing inefficiently, since the contribution of every single member is difficult to estimate. Without a control mechanism, someone may behave opportunistically (that is, he/she may work less). In this case he/she would enjoy all the advantages and would shift the disadvantages onto the other members. The structure of the incentives is thus characterized by a fundamental asymmetry and each member will find it advantageous to work a bit less (Alchian-Demsetz 1972). According to this analysis, in a self-managed firm, opportunistic tendencies prevail.[17]

In order to avoid this kind of opportunistic behaviour, someone must control individual productivity, being paid for that and receiving adequate incentives. According to this theory, the firm is divided into teams led by managers, whose task is arranging the inputs, fixing the wages, and controlling individual performance. The rule of marginal productivity still guarantees Pareto's optimum as to the efficiency within the firm, conceived as a particular kind of market. As long as the advantages of team production exceed the cost of control, it is convenient to enlarge the team, i.e. the firm.[18]

12.3.6 Williamson's synthesis

In 1975, Williamson makes an explicit attempt to integrate the main components of the contractual and the behaviouristic paradigms (Williamson 1975). According to him, the variety of organizations is due to the nature of organizations themselves. They are defined as a set of implicit and explicit contracts: in each situation, the most efficient organization prevails, that is, the one that is able to cut the transaction costs, arising from those contracts. Each *transaction* takes place when two or more agents exchange goods,

---

[17] Such risks have been reduced by means of the theory of moral hazard (Holmstrom 1982). If an individual takes out an insurance policy, he might be induced to be less cautious against accidents. To prevent this, insurance companies lower the cost of the next premiums for those who claim damages less frequently.

[18] Recently Demsetz (1988) has revised these statements, maintaining that "there is much more to the problem of economic organization than is plausibly subsumed under transaction and monitoring cost. Perhaps the transaction and monitoring approaches to the theory of the firm have confined our search too much. Firms would exist in a world in which transaction and monitoring costs are zero, although their organization might be considerably different" (Demsetz 1988, p. 154).

services, or information by means of a separate interface, that is, a "tool", which both contracting parts credit with such a role.[19]

Williamson observes that the efficiency of an organization depends on this management structure. The uncertainty of environmental factors, on the one hand, and opportunism and bounded rationality on the other, change the form of an organization. The problem, therefore, consists in carrying out transactions in such a way as to cut the costs due to bounded rationality, while safeguarding the firm against the risks of opportunism. According to this approach, markets and firms are the two major forms of transaction management, though a vast number of organizational structures exist between these two extremes (Richardson 1972).

12.4 Concluding remarks

This chapter contains a brief survey of the modern theory of the firm. Yet, the reader has certainly noticed that the contractualist theory (transaction costs), and the behaviouristic and evolutionary theories take up more space.[20] This happens because, among the manifold lines of research concerning the firm, these theories draw a particular attention, since they have developed the existing link between mental processes and organizations' nature, function and role.

These three theories start from observing the characteristics of human rationality and try to explain how organizations make up for the limitations of our minds. Moreover, in spite of remarkable differences, ·they all try to explain the workings of organizations by studying problem-solving processes through the development of routines.

---

[19] Each transaction consists of three elements: the object of the exchange, the parties taking part in the exchange, and the set of rules and acts making the exchange possible. This third element is also called Government structure or organizational structure of the transaction (Grillo-Silva 1989, p. 60).

[20] To cover this subject thoroughly, two more lines of research are to be mentioned: the one in which studies have been focused on the structural features of modern firms, referring particularly to the development of the capitalist system (Baran-Sweezy 1966; Galbraith 1967), and the one studying the growth and diversification processes of firms (Baumol 1959; Penrose 1959; Marris 1964).

13. Evolution, Organizations and Institutions

13.1 Introduction

Our analysis is drawing to an end, but there are still some open issues. We have seen that the source of change is to be found in the mechanisms of subjective perception, and that neurobiological and cognitive processes are, in turn, the humus from which the routines - used both in planned and unplanned decisions - emerge. Moreover, if we follow the teachings of neoinstitutionalism to the end, the emergence of rules becomes a crucial element, in order to understand organizational and institutional dynamics. Organizations are the fundamental context in which individuals play their social roles. Institutions are the framework within which such relations develop. Economic theory is now facing a double task: i) further studying the mechanisms by which individual behavioural rules are generated; ii) understanding what kind of relationship is created between organizations and institutions.

13.2 Institutions and organizations [1]

As mentioned above, institutions are the rules that give a structure to human interaction. They are established through formal (constitutions, laws, regulations) or informal (behavioural rules, conventions, conduct codes) constraints, and through the features of their enforcement, i.e. the series of procedures used to enforce them (North 1994, Schotter 1981; Horwitz 1993).

A set of rules can be considered an institution only if all the community members know them (Knight 1992; Uphoff 1993). Informal constraints play a major role, since they are the basis on which various informal institutions can be created. In other words, we can distinguish "material" institutions, which are spontaneous and informal, and "formal" institutions. The latter - after being made formal - support or replace the former, so as to improve their efficiency and guarantee their survival. As pointed out by North (1993), formal laws, in order to be effective, need to be supported by informal rules

---

[1] This section is a reviewed version of parts from the essay "Mente, organizzazioni e istituzioni (Mind, Organizations, and Institutions)" published in *Economia Politica*, n. 2, 1996.

or constraints, completing them and reducing their enforcement costs. North also points out that the problem of the evolution of informal laws is still open, since the comprehension of the evolution of rules is connected to the analysis of the relationship between formal rules and informal constraint.

Unlike institutions, organizations have no goals of their own; they are tools, created in order to reach goals that are compatible with the institutional context, The origin of the word organization is to be found in the Greek word "organon", meaning precisely instrument, means. Their being instrumental is the first, relevant difference between organizations and institutions. Institutions have a spontaneous origin, organizations are the result of a designing process.

This certainly is only a general definition, that does not describe the role of organizations completely. In fact, this is quite a complex phenomenon, concerning several disciplines. According to North (1990), institutions are the context within which organizations emerge. Yet, we must acknowledge that institutions need to be organizad - to a certain extent and at different levels - in order to work. Therefore, the difference is to be looked for between formal institutions and organizations, and, in my opinion, it can be found in the different fields of enforcement of the rules. Formal institutions are pervasive, their rules apply to all the members of a given society. On the contrary, the rules developed for the workings of organizations apply only to their own members and are subordinated to institutional rules. But, unlike institutions, organizations must be efficient since they compete on the market. This aspect is especially relevant if we want to understand how rules are developed within organizations. Within market constraints, and more generally within institutional constraints, each member's self-interest clashes with the others'. A mediation is then established: conflicts are settled by means of rules that undergo continuous processes of change, due to the dynamics of power.

These rules are - at least theoretically - more flexible as compared to institutional rules, since organizations must be ready to carry out innovating processes, in order to be competitive.

13.2.1 The features of institutions

As we have seen above, according to Hayek, institutions are necessary for two reasons: in order to simplify the context in which human rationality is exerted; so as to guarantee social order in the complex reality of an open society. The most recent literature starts from this assumption, to reach the conclusion that an institutional context is necessary in order to guarantee exchanges and economic processes in general. I am referring to Akerlof (1970), who, as mentioned above, thinks that institutions are created in order to guarantee exchanges, since the latter take place in a situation of asymmetrical information and may produce dishonesty. I am also referring to Arrow (1962) and Coase (1988b) and, more generally, to the whole literature on market failures and the necessity of institutions guaranteeing the workings of market itself. Also in these models, the origin of institutions is conceived as spontaneous, and it is linked to the problem of guaranteeing social order (taking into account, of course, all the already mentioned aspects connected with the transition from emergence to formalization). The connection I want to emphasize consists precisely in the emergence and function of institutions, with respect to the peculiar features of human behaviour, based on mental processes. According to Hayek, human mind and the theory of knowledge are at the basis of social processes and in particular of the economic ones. This concept helps him to explain market and competition realistically, and above all, to state that free individual behaviour produces a social order which is institutional order.[2]

13.2.2 The features of organizations

In the numerous works on the theory of the firm, the importance of studying hierarchical organizations for economic analysis is underlined. Starting from Coase, neoinstitutionalist analysis has often been in close contact with the various theories of the firm, which I have tried to outline above. I have also tried to point out the microfoundations of the emergence and function of hierarchical organizations. Marshall's and Simon's analyses showed the strict link existing between mind processes and organizations. Marshall underlined the analogy between the learning processes and the organizational efficiency of human mind; Simon emphasized the analogy between limits and potentiality of human mind and the structure of firms. Both of them shed light on the analogy between human problem-solving procedures and the organizational ones, between the processes of imitations and the emergence of new routines. Just like institutions, at the basis of the emergence and development of organizations we find neurobiological mechanisms.

The conclusion is that institutions and organizations are necessary and their common origin is to be found in mind processes. These are the two basic mechanisms on which the whole neoinstitutionalist approach is based. I think that Simon and Hayek dealt with these crucial problems with similar approaches, though from different points of view. They offer us sound solutions that converge on this new paradigm.

13.3 The emergence of rules: unplanned routines and decisions

From the analyses we have carried out so far, new perspectives have emerged regarding situations of uncertainty and cognitive incompleteness. These are the most interesting and the most often recurring situations. Both Hayek's ideas on the role of knowledge and on market, and Simon's ideas on the

---

[2] In fact, Hayek believes that market does not work outside a State. Hayek refers to a State, which has a monopoly of violence, coercion, and the defence of property rights, within which and only within which market can work (Hayek 1973; 1979; 1988b).

theory of the organization, imply a new approach to human behaviour within economic organizations. Economic agents' main problem is acquiring all the relevant knowledge by selecting information. The mechanisms concerning learning and problem-solving are the most interesting ones; they work by means of the processes of procedural rationality. Thus, while individuals' ability to formulate and solve problems is the core of microeconomic processes, the choice is nothing but the final act. From this point of view, it is necessary to draw the reader's attention to the important distinction - pointed out by Cyert, Simon and Trow (1956) - between planned decisions (routines) and unplanned decisions. They both concern economic action and refer both to individuals and organizations. When they act in a well-structured cognitive context, economic agents make their choices by following repetitive and already experienced criteria (routines). In any other circumstance, they face problems due to learning processes, problem-solving, procedural rationality, strategy and opportunism.

As regards planned decisions, the result of the most recent studies emphasize the fact that individuals do not seem to be able to make fully consistent choices (Kahneman-Tversky 1979, 1986). Today a new hypothesis is gaining ground: individual choices follow a regular pattern because, within economic organizations, the continuous interaction among individuals generates rules and procedures, and individuals follow them in their actions repetitively. These routines simplify the workings of human rationality, thus making it easy to take consistent decisions. The emergence of rules is connected to unplanned decisions. The process of acquisition of the knowledge necessary to solve problems (learning) is here crucial. The research into this aspect has been developing along three lines (recently also in Italy). The first line of research starts from the above-mentioned Newell and Simon studies on problem-solving;[3] the second one is connected with the models of neural nets; the last one is connected with the genetic algorithms developed by J. Holland (Holland-Holyoak-Nisbett-Thagard 1986; Holland-Miller 1991).[4]

---

[3] For a formalization of innovative behaviour with these methods, see Egidi 1992b.

[4] Marengo (1992) worked on the formalization of these models. In addition to these three main lines of research, at least another one must be mentioned: the research into the emergence of rules through the theory of games. Schotter (1981), for example, studies the emergence of rules in the traffic game and the telephone game. In the first game, two cars move towards a crossing at the same speed. Both drivers are in a hurry. One goes straight, the other one turns left. Only by means of an agreement between the drivers on who should pass first, can a situation of Pareto's optimum be reached. Within a pure market mechanism, where there are no rules and everybody pursues his/her own self-interest a crash is inevitable. In the telephone game two individuals are talking. If they are cut off, the best result can be reached only by means of an agreement on who should be calling back. If they both try to call back, they will not manage to talk to each other, since they both will find the line busy; the

The Economics of the Mind

With reference to the emergence of rules, in my opinion, the most relevant open problems are the following: i) the connection between social (or extracognitive) macrostructures; ii) the emergence of rules of cooperative or competitive behaviour.

The first problem concerns a very complex issue, which I have partly dealt with in Section 11.2.2, whose subject is institutional change. In next section, I will deal with other crucial aspects, concerning the concept of evolution, which are at the basis of institutional dynamics. Still, there are other elements, regarding the features of rules, that I want to mention here, though necessarily in brief.

One of the guidelines of this book is a sort of "laicization" of the concept of rule. Regardless of the context in which it has been analysed, this concept has been introduced free from the idea of "rule of pure reason". The rule has been here conceived as connected with human will, with human nature and its fallibility. What are the reasons inducing individuals to abide by the rules (be they tacit or formal)? I think that the answer may be summarized as follows. There are reasons concerning belonging, consideration, and approval. Abiding by common rules strengthens the individual awareness of belonging to a group, and it helps to consider oneself and to be considered as a member of that group. From this point of view a rule is an identifying tool, whether individual behaviour has a deontological or compensatory nature. But there is at least one more important reason, inducing individuals to abide by rules: I have already described it as the simplification of the context within which individual rationality is exerted. This is the instrumental dimension of the rule, linked to the identification of the relation individual-environment and to the attempt, on the part of individuals, to control and reduce environmental uncertainty. The second element is more relevant for economic theory, and not only because it can be extended from individuals to organizations. It is also important because it reveals a feature of the rules that is consistent both with individual rationality and with the macroeconomic role that recent neoinstitutionalist and neo-Austrian studies have attributed to rules. The fundamental element of this second feature can be found in the phenomenological concept of the relation between the individual and the outside world, which I have already dealt with in detail above. This element

---

same result will be achieved if none of them calls back for fear of finding the line busy.

With these examples, Schotter shows that rules and conventions limiting the pure principle of self-interest are necessary. Social conventions are defined as the regular behaviour, shared by all the members of a society, who behave in that specific way every time that specific situation recurs. The line of research dealing with the theory of games and institutions was started at the end of the 1970s by Ullman-Margalit (1977) and was followed by Schotter (1981 and 1990), Sugden (1986), who extended this approach to the analysis of law and the theory of welfare; and Walliser (1989) who mainly dealt with cooperative games.

implies a shift from the idea of the agent conceived as a "rule-follower" to that of a "rule-maker" and introduces a second open issue (ii).

It is my firm belief that the evolution of cooperative or competitive behaviour is to be studied by means of empirical tests, a method which has already yielded important results. I am referring to Axelrod's book (1984) mentioned above and to a few works on experimental economics. Yet, the most interesting contributions on the subject are probably being offered by the studies carried out by Cohen (1991), Cohen-Bacdayan (1991), and Egidi (1996). In brief, the question they try to find an answer to, is why some individuals tend to reach their own satisfaction by means of cooperation, while others by means of conflict. So far, it has emerged that the new routines, developed in problem-solving situations, have an open and incomplete nature. For this reason, cooperative behaviour - in the case of two individuals playing a game - allows the agents to offset the possible faults of the procedures they develop to solve a problem; they do so mutually and in a more effective way for both of them. Such procedures prove to be more effective than those developed in a situation of conflict between the agents (Egidi 1996).[5]

13.4 The evolution

Today, the natural course of the research in this field is heading towards the study of organizations, of their structure and evolution. By now, it seems inevitable to leave behind the simplified world of traditional economists. An individual, who is more and more real and limited in his/her cognitive abilities, but who uses his/her mind actively and creatively, is replacing *homo oeconomicus*. This individual behaves strategically; he/she is subject to environmental influences; he/she can also be an opportunist or an altruist. Above all, he/she acts and takes risks. Social interaction, in turn, is not due to a fortuitous mixture of a number of isolated individuals. In fact, it is at the same time organized and spontaneous.

At any rate, it is not possible to leave human mind out of consideration. As Marshall, Hayek and Simon taught us, mind is probably the most important element, if we want to understand both organizations and organic situations. As mentioned above, institutions are spontaneously established rules, within

---

[5] As underlined by Paolicchi (1991, p. 90), Piaget (1980) had already put forward the idea that in behaviour there are two primary invariants: organization and adjustment. An organism gets in touch with the world on the basis of its own schemes, through which it gathers and processes information, but also by means of its capability to modify those schemes on the basis of its relationship with the world and the feedback it receives, continuously researching and testing more complex, inclusive and balanced forms as adjusting. The behavioural rules emerging in Cohen's and in Egidi's experiments seem to complete Piaget's statement by adding the idea that cooperation strengthens and extends these capabilities.

which organizations operate. Organizations are the players (North 1992). The continuous interaction between institutions and organizations in a context characterized by scarcity and - consequently - by competition, is the key to institutional change. This element introduces our last subject. Is the dynamics of the relationship between organizations and institutions of a selective/evolutionary kind, like the dynamics used by Nelson and Winter, in their analysis of the firm? It is my firm belief that the correct answer is "No", and that Nelson and Winter's evolutionary theory should be integrated with Hayek's evolutionary theory.

13.4.1 The outcome of the selection process

The selection process in Nelson and Winter, in my opinion, presents itself as an ideological fallacy, consisting in the connection that seems to exist between evolution and progress. If we conceive selection as a process that somehow improves the state of the world, we fail to perceive the evident fact that evolution is neither a fact nor a theory, it is a way of organizing the knowledge of the world. The orderly arrangement of the successive stages of an evolutionary sequence involves a predetermined concept of order, a historically contingent idea of man. In the case of a deck of cards, given the equal probability of the different sequences, a heterogeneous distribution of 5 cards has exactly the same probability of a royal flush, and yet the appearance of the latter surprises us (and rewards us). The ideas about order are profoundly ideological and, consequently, the description of evolution as producer of order is necessarily ideological (Lewontin-Levins 1978, p. 999).

These considerations induce us to reconsider the process of evolution, outside an ideological dimension, in order to explain how it occurs, independently of its outcome. In order to reach this goal, it is necessary to refer to other evolutionary approaches, which I have only briefly mentioned above.

My formulation (derived from Hayek 1952a and 1963) rejects the idea that evolution always leads to a more desirable state (as in Spencer) or even to optimization (as in Alchian). It is coherent with the principles of procedural rationality, with cognitive psychology, with contemporary neurobiology, with path-dependent analyses, and with the neoinstitutionalist approach. Furthermore, it is built upon an idea of evolution which is neither positive nor negative in itself, but is based on a balance between ontogenesis and phylogenesis (see below). This approach takes into account random dynamics, as well as unitary evolution of the system, which does not coincide with the best of the possible worlds. It simply explains the mechanisms that lead to one of the possible words.

These results can only be reached by completely abandoning the use of misleading biological analogies in economic theory and by assuming, as typical characteristics of individual behaviour, the already mentioned psychological and neurobiological principles, which are also quite relevant in the explanation of the individual and organizational learning processes (Rizzello 1996b).

Most of the ideas I have mentioned here are the result of a second reading of Hayek, who has often been misunderstood on some important points. This is why it is important to point out two relevant aspects of his thought one more time: i) the methodological subjectivism and the processes of acquisition of knowledge; ii) the evolution of institutions and the acquisition of a spontaneous order. Here I will examine the second aspect, which allows us to deal with the above-mentioned problem of the reason why evolutionary theory remains confined to the context of industrial economics.

13.4.2 Evolution according to Hayek

Evolution is an important aspect in Hayek's theoretical approach. Yet, his idea of evolutionary processes differs significantly from Nelson and Winter's. Their approach - though with due caution - may be considered similar to Darwin's selection processes, while this is not possible for Hayek.

Let me outline the characteristic traits. They show several controversial aspects, which I would like to make clear.[6] A great deal of Hayek's theoretical efforts have been aimed towards two main goals: understanding the processes by which knowledge spreads in an economic system; the attempt to fully include the role of institutions in economic models. As mentioned above, the outcome of Hayek's thought is the abandonment of general economic equilibrium, which is replaced by a perspective of spontaneous order or catallaxis.

According to Hayek, the knowledge used by economic agents is the result of a process of endogenous development; in order to understand such development it is necessary to refer, first of all, to perception. This process, by means of which the mind is fed with perceptions, is mainly unconscious and affects two levels: the perceptive level itself, allowing us to attribute a meaning to new perceptions, by classifying stimuli; the level at which new stimuli settle on the existing patterns, partly modifying them. I think that this aspect should be emphasized: the role of previously acquired perceptions affects the perception of new stimuli remarkably. The process by which

---

[6] Recently, G. Hodgson (1993) has criticized Hayek. One of Hodgson's central ideas is that, though Hayek refers to a certain kind of philogenetic selective process, he does not go beyond an ontogenetic approach (pp. 152-53 and 161). Yet, this criticism cannot be accepted, if one remembers that Hayek underlines the importance and the role of experience in learning processes. As we shall better see below, Hayek keeps a certain balance between a philogenetic and an ontogenetic approach to change, which is not unsolved, as maintained by Hodgson (pp. 152 and 164). On the contrary, the balance is due to the fact that both approaches play a decisive role. Moreover, if one considers the importance of *The Sensory Order*, Hayek cannot be criticized (as Hodgson does) for not taking into account mental processes in his analysis (pp. 154-69). In fact, as we know, this is a central aspect in Hayek's theories.

knowledge is generated is thus the result of mainly unconscious mechanisms, the differentiated perceptions of identical external stimuli (due to the trifling or relevant differences in the previous experiences of each individual), and of conscious mechanisms, i.e. the ones by which an individual "builds" his knowledge on unconscious perceptions.

13.4.3 The role of learning

As recognized by standard evolutionary economics, learning is a crucial aspect for the understanding of economic processes (Nelson-Winter 1982). This branch of economics gives space especially to organizational learning, emphasizing the following dynamics. Learning is the most relevant aspect of the adjusting process and takes place through the readjustment of routines. The mechanism of imitation of the fittest keeps a prevailing role. The differences observed in reality are due to the process of imperfect imitation. For this reason, diversity is the source of creativity (Nelson 1987).

Let us try, however, to consider the extreme consequences of this mechanism. If we refer to the cognitivistic nature of learning processes, we cannot avoid seeing that at the basis of the motor of change there is not only imperfect imitation. Better stated, imperfect imitation is a "macro" aspect of a deeper mechanism. The true microfoundation of change can be found in imperfect perception, where imperfection is the outcome of individual peculiarities. This specification is not marginal. Imperfect perception cannot be plainly turned into imperfect imitation. The latter, in fact, is only compatible with adaptive learning processes, which refer mainly to organizations. Imperfect perception, instead, can be referred to both individual and organizational learning processes. Furthermore, it is generally compatible with traditional adaptive behaviour as well as with the behaviour that responds to the dynamics which try to reduce the unpredictability of the environment as much as possible.

Thanks to the acquisition of these micromechanisms, which are at the basis of the explanation of every context in which rationality is exerted, the idea of a common selection mechanism is emerging for individual, organizational and institutional processes of choice. If - as I believe - it is possible to demonstrate that individuals, organizations and institutions respond to the same evolutionary mechanism, though with differences, then the differentiation proposed by Nelson and Winter between individuals (stuck with their genes) and firms (not stuck with routines) vanishes. The consequences upon still open aspects of evolutionary economics are important. I shall come back to this concept in my conclusions. Before that, however, let me deal with selection a little further, making a comparison between the standard conception of Nelson and Winter and the standard conception of F. von Hayek.

13.4.4 A brief comparison between two different conceptions of evolution

As we have seen, evolution as conceived by Nelson and Winter is phylogenetic. The outcome of the selection process permits the survival of those who are able to adjust well to environmental mutations, while those who are unable to, will perish (Nelson-Winter, 1982). According to this model, it is the environmental stimuli which trigger off processes of mutations of routines within the firms, whose success depends on the ability and the readiness to restructure themselves. The *motus* is of an external-internal kind and is typical of organizations and not of individuals. In fact, the former must structure themselves in a way that allows them to be very elastic in responding to environmental stimuli, while the latter are far less elastic, since the genes are much more rigid.

In Hayek the approach is different. There is a better balance between ontogenesis and phylogenesis. On one side, the innatism of mental schemes plays an important role, but not in the sense that it sclerotizes the future individual development, as development of what is already potentially inside the individual at the moment when the genes are given their wealth of information. On the contrary, it is important because it stresses the prevailing dimension of individual diversity, that same diversity which is so important in more traditional evolutionary approaches such as Darwin's, and which has been taken up again and underlined also by Nelson.[7]

On the other side, one can stress the passage from the ontogenetic dimension to the phylogenetic one and to the interaction between the two. The role of mental schemes is relevant because they give a meaning to perceptions, but without perceptions they are useless. Knowledge is the outcome of the interaction between subjectivity and objectivity, between schemes and data. Moreover, every sensorial experience becomes sediment in the individual perceptive processes, that is, it modifies their schemes, and this further strengthens individual diversity. Therefore, in Hayek's opinion, the relationship agent-environment is primarily characterized by feedback (Hayek 1952a). Mental schemes perceive, organize, and give meaning to environmental stimuli. Even though they are ever-changing, through feedback they are gradually reduced to classes of stimuli and already experienced classes of responses, until they can be structured into a meaning. At this point one acts by making choices which may prove more or less successful, depending on the meaning given to the external stimuli. The direction of the

---

[7] The capitalistic driving-force allows the market to understand, ex post, which ideas are good and which are not (Nelson 1987, p. 120). Again, this is the idea of market as a cybernetic mechanism, somehow improving the system; I think that market does not necessarily play such a role. Market does select, but it does not always select good ideas eliminating the bad ones. Yet, the capitalistic driving-force has the advantage that the nature of its dynamics is continuously tested by its organizations, within which multiple and independent sources of initiative are present (ibid., p. 121).

motus, in this case, is of an internal-external-internal kind.

The differences are relevant. First of all the environment is not completely exogenous but it is the result of subjective interpretations; these interpretations, therefore, must play an important role in the analysis. Thus, the selection process is not tied to a completely external and impersonal mechanism. More precisely, in a sense this dimension continues to exist. The selection is carried out by the agents, who keep the routines which have proven efficient, as in the case of Nelson and Winter. Yet, whenever between the perception of external data and the efficiency of actions dyscrasiae intervene, which are not due to errors in perception but to very stringent environmental constraints, this may stir a drive towards environmental change. In fact, the environment may be conceived as an institutional environment, with its rules concerning selections, which are themselves subject to selection. The result is a heap in which individuals, organizations and institutions are mutually linked, by means of feedback, in processes of continuous adjustment.

In this case, we evidently move beyond the mere context of the firm, in which the traditional evolutionary theory is confined. Above all, it becomes possible to find a unique evolutionary principle that concerns the whole system, from individual to collective behaviour and to the role of organizations and institutions.

This means that the outcome of evolutionary processes does not necessarily (as in Spencer) lead to a better solution, compared to the previous state. The outcome is only one among the many possible outcomes. At times, it might also be an involution, due to an adverse mixture of distorted information and generation of erroneous knowledge. However, if - as I have already written - involution and evolution are ideological concepts, perhaps all that can be said is simply that evolution occurs because it occurs.

13.5 Concluding remarks

I believe that the results emergin in this chapter may be summed up as follows:

i) there is one single principle that can explain economic change in individual, organizational, and institutional processes;
ii) the criteria underlying evolutionary economics are extended, and a different principle of economic evolution is proposed, making no use of biological analogies.

As regards the first aspect, Hayek's approach to the theory of knowledge, I believe, makes sufficiently clear the endogenous and path-dependent nature of the individual processes of choosing. However, there is a very strong relationship between individuals and institutions. Institutions can be considered as common schemes of behaviour, which simplify the complexity of the world (they lower its level of entropy) and enable us to operate with a certain degree of predictability (though they do not allow us to predict the single individual action perfectly, because of the peculiarities of individual behaviour). Institutions standardize the world; each individual acts inside the world and within its limits, which ensure order and a certain regularity through simplification.

As concerns organizations, if we accept the idea that organizational learning has much in common with individual learning, then we can conclude that between the three dimensions that are typical of the heterodox approach (individuals, organizations and institutions) the following relationship may be established. Organizations, spurred by competition, in a context of uncertainty, continuously invest in knowledge and skills, in an effort to respond to environmental problems in the most efficient way, or in an effort to control and determine the environment. These choices, as well as the structure of organizations, are always affected by the institutional environment.

Moreover, as Bianchi (1995) pointed out, firms and markets never stop creating new knowledge, since they arrange learning. This statement is consistent with all the microeconomic principles I have dealt with in this book and show, one more time, the link between learning processes, the role of organizations and the nature of institutions. Therefore, in the case of the traditional environmental variations, Nelson and Winter's theory remains valid. Yet, by removing the use of biological analogies, it is possible to account for the processes of change that do not depend on stochastic shocks and to extend coherently the processes of change also to the individual and institutional context.

This result may be reached by disclosing another aspect, which, in my opinion, remains ambiguous: standard evolutionary economics is not immediately coherent with path-dependency. While the former considers change as a mainly exogenous phenomenon, the latter sees it as an endogenous phenomenon. Since the microfoundations of human behaviour seem to confirm the second interpretation, I think that the adaptation of standard evolutionary economics to the theoretical framework of path-dependent models strengthens and extends it.

There is one last aspect to consider. The definitive abandonment of biological analogies, implies the need for a new evolutionary principle, different from Darwin's view. The idea of evolution derived from Hayek, allows us to state that evolution does not necessarily coincide with continuity, order, or a better state than the preceding one. The outcome is left undefined. The most relevant idea is that the source of change is a part of human nature, which is at the same time individual and holistic. For this reason, the onto-phylogenetic balance between mental schemes and institutions emerges as the foundation of social order.

As a conclusion of this picture of the unorthodox literature, I would like to point out what I consider the most relevant result I have achieved. The foundations of human behaviour are inside our minds. Understanding the dynamics of the processes of choice and decision means coherently accepting what neurobiology and psychology teach us and being able to introduce such processes into the organizational and institutional context where they take place. But there are preconditions ensuring the development of human creativity, which - as I have stated - is the basis of any evolutionary process. These preconditions are individual freedom and diversity. In fact, as maintained especially by Hayek and Marshall, only a free spirit and a free mind can reorganize external stimuli creatively, thus generating the new procedures that are at the basis of individual and social progress. And as maintained especially by Coase, Simon, and Williamson, economic theory cannot leave reality out of consideration; in the reality individuals are not isolated, but they are organized in a complex net of relations, governed by explicit and tacit rules.

In this book I have advised economists to take a step leading them beyond a legitimate attachment for their scientific tradition and to tolerate the idea that alternative and equally valid approaches to the analysis of these problems may exist. By doing so, I hope I have found a few tesserae of the complex mosaic of the analysis of the economics of complexity, creativity, and uncertainty, i.e. of the economics of the mind.

References

Akerlof, G. A. (1970), "The Market For 'Lemons': Quality, Uncertainty and the Market Mechanism", *Quarterly Journal of Economics,* 84, 488-500.

Akerlof, G. A. and W. T. Dickens (1982), "The Economic Consequences of Cognitive Dissonance", *American Economic Review,* LXXII, 307-319.

Alchian, A. A. (1950), "Uncertainty, Evolution and Economic Theory", *Journal of Political Economy,* 58, 211-221.

Alchian, A. A. (1953), "Biological Analogies in the Theory of the Firm: Comment", *American Economic Review,* 43 (4), 600-603.

Alchian, A. A. and H. Demsetz (1972), "Production, Information Costs and Economic Organization", *American Economic Review,* 62, 777-795.

Aleksander, I. and H. Morton (1990), *An Introduction to Neural Computing,* London: Chapman and Hall.

Allais, M. (1952), "Le comportament de l'homme rationnel devant le risque: Critique des postulats de l'école Américaine", *Econometrica,* 21, pp. 503-46.

Allen, R. (1990), *Polanyi,* London: The Claridge Press.

Alter, M. (1990), *Carl Menger and the Origins of the Austrian Economics,* Boulder: Westview Press.

Amendola, M. (ed.) (1990), *Innovazione e progresso tecnico,* Bologna: Il Mulino.

Anderson J. and E. Rosenfeld (1988), *Neurocomputing. Foundations of Research,* Cambridge (Ma.): MIT Press.

Anderson, P., K J Arrow and Pines D. (eds.) (1988), *The Economy as an Evolving Complex System,* Reading (Ma.): Addison-Wesley Publishing Company.

Anokhin, P. K. (1974), *Biology and Neurophisiology of the Conditioned Reflex and its Role in Adaptive Behavior,* Oxford: Pergamon. Or. Ed. (1968).

Antonelli, C. (ed.) (1988), *New Information Technology and Industrial Change: the Italian Case,* Dordrecht - Boston - London: Kluwer Academic Publishers.

Antonelli, C. (1995a), *The Economics of Localized Technological Change and Industrial Dynamics,* Dordrecht - Boston - London: Kluwer Academic Publishers.

Antonelli, C. (1995b), "Dynamic Structuralism and Path-Dependence", *Revue d'Economie Industrielle*, 73, 65 - 90.

Antonides, G. (1991), *Psychology in Economics and Business. An Introduction to Economic Psychology*, Dordrecht-Boston-London: Kluwer Academic Publishers.

Aoki, M. (1984), *The Co-operative Game Theory of the Firm*, Oxford: Oxford University Press.

Arrow, K. J. (1962), *Economic Welfare and the Allocation of Resources for Invention*, in *NBER The Rate and Direction of Incentive Activity: Economic and Social Factors*, Princeton: Princeton University Press.

Arrow, K. J. (1969), *The Organizations of Economic Activity: Issues Pertinent to the Choice of Market versus Nonmarket Allocation, The Analysis and Evaluation of Public Expenditure: The PPB System.* Vol. 1, U. S. Joint Economic Committee, 91st Congress, 1st session, Washington: Government Printing Office, 50-73.

Arrow K. J. (1971), "The Firm in General Equilibrium Theory", in Marris and Wood (eds.) (1971).

Arrow, K. J. (1972), "Exposition of the Theory of Choice under Uncertainty", in McGuire and Radner (eds.)(1986).

Arrow, K. J. (1974), *The Limits of Organization*, New York: Norton.

Arrow, K. J. (1983), *Collected Papers of Kenneth J. Arrow,* vol. II, Cambridge (Ma.): Harvard University Press.

Arrow, K. J. (1984), "The Economics of Agency", in Zeckhauser and Pratt (eds.) (1984).

Arrow, K. J. (1994), "Methodological Individualism and Social Knowledge", *American Economic Review*, 84 (2), 1-9.

Arrow, K. J. and G Debreu (1954), "Existence of an Equilibrium for a Competitive Economics", *Econometrica*, 22, 265-290.

Arrow, K. J. et al. (eds.) (1996*), The Rational Foundations of Economic Behaviour*, London: Macmillan.

Arthur, W. B. (1988), "Self-Reinforcing Mechanism in Economics", in Anderson, Arrow and Pines (eds.) (1988).

Arthur, W. B. (1989), "Competing Technologies, Increasing Returns, and Lock-in by Historical Events", *Economic Journal*, 99, 116-131.

Ashby, W. R. (1960), *Design for a Brain: the Origin of Adaptive Behavior,* London: Chapman and Hall.

Aspray, W. (1985), "The Scientific Conceptualization of Information: A Survey", *Annals of the History of Computing*, 7 (2), 117-140.

Atkinson, R. C. and R.M. Shiffrin (1968), "Human Memory: A Proposed System and its Control Processes", in K. W. Spence and J. W. Spence (eds.) (1968), II, pp. 89-195.

Axelrod, R. (1984), *The Evolution of Cooperation*, New York: Basic Books.

Axelrod R. and W. D. Hamilton (1981), "The Evolution of Cooperation", *Science,* 211, 1390-1396.

Babbage, C. (1832), *On the Economy of Machinery and Manifactures,* III ed., London, Charles Knight.

Baran, P. and P. Sweezy (1966), *Monopoly Capital,* New York: Monthly Review Press.

Barnard, C. I. (1938), *The Functions of the Executive,* Cambridge: Harvard University Press.

Barry, N. (1979), *Hayek's Social and Economic Philosophy,* London: Macmillan.

Bartlett, F. C. (1932), *Remembering,* Cambridge (Ma): Cambridge University Press.

Baumol, W. (1967), *Business Behaviour, Value and Growth,* New York: Harcourt.

Becattini, G. (1990), *Il pensiero economico: temi, problemi e scuole,* vol. III, Torino: UTET.

Becattini, G. and Vaccà S. (eds.) (1994), *Prospettive degli studi di economia e politica industriale in Italia,* Milano: F. Angeli.

Becker, G. S. (1962), "Irrational Behavior and Economic Theory", *Journal of Political Economy,* 70, 1-13.

Beltratti, A., S. Margarita and P. Terna (1996), *Neural Network for Economic Financial Modelling,* London: ITCP.

Berns, G.S. and T.J. Sejnowskj (1995), *How the Basal Ganglia Make Decisions,* in Damasio, Damasio and Christen (eds.)(1995).

Bianchi, M. (1995), "Markets and Firms Transaction Costs versus Strategic Innovation", *Journal of Economic Behavior and Organization,* 28, 183-202.

Birner J. and R. van Zijp (eds.) (1993), *Hayek, Co-ordination and Evolution: his Legacy in Philosophy, Politics, Economics, and the History of Ideas,* London: Routledge.

Boettke, J. (ed.) (1994), *The Elgar Companion to Austrian Economics,* Aldershot: Edward Elgar.

Bombi, A. S. (ed.) (1991), *Economia e processi di conoscenza,* Torino, Loescher.

Boring, E. (1933), *The Physical Dimension of Consciousness,* London,: The Century Co.

Brehm, J. W. and A. R. Cohen (1962), *Explorations in Cognitive Dissonance,* New York: Wiley & Sons.

Broadbent, D. E. (1954), "A Mechanical Model of Human Attention and Immediate Memory", *Psychological Review,* 64-205.

Broadbent, D. E. (1958), *Perception and Communication,* London: Pergamon.

Brosio, G. (ed.) (1989), *La teoria economica dell'organizzazione*, Bologna: Il Mulino.

Brosio, G. (1995), *Introduzione all'economia dell'organizzazione*, Roma, Nuova Italia Scientifica

Buchanan, J. and V. Vanberg (1991), "The Market as a Creative Process", *Economics and Philosophy*, 7, 167-186.

Burczak, T. A. (1994), The Postmodern Moments of F. A. Hayek's Economics, *Economics and Philosophy*, 10, pp. 31-58.

Cagliozzi, R. (1990), *Oggettività e intenzione nell'analisi economica*, Napoli: Liguori Editore.

Calabrò, G. (1980), *Ragione*, in *Enciclopedia*, vol. XI, Torino: Einaudi.

Caldwell, B. J. (1988), *"Hayek's Transformation"*, *History of Political Economy*, 20, (4), 513-541.

Calissano, P. (1992), *Neuroni, mente ed evoluzione*, Milano: Garzanti.

Camagni, R., R. Cappellin and G. Garolfi (eds.) (1984), *Cambiamento tecnologico e diffusione territoriale*, Milano: F. Angeli.

Cammarata, S. (1990), *Reti neurali. Una introduzione all'"altra" intelligenza artificiale*, Milano: Etas.

Campanella, M. (ed.) (1988), *Between Rationality and Cognition*, Torino: A. Meyner.

Castellan, N. J., D. B. Pisoni and G. R Potts (eds.) (1977), *Cognitive Theory*, vol. II, Hillsdale, Lawrence Erlbaum Associates.

Chamberlin, I. E. (1948), "An Experimental Imperfect Market", *Journal of Political Economy*, 56, 95-108.

Chapanis, N. P. and A. Chapanis (1964), "Cognitive Dissonance: Five Years Late", *Psychological Bulletin*, vol 64, 1-22.

Civita, A. (1993), *Saggio sul Cervello e sulla Mente*, Milano: Guerini Associati.

Coase, R. (1937), The Nature of the Firm, *Economica*, n. s. IV, 386-405.

Coase, R. (1960), The Problem of the Social Cost, *Journal of Law and Economics*, 3, 1-44.

Coase, R. (1988a), "Lectures on: The Nature of the Firm", *Journal of Law, Economics, & Organization*, 4, 3-47.

Coase, R. (1988b), *The Firm, the Market and the Law*, Chicago: University of Chicago Press.

Cofer, C. (ed.) (1969), *The Structure of Human Memory*, S. Francisco: Freeman.

Cohen, M. D. (1991), "Individual Learning and Organizational Routines: Emerging Connections", *Organization Science*, 2 (1), 135-139.

Cohen, M. D. and P. Bacdayan (1991), *Organizational Routines are Stored as Procedural Memory: Evidence from a Laboratory Study*, University of Michigan, mimeo.

Commons, J. R. (1934), *Institutional Economics*, Madison: University of Wisconsin Press.

Conte, R. (ed.) (1991), *La norma. Mente e regolazione sociale*, Roma: Editori Riuniti.

Cooper ,W. W., H. Leavitt, M. W. Shelly and F. J. Wiley (eds.) (1964), *New Perspectives in Organization Research*, New York: Wiley.

Cubeddu, R. (1986), "Dal 'Metodo compositivo' all'Individualismo metodologico'. Naturalità, oggettivismo e spontaneità nel concetto di "ordine politico" di C. Menger, L. von Mises, F. von Hayek", *Quaderni di Storia dell'Economia Politica*, IV (3), 25-31.

Cubeddu, R. (1993), *The Philosophy of the Austrian School*, London: Routledge.

Cubeddu, R. (1996), *Tra scuola austriaca e Popper*, Napoli: ESI.

Cunningham, R. L. (ed.) (1979), *Liberty and Rule of Law*, College Station (Texas): Texas A. & M. University Press.

Cyert, R. M. and J. G. March (1963), *A Behavioral Theory of the Firm*, Englewood Cliffs (N. J.): Prentice-Hall.

Cyert, R. M. and J. G. March (1964), *The Behavioral Theory of the Firm: a Behavioral Science*, in Cooper, Leavitt, Shelly and Wiley (eds.) (1964).

Cyert, R. M., H. A Simon and D. B. Trow (1956), "Observation of a Business Decision", *Journal of Business*, 29, 237-248.

Dahl, R. A. and C. E. Lindblom (1953), *Politics, Economics, and Welfare*, New York: Harper.

Damasio, A. R. (1995), *Descartes' Error. Emotion, Reason and the Human Brain*, London: Picador.

Damasio, A. R., H. Damasio and Y. Christen (eds.)(1995), *The Neurobiology of Decision Making*, Berlin - New York: Springer Verlag.

Darwin, C. (1859), *On the Origin of Species by Means of Natural Selection*, London: Murray.

David, P. (1985), "Clio and the Economics of QWERTY", *American Economic Review*, 75, 332-337.

David, P. (1988),"Path-dependence: Putting the Past into the Future of Economics", *Technical Report N. 553. The Economic Series. Institute for Mathematical Studies in the Social Sciences*, Stanford: Stanford University Press.

Day, R. and Groves T. (eds.) (1975), *Adaptive Economic Models*, New York: Academic Press.

Deaton A. and J. Muellbauer (1980), *Economics and Consumer Behaviour*, Cambridge: Cambridge University Press.

De Finetti, B. (1974), *The Theory of Probability*, London: Wiley.

Demaria, G. (1962), *Trattato di logica economica*, vol. I, Padova: Cedam.

Demsetz, H. (1988), "The Theory of the Firm Revisited", *Journal of Law, Economics and Organization*, 4 (1), 141-162.

De Vecchi, N. (1986a), "Da Menger ai viennesi. Il rapporto tra individuo e istituzioni nella spiegazione del processo capitalistico", *Quaderni di Storia dell'Economia Politica*, IV (3), 5 - 22.

De Vecchi N. (1986b), "La scuola viennese di· economia", in Becattini (1990).

De Vries, R. P. (1993), "The Place of Hayek's Theory of Mind and Perception in the History of Philosophy and Psychology", in Birner - van Zijp (eds.) (1993).

Dewey, J. (1933), *How We Think*, Boston: Heath.

Dewey, J. (1946), *Problems of Men*. reprint. (1958), *Philosophy of education*, Paterson (N. J.): Littlefield Adams.

Dewey, J. and A. F. Bentley (1949), *Knowing and the Known*, Boston: Beacon Press.

Diamond, A. M. Jr. (1980), "F. A. Hayek on Constructivism and Ethics", *Journal of Libertarian Studies*, 4, 353 - 665.

Doise, W. and G. Mugny (1981), *Le développement social de l'intelligence*, Paris: Inter Editions.

Donzelli, F. (1986), *Il concetto di equilibrio nella teoria economica neoclassica*, Roma: La Nuova Italia Scientifica.

Donzelli, F. (1988), "Introduzione" to Hayek (1988b).

Dosi, G. (1988), "Sources Procedures and Microeconomic Effects of Innovation", *Journal of Economic Literature*, 26, pp. 1120-1171.

Dosi, G. and M. Egidi (1988), "A Bounded Rationality Approach to Uncertainty and Innovation", in Campanella (ed.)(1988).

Dosi, G. and M. Egidi (1991), "Substantive and Procedural Uncertainty. An Exploration of Economic Behaviours in Changing Environments", *Journal of Evolutionary Economics*, 1, 145-168.

Dosi, G. and Y. Kaniovski (1994), "On "badly behaved" Dynamics. Some Application of Generalized Urn Schemes to Technological and Economic Change", *Journal of Evolutionary Economics*, 4, 93-123.

Dosi, G. and Nelson R. (1994), "An Introduction to Evolutionary Theories in Economics", *Journal of Evolutionary Economics*, n. 4 (3), pp. 153-72.

Douglas, M. (1990), *The Scottish Contribution to Modern Economic Thought*, Aberdeen: Aberdeen University Press.

Dow, S. (1987), "The Scottish Political Economy Tradition", *Scottish Journal of Political Economy*, 34 (4), 335-48.

Droz, R. (1977), Apprendimento, in *Enciclopedia*, vol. I, Torino, Einaudi.

Droz, R. (1978), *Cognizione*, in *Enciclopedia*, vol. III, Torino, Einaudi.

Duesenberry, J. S. (1949), *Income, Saving and the Theory of Consumer Behavior*, Cambridge (Mass.): Harvard University Press.

Dufourt, D. and P. Garrouste (1993), "Criteria of Scientificity and Methodology of the Social Sciences: Menger, Mises and Hayek", in Herbert (ed.) (1993).

Dunker, K. (1945), "On Problem Solving", *Psychological Monographs*, 58-65.

Earl, P. E. (1983), *The Economic Imagination. Towards a Behavioural Analysis of Choice*, New York: M. E. Sharpe Armonk.

Eatwell, J., M. Milgate and P. Newman (eds.) (1987), *The New Palgrave. A Dictionary of Economics*, Voll. I-IV, London: Macmillan.

Egidi, M. (1981), *Schumpeter: lo sviluppo come trasformazione morfologica*, Milano: Etas Libri.

Egidi, M. (1989a), "Note su: causalità, prevedibilità, incertezza", *Quaderni di Storia dell'Economia Politica*, V/1987/3 - VI/1988/1, 77 - 101.

Egidi, M. (1989b), "L'impresa come organizzazione e la funzione di produzione, un binomio impossibile", in Zamagni (ed.)(1989).

Egidi, M. (1991), *Innovazione, tecnologia ed organizzazione come attività di Problem Solving*, in Egidi, Lombardi and Tamborini (eds.)(1991).

Egidi, M. (1992a), *Dalla razionalità all'apprendimento organizzativo: l'analisi del comportamento umano nelle organizzazioni economiche*, Università di Trento, Dipartimento di Economia, mimeo.

Egidi, M. (1992b), "Organizational Learning and the Division of Labour", in Egidi and Marris (ed.) (1992).

Egidi, M. (1996), *Routines, Hierarchies of Problems, Procedural Behaviour: Some Evidence from Experiments*, in Arrow et al. (eds.) (1996).

Egidi, M., M. Lombardi and R. Tamborini (1991), *Conoscenza, incertezza e decisioni economiche. Problemi e ipotesi di ricerca*, Milano: F. Angeli.

Egidi, M. and R. Marris (eds.) (1992), *Economics, Bounded Rationality and the Cognitive Revolution*, Aldershot: Edward Elgar.

Enke, S. (1951), "On Maximizing Profits: a Distinction between Chamberlin and Robinson", *American Economic Review*, XLI (4), 566-578.

Fabbri, G. and R. Orsini (1991), "Una rete neurale per studiare l'avversione al rischio", *Giornale degli economisti e annali di economia*, 50 (3-4), 163-177.

Fabbri, G. and R. Orsini (1993), *Reti Neurali per le Scienze Economiche*, Padova: Muzzio.

Fama, E. (1980), Agency Problems and the Theory of the Firm, *Journal of Political Economy*, 88(2), pp. 288- 307.

Feiwel, J. R. (ed.) (1985), *Issues in Contemporary Macroeconomics and Distribution*, New York: Macmillan.

Ferry, J. (1990), *Friedrich A. Hayek: les élémentes d'un liberalisme radical*, Nancy: Presses Universitaires de Nancy.

Festinger, L. (1957), *A Theory of Cognitive Dissonance*, Stanford: Stanford University Press.

Filippi, F. (1985), "Introduzione" to Simon (1985).

Fishburn, P. C. (1983), "Transitive Measurable Utility", *Journal of Economic Theory*, 31, 293-317.

Foster, J. (1991), "The Institutionalist (Evolutionary) School", in Mair and Miller (1991).

Friedman, M. (1953), *Essays in Positive Economics*, Chicago: The University Press.

Frowen, S. F. (ed.) (1990), *Unknowledge and Choice in Economics*, Basingstoke: Macmillan.

Galbraith, J. (1967), *The New Industrial State*, London: H. Hamilton.

Gallant, S.I. (1993), *Neural Network Learning and Experts System*, Cambridge: MIT Press.

Gallino, L. (1984), *Mente, comportamento e intelligenza aritificiale*, Milano: Edizioni di Comunità.

Gardner, H. (1985), *The Mind's New Science*, New York: Basic Books.

Garofalo, G. (1990), *Equilibrio Razionalità Causalità. Ricerche sui fondamenti della teoria economica*, Milano: F. Angeli.

Gee, J. M. A. (1991), "The Neoclassical School", in Mair and Miller (eds.) (1991), 71-108.

Giddens, A. (1982), *Profiles and Critiques in Social Theory*, London: Macmillan.

Gissurarson, H. H. (1987), *Hayek's Conservative Liberalisme*, New York: Garland.

Giva, D. (1985), "Economia, razionalità e scienza dell'artificiale: Herbert Simon", *Quaderni di Storia dell'Economia Politica*, III (3), 159 - 213.

Goldberg, D. E. (1989), *Genetic Algorithms in Search, Optimization and Machine Learning*, Reading (MA.): Addison-Wesley.

Goulg, J. and Kolb L. (eds.) (1964), *A Dictionary of the Social Sciences*, New York: The Free Press.

Grassl, W. and B. Smith (eds.) (1986), *Austrian Economics Historical and Philosophical Background*, London - Sidney: Croom Helm.

Gray, J. (1980), "F. A. Hayek on Liberty and Tradition", *Journal of Libertarian Studies*, 4, 119 -37.

Gray, J. (1983), *Hayek*, "The Salisbury Review. A Quarterly Magazine of Conservative Thought", vol 1, n. 4; in Scruton (ed.) (1988).

Gray, J. (1988), "Hayek, the Scottish School, and Contemporary Economics", in Winston and Teichgraeber (eds.) (1988).

Gray, J. (1990), *Hayek, the Scottish School, and Contemporary Economics*, in Douglas (1990).

Gray, J. (1994),"Hayek's Scientific Subjectivism?", *Economics and Philosophy*, 10, 305-313.

Greenberger, M. (1971), *Computers, Communications, and the Public Interest*, Baltimore: J. Hopkins Press.

Greenwald, B. and J. Stiglitz (1986), "Externalities in Economies with Imperfect Information and Incomplete Market", *Quarterly Journal of Economics*, pp. 229-264.

Gregg, L. W. (ed.) (1974), *Knowledge and Cognition*, Potomac: Lawrence Erlbaum Associates.

Gregory, R. L. (1987), *The Oxford Companion to the Mind*, Oxford: Oxford University Press.

Grillo M. and F. Silva (1989), *Impresa, concorrenza e organizzazione*, Roma: Nuova Italia Scientifica.

Groenewegen J., C. Pitelis and S. E: Sjostrand (1995), *On the Theory of Institutions and Institutional Change*, Aldershot: E. Elgar.

Grunert, K. G. and F. Olander (eds.) (1989), *Understanding Economic Behavior*, Boston: Kluwer.

Haley, B. F. (ed.)(1952), *A Survey of Contemporary Economics*, II, Homewood: Rd Irwin.

Harris, M. and A. Raviv (1978), "Some Results on Incentive Contracts with Application to Education and Employment, Health Insurance and Law Enforcement", *American Economic Review*, 68 (1), 20-30.

Haugeland, J. (1981), *Mind, Design: Philosophy, Psychology, Artificial Intelligence*, Cambridge (MA): MIT Press.

Hayek, F. A. (1934), "Carl Menger", *Economica*, n.s. IV, 1, 393-420.

Hayek, F. A. (1937), "Economics and Knowledge", *Economica*, n.s. IV, n. 13, 96-105.

Hayek, F. A. (1942), "Scientism and the Study of Society", *Economica*, n.s. IX, 35, 267-291.

Hayek, F. A. (1945), "The Use of Knowledge in Society", *American Economic Review*, 35 (4), 519-530.

Hayek, F. A. (1946), "The Meaning of Competition", in Hayek (1949), Chapter 5.

Hayek, F. A. (1949), *Individualism and Economic Order*, London: Routledge & Sons.

Hayek, F. A. (1952a), *The Sensory Order. An Inquiry into the Foundations of Theoretical Psychology*, London : Routledge & Kegan Paul.

Hayek, F. A. (1952b), *The Counter-Revolution of Science: Studies on the Abuse of Reason*, Glencoe: The Free Press.

Hayek, F. A.(1958), "The Austrian School", in *International Encyclopaedia of the Social Sciences*, vol. 10, 458-462, Sills D. (ed.), New York: The Free Press.

Hayek, F. A. (1960), *The Constitution of Liberty*, London: Routledge & Kegan Paul.

Hayek, F. A. (1963), "Rules, Perception and Intelligibility", *Proceedings of the British Academy*, XLVIII, 321-344.

Hayek, F. A. (1967a), *Studies in Philosophy, Politics and Economics*, London: Routledge & Kegan Paul.

Hayek, F. A. (1967b), "The Results of Human Action but not of Human Design", in Hayek (1967a).

Hayek, F. A. (1968), "Competition as a Discovery Procedure", in Hayek (1978), Chapter 12.

Hayek, F. A. (1973), *Law, Legislation and Liberty. A New Statement of the Liberal Principles of Justice and Political Economy*, vol I, *Rules and Order*, London: Routledge & Kegan Paul.

Hayek, F. A. (1976), *Law, Legislation and Liberty. A New Statement of the Liberal Principles of Justice and Political Economy*, vol II, *The Mirage of Social Justice*, London: Routledge & Kegan Paul.

Hayek, F. A. (1978), *New Studies in Philosophy, Politics and the History of Ideas*, London: Routledge & Kegan Paul.

Hayek, F. A. (1979), *Law, Legislation and Liberty. A New Statement of the Liberal Principles of Justice and Political Economy*, vol III, *The Political Order of a Free People* London: Routledge & Kegan Paul.

Hayek, F. A. (1983), *Knowledge, Evolution and Society*, London: Adam Smith Institute.

Hayek, F. A. (1988a), *The Fatal Conceit. The Errors of Socialism*, London: Routledge.

Hayek, F. A. (1988b), *Conoscenza, mercato, pianificazione*, Bologna: Il Mulino.

Hayek, F. A. (1994), *Hayek on Hayek. An Autobiographical Dialogue*, London: Routledge.

Hayes, J. R. and H. A. Simon (1974), *Understanding Written Problem Instructions*, in Gregg, L. W. (ed.) (1974).

Hayes, J. R. and H.A. Simon (1976a), *Understanding Complex Task Instructions*, in Klahr, D. (ed.) (1976).

Hayes, J. R. and H.A. Simon (1976b), "The Understanding Process: Problem Isomorphs", *Cognitive Psychology*, 8, 165-190.

Hayes, J. R. and H.A. Simon (1977), *Psychological Differences among Problem Isomorphs*, in Castellan, Pisoni and Potts (eds.) (1977), vol. II.

Hayes, S. P. (1950), "Some Psychological Problems of Economics", *Psychological Bulletin*, 47, 289-330.

Herbert, R. F. (ed.)(1993), *Perspectives on the History of Economic Thought*, vol. IX, Aldershot: Edward Elgar.

Hey, J. D. (1991), *Experiments in Economics,* Oxford (UK) - Cambridge (Mass.): Basil Blackwell.

Hill, W. F. (1963), *Learning: A Survey of Psychological Interpretations*, S. Francisco: Chandler Publishing Company.

Hirschman, A. O. (1965), "Obstacles to Development: a Classification and a Quasi-vanishing Act", *Economic Development and Cultural Change*, vol. XIII, (4), part I, 385-393.

Hodgson, G. M. (1988), *Economics and Institutions, A Manifesto for a Modern Institutional Economics*, Oxford: Basil Blackwell.

Hodgson, G. M. (1991), "Hayek's Theory of Cultural Evolution. An Evaluation in The Light of Vanberg's Critique", *Economics and Philosophy*, 7, 67-82.

Hodgson, G. M. (1993), *Economics and Evolution*, Cambridge, Polity Press.

Hogarth, R. M. and M. W. Reder (1986a), "The Behavioral Foundations of Economic Theory", in Hogarth and Reder (1986b).

Hogarth, R. M. and M. W. Reder (eds.) (1986b), *Rational Choice: The Contrast between Economics and Psychology*, Chicago: University of Chicago Press.

Holland, J. H., J. Holyoak, R. E. Nisbett and P. R.Thagard (1986), *Induction - Processes of Inference, Learning and Discovery*, Cambridge (MA.): MIT Press.

Holland, J. H. and J. H. Miller (1991), "Artificial Adaptive Agents in Economic Theory", *American Economic Review,* 81(2), 365-370.

Holmstrom, B. (1982), "Moral Hazard in Teams", *The Bell Journal of Economics*, 13, 324-330.

Holmstrom, B. and J. Tirole (1989), *The Theory of the Firm*, in Schmalensee R. and R. Willig (eds.) (1989).

Horwitz, S. (1993), "Spontaneity and Design in the Evolution of Institutions: the Similarities of Money and Law", *Journal des Economistes et des Etudes Humaines*, 4 (4), 571-587.

Hutchison, T. W. (1981), *The Politics and Philosophy of Economics: Marxians, Keynesians and Austrians*, Oxford: Basil Blackwell.

Innocenti, A. (1995), "Oskar Morgenstern and the Heterodox Potentialities of the Application of Game Theory to Economics", *The Journal of the History of Economic Thought,* 17, 205-227.

Jensen, M. and W. Meckling (1976), "Theory of the Firm: Managerial Behaviour, Agency Costs and Ownership Structure", *Journal of Financial Economics*, 3, 305-60.

Jossa, B. (1993), "Ordine spontaneo e liberalismo secondo Hayek", *Studi Economici,* 48(49), 5-45.

Kahneman, D. and A. Tversky (1973), "On the Psychology of Prediction", *Psychological Review*, 80, 237-251.

Kahneman, D. and A. Tversky (1979), "Prospect Theory: an Analysis of Decision under Risk", *Econometrica*, 47, 263-291.

Kahneman, D. and A. Tversky (1986), "Rational Choice and the Framing of Decisions", in Hogarth and Reder (eds.) (1986b), 67-94.

Katona, G. (1940), *Organizing and Memorizing*, New York: Columbia University Press.

Katona, G. (1951), *Psychological Analysis of Economic Behavior*, New York: McGraw-Hill.

Katona, G. (1975), *Psychological Economics*, New York: Elsevier.

Kay, N. M. (1984), *The Emergence of the Firm: Knowledge, Ignorance and Surprice in Economic Organization*, London: Macmillan.

Kirzner, I. M. (ed.) (1979), *Perception, Opportunity and Profit,* Chicago-London: University of Chicago Press.

Kirzner, I. M. (ed.) (1986), *Subjectivism, Intelligibility and Economic Understanding,* New York: Macmillan.

Kirzner, I. M. and L. von Mises (eds.) (1982), *Method, Process, and Austrian Economics: Essays in Honor of L. v. Mises*, Lexington (MA.): Lexington Books.

Klahr, D. (ed.) (1976), *Cognition and Instruction*, New York: Hillsdale.

Knight, F. H.(1921), *Risk, Uncertainty and Profit*, Boston: Houghton Mifflin Company.

Knight, F. H. (1947), *Freedom and Reforms: Essays in Economics and Social Philosophy*, New York: Harper.

Knight, J. (1992), *Institutions and Social Conflict. The Political Economy of Institutions and Decision Series*, Cambridge - New York - Melbourne: Cambridge University Press.

Koch, S. (ed.) (1963), *Psychology as a Study of a Science*, vol. VI, New York: McGraw-Hill.

Kohler, W. (1947), *Gestalt Psychology*, New York: Liveright Publishing Corporation.

Kohonen, T. (ed.) (1991), *Artificial Neural Network,* Amsterdam: Elsevier.

Kreps, D. M. (1988), *Notes on the Theory of Choice*, Boulder-London: Westview Press.

Krugman, P. (1991a), *Geography and Trade*, Cambridge: MIT Press.

Krugman, P. (1991b), "History and Industry Location: the Case of the Manufacturing Belt", *American Economic Review*, 81, n.2, 80-83.

Krugman, P. (1991c), "Increasing Returns and Economic Geography", *Journal of Political Economy*, 99 (3), 483-99.

Kulkarni, D. and H. A. Simon (1988), "The Processes of Scientific Discovery: the Strategy of Experimentation", *Cognitive Science*, 12, 139-76.

Lachmann, L. M. (1990), "G. L. S. Shackle's Place in the History of Subjectivist Thought", in Frowen (1990).

Lakatos, I., J. Worral and G. Currie (1978), *The Methodology of Scientific Research Programmes. Philosophical Papers*, vol. I., Cambridge: Cambridge University Press.

Langley, P. W., H. A. Simon, G. Bradshaw and J. Zytkow (1987), *Scientific Discovery: Computational Explorations of the Creative Processes*, Cambridge (MA.): MIT Press.

Langlois, R. N. (1986), *Economics as a Process. Essays in The New Institutional Economics*, Cambridge (MA.): Cambridge University Press.

Latsis, S. (ed.) (1976), *Method and Appraisal in Economics*, Cambridge, (MA.): Cambridge University Press.

Lavoie, D. (1985), *Rivalry and Central Planning. The Socialist Calculation Debate Reconsidered*, Cambridge, (MA.): Cambridge University Press.

Legrenzi, P. (1984), "Introduzione" to italian ed. Simon (1983).

Legrenzi, P. (1991), "Psicologia ed economia ingenue", in Bombi (1991).

Lewontin, R. C. and R. Levins R. (1978), "Evoluzione", in *Enciclopedia*, vol 5, Torino: Einaudi.

Loasby, B. J. (1967), "Management Economics and Theory of the Firm", *Journal of Industrial Economics*, 15, 165-176.

Loasby, B. J. (1976), *Choice, Complexity and Ignorance. An Inquiry into Economic Theory and the Practice of Decision Making*, Cambridge, (MA.): Cambridge University Press.

Loasby, B. J. (1989), *The Mind and Method of the Economist. A Critical Appraisal of Major Economists in the 20th Century*, Aldershot: Edward Elgar.

Loasby, B. J. (1991), *The Austrian School*, in Mair and Miller (eds.) (1991), 40-70.

Lucas, R. E. Jr. (1981), *Studies in Business-Cycles Theory*, Oxford: Basil Blackwell.

Luce, R. D. and L. Narens (1985), "Classification of Concatenation Measurement Structures According to Scale Type", *Journal of Mathematical Psychology*, 29, 1-72.

Luce, R. D. and H. Raiffa (1957), *Games and Decisions. Introduction and Critical Survey*, New York: J. Wiley & Sons.

Luini, L. (1994), *Economia dell'informazione. Mercato, tecnologia, organizzazione*, Roma: Nuova Italia Scientifica.

Lurija, A. R. (1976), *La storia sociale dei processi cognitivi*, Firenze: Giunti Barbera.

Macfie, A. L. (1955), "The Scottish Tradition in Economic Thought", *Scottish Journal of Political Economy*, 2, 81-105.

Machina, M. J. (1982), "Expected Utility Analysis without the Independent Axiom", *Econometrica*, 50, 277-323.

Machlup, F. (1946), "Marginal Analysis and Empirical Research", *American Economic Review*, 36, 519-554.

Machlup, F. (1974), "Friedrich von Hayek's Contribution to Economics", *Swedish Journal of Economics*, 76 (4), 498-531.

Magnusson, L. and Ottosson I. (eds.) (1997), *Evolutionary Economics and Path-dependency*, Aldershot: Edward Elgar.

Mair, D. and G. A. Miller (eds.) (1991), *A Modern Guide to Economic Thought. An Introduction to Comparative Schools of Thought in Economics*, Aldershot: Edward Elgar.

Malerba, F. and Orsenigo L. (1990), "Teoria evolutiva e innovazione industriale: risultati empirici degli anni '80", in Amendola (1990).

March, J. C. (1991), "How Decisions Happen in Organizations", *Human Computer Interaction*, 6, 95 - 117.

March, J. C. and H. A. Simon (1958), *Organizations*, New York: John Wiley.

Marchionatti, R. and F. Silva (1994), "Teoria economica e contesto istituzionale. Il caso dell'economia industriale italiana", in Becattini and Vaccà (eds.)(1994).

Marengo, L. (1992), "Coordination and Organizational Learning in the Firm", *Journal of Evolutionary Economics*, 2, 313-326.

Marhaba, S. (1976), *Antinomie epistemologiche nella psicologia contemporanea*, Firenze: Giunti Barbera.

Marris, R. (1964), *The Economic Theory of "Managerial" Capitalism*, London: Macmillan.

Marris, R. (1992), "Implications for Economics", in Egidi and Marris (eds.) (1992), 194-224.

Marris, R. and A. Wood (eds.) (1971), *The Corporate Economy Growth Competition and Innovative Potential*, London: Macmillan.

Marschak, J. and R. Radner (1972), *Economic Theory of Teams*, New Haven: Yale University Press.

Marshall, A. (1867-8), *Ye Machine*, in Raffaelli (1994).

Marshall, A. (1961), *Principles of Economics*, (9th ed.), London: Macmillan.

Mason, E. S. (1952), "Comment", in Haley (1952).

Maturana H. and F. Varela (1984), *El árbol del conocimiento*, Madrid: Editorial debate.

McClelland, J. L. and D. E. Rumelhart (1988), *Explorations in Parallel Distributed Processing - A Handbook of Models, Programs, and Exercises*, Cambridge (MA.): MIT Press.

McCulloch, W. and W. Pitts (1943), "A Logical Calculus of the ideas Immanent in Nervous Activity", *Bulletin of Mathematical Biophysics*, 5, 115-137.

McGuire, C. B. and R. Radner (eds.) (1986), *Decision and Organization: A Volume in Honour of Jacob Marschak*, Minneapolis: University of Minnesota Press.

Mecacci, L. (1977), *Cervello e storia. Ricerche sovietiche di neurofisiologia e psicologia*, Roma: Editori Riuniti.

Menger, C. (1883), *Untersuchungen ueber die Methode der Socialwissenschaften der politischen Oekonomie insbesondere*, Leipzig: Dunker Humblot.

Milgrom, P. and J. Roberts 1988, "Economic Theory of the Firm: Past, Present and Future", *Canadian Journal of Economics*, XXI, 444-458.

Miller, G. A. (1956), The Magical Number Seven, Plus or Minus Two, *Psychological Review*, 63, 81-97.

Miller, G. A. and A. Frick (1949), "Statistical Behavioristics and Sequences of Responses", *Psychological Review*, 56, 311-329.

Miller, G. A., Galanter E. and K. H. Pribam (1960), *Plans and the Structure of Behavior*, New York: Rinehart & Winston.

Miller, H. (1979), "The Cognitive Basis of Hayek's Political Thought", in Cunningham (1979).

Minsky, L. M. (1975), *The Society of Mind*, New York: Simon & Schuster.

Mises, L. v. (1969), *The Historical Setting of the Austrian School*, New Rochelle (NY): Arlington House.

Mises, L. von (1981), *Socialism*, Indianapolis: Liberty Classics.

Moe, T. (1984), "The New Economics of Organizations", *American Journal of Political Science*, 28.

Momigliano, F. (1975), *Economia industriale e teoria dell'impresa*, Bologna: Il Mulino.

Morgenstern, O. (1935), *Perfect Foresight and Economic Equilibrium*, in Schotter (1976).

Nadeau, R. (1987), "La thèse subjective de Hayek. Sur la nation d'ordre sensoriel et son rapport à la methodologie economique", *Cahiers d'épistèmologie*, n. 8706, Montreal.

Napoleoni, C. and F. Ranchetti (1990), *Il pensiero economico del novecento*, Torino: Einaudi.

Negishi, T. (1985a), "Non Walrasian Foundations of Macroeconomics", in Feiwel (ed.) (1985).

Negishi, T. (1985b), *Economic Theories in a non Walrasian Tradition*, Cambridge: Cambridge University Press.

Negishi, T. (1989), *History of Economic Theory*, Amsterdam: North-Holland.

Neisser, U. (1967), *Cognitive Psychology*, New York: Appleton Century Crofts.

Nelson, R. R. (1981), "Assessing Private Enterprise: An Exegesis of Tangled Doctrine", *The Bell Journal of Economics,* 12 (1), 93-111.

Nelson, R. R. (1987), *Understanding Technical Change as Evolutionary Process*, Amsterdam: North-Holland.

Nelson, R. R. (1995), "Recent Evolutionary Theorizing about Economic Change", *Journal of Economic Literature*, 33 (1), 48-90.

Nelson, R. R. and S. G. Winter (1982), *An Evolutionary Theory of Economic Change*, Cambridge (MA.): Harvard University Press.

Neumann, J. von (1958), *The Computer and the Brain*, New Haven: Yale University Press.

Neumann, J. von and O. Morgerstern (1944), *Theory of Games and Economic Behavior,* Princeton: Princeton University Press.

Newcomb, T. M. (1972), "Expectation as a Social Psychological Concept", in Strumpel, Morgan and Zahan (eds.) (1972).

Newell, A., J. C. Shaw and H. A. Simon (1958a), "Elements of a Theory of Human Problem Solving", *Psychological Review*, 65, pp. 151-66.

Newell, A. J. C. Shaw and H. A. Simon (1958b), "Chess-playing Programs and the .Problem of Complexity", *IBM Journal of Research and Development*, 2, 320-335.

Newell, A. and H. A. Simon (1965), "An Example of Human Chess Play in the Light of Chess Playing Programs", in Wiener and Schade (eds.) (1965), vol. II.

Newell, A. and H. A. Simon (1972), *Human Problem Solving*, Englewood Cliffs: Prentice Hall.

Newell, A. and H. A. Simon (1981), "Computer Science as Empirical Inquiry: Symbol and Search", in Haugeland (ed.) (1981).

Norman, D. A. (1969), *Memory and Attention*, Wiley: New York.

Norman, D. A. and D. G. Bobrow (1976), "On the Role of Active Memory Processes", in Cofer (1969).

North, D. C. (1990), *Institutions, Institutional Change and Economic Performance*, Cambridge (MA.), Cambridge University Press.

North, D. C. (1991), "Institutions", *Journal of Economic Perspectives*, 5 (1), 97-112.

North, D. C. (1992), "Institutions and Economic Theory", *The American Economist*, XI, n. 1, pp. 3-6.

North, D. C. (1993), "Institutions and Credible Commitment", *Journal of Institutional and Theoretical Economics*, 149 (1), 11-23.

North, D. C. (1994), "Economic Performance through Time", *American Economic Review*, (84) 3,.359-368.

Oakeshott, M. (1962), *Rationalism in Politics*, London: Methuen.

O'Driscoll, G. P. and M. J. Rizzo (1985), *The Economics of Time and Ignorance*, Oxford: Basil Blackwell.

O'Driscoll, G. P. and M. J. Rizzo (1986), "Subjectivism, Uncertainty and Rules", in Kirzner (ed.) (1986).

Paolicchi, P. (1991), "Perchè gli individui obbediscono alle norme"?, in Conte (ed.) (1991).

Parisi, D. (1991), "Cognitivismo-connessionismo e il legame micro-macro", in Conte (ed.) (1991).

Parisi, D., F. Cecconi, and S. Nolfi (1990), "Econets: Neural Networks that Learn in an Environment", *Network*, vol. 2, 149-168.

Patterson, P. and H. Nawa (1993), "Neuronal Differentiation Factors/Cytokines and Synaptic Plasticity", *Cell*, 72/Neuron, 10 (suppl.), 123-137.

Pavlov, I. P. (1928), *Lectures on Conditioned Reflexes*, London: Martin Lawrence.

Penrose, E. T. (1952), "Biological Analogies in the Theory of the Firm", *American Economic Review*, 42(5), 804-819.

Penrose, E. T. (1959), *The Theory of the Growth of the Firm*, Oxford: Blackwell.

Pessa, E. (1992), *Intelligenza artificiale. Teorie e sistemi*, Torino: Bollati Boringhieri.

Piaget, J. (1967), *Biologie et conneissance*, Paris: Gallimard.

Piaget, J. (1969), *The Mechanism of Perception*, London: Routledge & Kegan Paul.

Piaget, J. (1970), *L'épistémologie génétique*, Paris: Presses Universitaires de France.

Piaget, J. (1980), "The Psychogenesis of Knowledge and its Epistemological Significance", in Piattelli and Palmarini (eds.) (1980).

Piaget, J. and B. Inhelder (1968), *Memoire et intelligence*, Paris: Presses Universitaires de France.

Piattelli, M. and C. Palmarini (1980), *Language and Learning: the Debate Between J. Piaget and N. Chomsky*, Cambridge (MA.): Harvard University Press.

Pigou, A. C. (1952) *The Economics of Welfare*, London: Macmillan.

Polanyi, M. (1951), *The Logic of Liberty*, London: Routledge & Kegan Paul.

Polanyi, M. (1967), *The Tacit Dimension*, London: Routledge & Kegan Paul.

Popper, K. R. (1965), "Clouds and Watches", in Popper (1979).

Popper, K. R. (1979), *Objective Knowledge: an Evolutionary Approach*, Oxford: Clarendon Press.

Popper, K. R. and J. C. Eccles (1977), *The Self and Its Brain. An Argument for Interactionism*, Berlin - New York: Springer International.

Pounds, W. F. (1969), "The Process of Problem Finding", *Industrial Management Review*, 11, 1-19.

Rachlin, H. (1980), "Economics and Behavioral Psychology", in Staddon (1980).

Raffaelli, T. (1994), "Alfred Marshall's Early Philosophical Writings", *Research in the History of Economic Thought and Methodology: Archival Supplement*, n. 4, 53 - 159.

Rapoport, A. (1962), "The Use and Misuse of Game Theory", *Scientific American*, vol. 207, (6), 108-118.

Richardson, G. B. (1972), "The Organization of Industry", *Economic Journal*, 82, pp. 883-896.

Richardson, G. P. (1991), *Feedback Thought in Social Science and Systems Theory*, Philadelphia: University of Pennsylvania Press.

Ricketts, M. (1987), *The economics of business enterprise: An introduction to economic organisation and the theory of the firm*, New York - London and Toronto: Simon and Schuster International, Harvester Wheatsheaf.

Rizzello, S. (1993), *Conoscenza, razionalità, e organizzazione: Hayek, Simon e i microfondamenti della teoria economica*, PhD Thesis, Firenze.

Rizzello, S. (1995), "The Endogenous Asymmetrical Information", *Quaderni di Ricerca,* Università di Torino, Dipartimento di Economia, n. 11.

Rizzello, S. (1996a), "Mente, organizzazioni, istituzioni. I microfondamenti del neoistituzionalismo", *Economia Politica,* XIII (2), 225 - 263.

Rizzello, S. (1996b), "The Microfoundations of Path-dependency", in Magnusson - Ottosson (eds.) (1997).

Robinson, J. V. (1980a), "Time in Economic Theory", in Robinson (1980b).

Robinson, J. V. (1980b), *Further Contributions to Modern Economics,* Oxford: Blackwell.

Rosenberg, N. (ed.)(1971), *The Economics of Technological Change,* Harmondsworth: Penguin Book.

Runde, J. H. (1988), *Subjectivism, Psychology, and the Modern Austrians: Development, Tensions, Prospects,* Dordrecht: Kluwer Academic.

Russel, B. (1921), *The Analysis of Mind,* London: Allen & Unwin.

Ryle, G. (1949), *The Concept of Mind,* London: Hutchinson.

Savage, L. J. (1954), *The Foundations of Statistics,* New York: Dover Publications.

Schmalensee, R. (1992), "Sunk Costs and Market Structure: A Review Article", *Journal of Industrial Economics,* 40 (2), 125-134.

Schmalensee, R. and R. Willig (eds.) (1989), *The Handbook of Industrial Organization,* Amsterdam: North Holland.

Schoemaker, P. J. H. (1982), "The Expected Utility Model: Its Variants, Purposes, Evidence and Limitations", *Journal of Economic Literature,* 20(2), 529-63.

Schotter, A. (ed.) (1976), *Selected Economic Writings of Oskar Morgenstern,* New York : New York University Press.

Schotter, A. (1981), *The Economic Theory of Social Institution,* Cambridge: Cambridge University Press.

Schotter, A., (1990), *Free Market Economics: a Critical Appraisal,* New York: St. Martin Press.

Schultz, D. P. (1974), *Storia della psicologia moderna,* Firenze: Giunti Barbera.

Schumpeter, J. A. (1912), *Theorie der Wirtschaftlichen Entwicklung,* Leipzig: Verlag von Dunker & Humblot.

Schumpeter, J. A. (1943), *Capitalism, Socialism, Democracy,* London: Allen & Unwin.

Schumpeter, J. A. (1954), *History of Economic Analysis,* Oxford: Oxford University Press.

Schumpeter, J. A. (1971), "The Instability of Capitalism", in Rosemberg N. (ed.) (1971).

Scitovsky, T. (1977), *The Joyless Economy,* Oxford: Oxford University Press.

Screpanti, E. and S. Zamagni (1989), *Profilo di storia del pensiero economico*, Roma: Nuova Italia Scientifica.

Scruton, R. (ed.) (1988), *Conservative Thinkers: Essays from the "Salisbury Review"*, London: Claridge Press.

Seltzer, L. H. (ed.) (1964), *New Horizons of Economic Progress, The Franklin Memorial Lectures*, vol. 12, Detroit: Wayne State University Press.

Shackle, G. L. S. (1972), *Epistemics and Economics: A Critique of Economic Doctrine*, Cambridge: Cambridge University Press.

Shannon, C. (1938), "A Symbolic Analysis of Relay and Switching Circuits", *Transactions of the American Institute of Electrical Engineers*, 57, 1-11.

Shearmur, J. (1986), "The Austrian Connection: Hayek's Liberalism and the Thought of Carl Menger", in Grassl - Smith (1986).

Silberston, A. (ed.) (1989), *Technology and Economic Progress*, London: Macmillan.

Silva, F. (1985), "Qualcosa di nuovo nella teoria dell'impresa?", *Economia Politica*, 2(1), 95-134.

Simon, H. A. (1944), "Decision Making and Administrative Organization", *Public Administration Review*, 4, 16-31.

Simon, H. A. (1946), "The Proverbs of Administration", *Public Administration Review*, 6, 53-67.

Simon, H. A. (1947), *Administrative Behavior*, New York: Macmillan.

Simon, H. A. (1955), "A Behavioral Model of Rational Choice", *Quarterly Journal of Economics*, 69, 99-118.

Simon, H. A. (1956), "Rational Choice and the Structure of the Environment", *Psychological Review*, 63, 129-38.

Simon, H. A. (1957), *Models of Man*, New York: Wiley.

Simon, H. A. (1959), "Theories of Decision-Making in Economics and Behavioural Science", *American Economic Review*, XLIX (3), 253-283.

Simon, H. A. (1962), "New Developments in the Theory of the Firm", *American Economic Review*, 52, 1-15.

Simon, H. A. (1964a), "Decision Making as Economic Resource", in Seltzer (ed.) (1964).

Simon, H. A. (1964b), *Rationality*, in Goulg and Kolb (eds.) (1964).

Simon, H. A. (1965), *The Shape Automation. For Men and Management*, New York: Harper & Row.

Simon, H. A. (1967), "Programs as a Factor of Production", *Proceedings of the Nineteenth Annual Winter Meeting* (1966), Industrial Relations Research Association.

Simon, H. A. (1969), *The Science of the Artificial*, Cambridge (MA.): MIT Press.

Simon, H. A. (1971), "Designing Organizations for an Information Rich World", in Greenberger (ed.) (1971).

Simon, H. A. (1972), "Theories of Bounded Rationality", in McGuire and Radner (eds.) (1986).

Simon, H. A.(1973), "The Structure of Ill-Structured Problems", *Artificial Intelligence*, 4, 181-201 .

Simon, H. A. (1976), "From Substantive to Procedural Rationality", in Latsis (ed.) (1976).

Simon, H. A. (1978), "On How to Decide What to Do", *Bell Journal of Economics*, 9(2), 494-507.

Simon, H. A. (1979a), "Rational Decision Making in Business Organizations", *American Economic Review*, 69, 493-512.

Simon, H. A.(1979b), *Models of Thought*, vol. 1, New Haven: Yale University Press.

Simon, H. A. (1983), *Reason in Human Affairs*, Stanford: Stanford University Press.

Simon, H. A. (1985), *Causalità, razionalità, organizzazione*, Bologna: Il Mulino.

Simon, H. A. (1987a), "Bounded Rationality", in Eatwell, Milgate and Newman (eds.) (1987), Vol. I, 266-7.

Simon, H. A. (1987b), "Satisficing", in Eatwell, Milgate and Newman (eds.) (1987), vol. IV, 243- 244.

Simon, H. A. (1991), *Models of My Life*, New York: Basic Books.

Simon, H. A. (1992), *Introduzione* to Egidi and Marris (eds.)(1992).

Simon, H. A. and A. Newell (1959), *The Simulation of Human Thought*, S. Monica (Ca): The Rand Corporation, Research memorandum n. 2506.

Simon, H. A.and L. Siklóssy (1972), *Representation and Meaning*, Englewood Cliffs: (N. J.) Prentice Hall.

Slote, M. (1989), *Beyond Optimizing. A Study of Rational Choice*, Cambridge (MA): Harvard University Press.

Smith, V. L. (ed.) (1990), *Experimental Economics*, Aldershot: Edward Elgar.

Spence, J. T. and K. W. Spence (eds.) (1968), *The Psychology of Learning and Motivation: Advances in Research and Theory*, vol. 2, New York: Academic Press.

Spencer, H. (1857), "Progress: Its Law and Cause", *Westminster Review*, n. s., XI, 445-485.

Staddon, J. E. R. (ed.) (1980), *Limits to Action. The Allocation of Individual Behavior*, New York: Academic Press.

Stigler, G. J. (1961), "The Economics of Information", *Journal of Political Economy*, 69, 213-215.

Stigler, G. J. (1966), *The Theory of Price*, New York: Macmillan.

Stiglitz, J. E. (1987a), "The Causes and Consequences of the Dependence of Quality on Price", *Journal of Economic Literature*, XXV (1), 1-48.

Stiglitz, J. E. (1987b), "Technological Change, Sunk Costs, and Competition", *Brookings Papers*, 18 (3), 883-937.

Stiglitz, J. (1989), *The Economic Role of the State*, Oxford: Basil Blackwell.

Strumpel, B., J. N. Morgan and E. Zahan (eds.) (1972), *Human Behavior in Economic Affairs*, Amsterdam - London: Elsevier.

Sugden, R. (1986), *The Economics of Rights, Co-operation and Welfare*, Oxford: Basil Blackwell.

Sutton, J. (1989), "Endogenous Sunk Costs and the Structure of Advertising Intensive Industries", *European Economic Review*, 33(2/3), 335-344.

Tamborini, R. (1991), "Conoscenza e previsione del comportamento economico per un approccio costruttivista", in Egidi, Lombardi and Tamborini (1991).

Tarde, G. (1902), *La Psychologie Economique*, Paris: Alcan.

Terna, P. (1991), "Labour Consumption and Family Assets: A Neural Network Learning from its own Cross-Targets", in Kohonen (ed.)(1991).

Terna, P. (1995), "Reti neurali artificiali e modelli con agenti adattivi", *Rivista Italiana di Economia*, 0, 71-106.

Tolman, E. C. (1932), *Purposive Behavior in Animals and Men*, New York: Century Co.

Tomlinson, J. (1990), *Hayek and the Market*, London: Pluto Press.

Turing, A. M. (1950), "Computing Machinery and Intelligence", *Mind*, 59, 433-50.

Tversky, A. (1969), "Intransitivity of Preferences", *Psychological Review*, 76, 1, 31-48.

Ullmann-Margalit, E. (1977), *The Emergence of Norms,* Oxford: Clarendon Press.

Uphoff, N. (1993), "Grassroots Organization and NGO's Rural Development: Opportunity with Diminishing States and Expanding Markets", *World Development*, 21(4), 607-622.

Vanberg, V. (1986), "Spontaneous Market Order and Social Rules: A Critical Examination of Hayek's Theory of Cultural Evolution", *Economics and Philosophy*, 2, 75-100.

Vanberg, V. (1994), *Rules and Choice in Economics*, London - New York: Routledge.

Vannucci, A. (1990), "La Rivoluzione marginalista nelle scienze sociali: alcune osservazioni", *Quaderni di Storia dell'Economia Politica*, VIII (1), 141 - 177.

Van Raaij, W. F., G. M. Van Veldhoven and K. E. Warneryd (eds.) (1988), *Handbook of Economic Psychology*, Dordrecht: Kluwer Academic.

Veblen, T. B. (1899), *The Theory of Leisure Class: an Economic Study of Institutions*, New York: Thoemmes Press.

Walliser, B. (1989), "Théorie des jeux et génèse des institutions", *Recherches economiques de Louvain*, 55 (4), 339-364.

Walras, L. (1889), *Eléments d'Economie Politique Pure*, Lausanne: F. Rouge Editeur.

Walter, W. F. (1953), *The Living Brain*, New York: Duckworth.

Watzlawick, P. (1981), *The Invented Reality,* New York: Norton.

Wertheimer, M. (1945), *Productive Thinking*, Westport (Conn.): Greenwood Press.

Wiener, N. (1948), *Cybernetics or Control and Communication in the Animal and the Machine*, Cambridge (MA.): MIT Press,.

Wiener, N. and J. P. Schade (1965), *Progress in Biocybernetics*, vol. II, Amsterdam: Elsevier.

Williamson, O. E. (1975), *Market and Hierarchies: Analysis and Antitrust Implications*, New York: The Free Press.

Williamson, O. E. (1986), *The Economic Institutions of Capitalism. Firms, Markets, Relational Contracting*, New York: The Free Press.

Williamson, O. E. (1988), "The Logic of Economic Organization", *Journal of Law, Economics, and Organization*, 4, 65-94.

Winston, G. C. and R. F. Teichgraeber (eds.) (1988), *The Boundaries of Economics*, Cambridge - New York - Melbourne: Cambridge University Press.

Winter, S. G. (1964), "Economic, Natural Selection and the Theory of the Firm", *Yale Economic Essay*, 4, 225-272.

Winter, S. G. (1971), "Satisficing, Selection and the Innovating Remnant", *Quarterly Journal of Economics*, 85 (2), 237-261.

Winter, S. G. (1975), "Optimization and Evolution in the Theory of the Firm", in Day and Groves (eds.) (1975).

Witt, U. (1989), "Subjectivism in Economics. A Suggested Reorientation", in Grunert and Olander (eds.) (1989), 409-31.

Witt, U. (1992), "Evolutionary Concepts in Economics", *Eastern Economic Journal*, 18 (4), 405-419.

Wood, J. C. and R. N. Woods, (eds.) (1991), *Friedrich A. Hayek Critical Assessments,* vol. IV, London and New York: Routledge.

Zamagni, S. (1982), "Sui fondamenti metodologici della scuola austriaca", *Note Economiche*, 3, 63-93.

Zamagni, S. (1986), "La teoria del consumatore nell'ultimo quarto di secolo", *Economia Politica*, 3, 409-466.

Zamagni, S. (ed.)(1989), *Le teorie economiche della produzione*, Bologna: Il Mulino.

Zeckhauser, R. J. and Pratt J. W. (1984), *Principals and Agents: The Structure of Business*, Boston (MA.): Harvard Business School Press.

Index

Printed and bound by CPI Group (UK) Ltd, Croydon, CR0 4YY

23/04/2025

14660962-0001